BACK

TO THE

BASICS

Follow-up for Followers of Christ
Johnny A Palmer Jr.

INTRODUCTION:

Vince Lombardi was one who knew the importance of the basics. He once said to his Green Bay Packers holding the pigskin high in the air, he shouted, "Okay, gentlemen, today we go back to the basics. You guys, look at this. This is a football!"[1] This book is about basic truth that both new and mature believers in Christ need. We have often become too complicated and far removed from our foundation. In fact, part of the problem is that many Christians have never been taught these basic truths. My prayer is that this book will at least give us a glimpse of these vital and timeless basics of the Christian life.

OUTLINE:

I. THE *SITUATION*.

A. God's Perfection.

1. Holy, Holy, Holy.

---

[1] Swindoll, Charles R.. The Tale of the Tardy Oxcart (Swindoll Leadership Library) (p. 521). Thomas Nelson. Kindle Edition.

2. Just As He is.

3. I Love to Tell the Whole Story.

B. God's Creation.

1. The Inception of spirit beings.

2. The Introduction of sin into the universe.

C. God's Demonstration of grace through project humanity.

1. Creation.

2. Obligation.

II. THE *SEPARATION* OF MAN.

A. God is the *Standard of Deity.*

B. Man has a *Sin Debt.*

C. Man is in *Slavery to the Devil.*

D. Man's *Spiritual Death.*

III. THE *SOLUTION* BY GOD.

A. Representation.

B. Incarnation.

C. Substitution.

D. Satisfaction.

IV. THE *SALVATION* FOR MAN.

A. Justification.

1. Pardon.

2. ImPutation.

B. Redemption.

C. Regeneration.

D. Relocation.

V. THE *STIPULATION* OF MAN.

Bonus Material: Follow-up especially for new Christians.

Chapter One

I. THE SITUATION

A. God's Perfection

Intro:

1. The March/April 2016 issue of *Psychology Today* attempted to give readers several reasons to cultivate a sense of awe and wonder with their article "It's Not All About You!" The article mentioned the following secular sources about our need for awe and wonder:

- University of Pennsylvania researchers defined awe as the "emotion of self-transcendence, a feeling of admiration and elevation in the face of something greater than the self."

- A popular theoretical physicist wrote: "Awe gives you an existential shock. You realize that you are hardwired to be a little selfish, but you are also dependent on something bigger than yourself." Being enraptured is a way "to remove the tyranny of the ego."

- Therapist Robert Leahy, PhD writes: "Awe is the opposite of rumination. It clears away inner turmoil with a wave of outer immensity."

- Social scientists have found that when people experience a sense of awe, they feel more empathetic and more connected with others. One scientist concluded, "Wonder pulls us together—a counterforce to all that seems to be tearing us apart."

- The Wharton School of Business evaluated the *New York Times*' most emailed articles and found that the ones that evoked awe were the most shared. [2]

2. In reality there is only one thing, one person that lives up to that name "awe" and that would be God! This book is not about the attributes of God that would

---

[2] Carlin Flora, "It's Not All About You!" Psychology Today, (March-April, 2016); submitted by Jerry De Luca, Montreal, Canada.

take another entire series of books. So we must limit ourselves to just a few basic truths about God, that are relevant to our present study.

But we have to keep in mind that at one time, if you want to call it time, there was the Triune God, Father, Son, and Holy Spirit – and no one else! I love the way Arthur Pink puts it in The Attributes of God;

"In the beginning God." There was no heaven, where His glory is now particularly manifested. There was no earth to engage His attention. There were no angels to hymn His praises; no universe to be upheld by the word of His power. There was nothing, no one, but God; and that, not for a day, a year, or an age, but "from everlasting." During eternity past, God was alone: self-contained, self-sufficient, self-satisfied; in need of nothing. Had a universe, had angels, had human beings been necessary to Him in any way, they also had been called into existence from all eternity. The creating of them when He did, added nothing to God essentially. He changes not (Mal 3:6), therefore His essential glory can be neither augmented nor diminished.[3]

Read that again and let it soak in! Wow! You talk about awesome and stunning and breathtaking and...That would be God! As usual A. W. Tozer in his book The Knowledge of the Holy makes a needed application:

To admit that there is One who lies beyond us, who exists outside of all our categories, who will not be dismissed with a name, who will not appear before the bar of our reason, nor submit to our curious inquiries: this requires a great deal of humility, more than most of us possess, so we save face by thinking God down to our level, or at least down to where we can manage Him. Yet how He eludes us! For He is everywhere while He is nowhere, for "where" has to do with matter and space, and God is independent of both. He is unaffected by time or motion, is wholly self-dependent and owes nothing to the worlds His hands have made.[4]

---

[3] Pink, Arthur W.. The Attributes of God (p. 7). . Kindle Edition.

[4] Tozer, A.W.. The Knowledge of the Holy (p. 26). Fig. Kindle Edition.

I have to resist the temptation to go on and on and discipline myself to focus on the purpose of this book. So let's begin.

1. Holy Holy Holy.

a. *Definition* of holiness.

Charles Ryrie in Basic Theology notes:

In respect to God, holiness means not only that He is separate from all that is unclean and evil but also that He is positively pure and thus distinct from all others. An analogy may help in understanding this concept. What does it mean to be healthy? It is the absence of illness, but also a positive infusion of energy. Holiness is the absence of evil and the presence of positive right... The absolute, innate holiness of God means that sinners have to be separated from Him unless a way can be found to constitute them holy. And that way has been provided in the merits of Jesus Christ.[5]

---

[5] Charles Ryrie, *Basic Theology: A Popular Systematic Guide to Understanding Biblical Truth*, (Chicago: Moody Press, 1986), WORD*search* CROSS e-book, 41.

We can say at least two things about God's holiness:

- Transcendency.
- Absolute moral Purity.

Herbert Lockyer in All the Doctrines of the Bible notes:

God possesses *intrinsic* holiness.

He is holy in His nature. As light is the essence of the sun, so holiness is God's very being.

God possesses *original* holiness.

He is primarily holy. He can present Himself as the pattern of holiness because He is the origin and source of it. From the dateless past.

God possesses *transcendent* holiness.

The holiest angel above, or the holiest man on earth cannot measure the just dimensions of God's holiness. "There is none as holy as the Lord" (1 Sam. 2:2)...because God's holiness is His essence, He can never forfeit it. His is an infinite and unchangeable moral excellence.

God possesses *efficient* holiness.

This facet of the diamond of divine holiness implies that He is the Cause of all that is holy in others...[6]

Tony Evans gives this easy to understand Illustration in Understanding God:

Last fall, we had a problem with our television picture. Both sets transmitted a lot of fuzz. I got it looked into, and the repairman told me we had a reception problem. Our antenna and wiring were just not doing the job. I about had cardiac arrest when the repairman told me what it was going to cost for the rewiring we needed to get good reception. So every time I watch TV, the focus is not that clear. It's not sharp. It's somewhat distorted, and I'm sure you know how irritating that can be. That's what may happen when you try to study God. If your antenna is not

---

[6] All the Doctrines of the Bible, Herbert Lockyer, p. 31. ZondervanPublishingHouse.

working right, you won't get a clear picture. He won't come in clear. He won't be sharp, not because something is wrong with Him, but because something has gone wrong with your receiver. Since Adam's fall, our ability to pick up the "God channel" has been greatly disturbed.[7]

b. The *Declaration* of God's Holiness.

The declaration of God's holiness as found in Scripture, in both the Old and New Testament would take the rest of this book, and then some, to look at all of them.

See Ex. 3:5-6; 19:10-24; 40:9-16/Lev. 11:44-45/Num. 20:6-13/Deut. 23:18 /Josh. 3:4; 5:15; 24:19/1 Sam. 2:2/1 Chron. 13:10-12/Ezra 9:2/Lu. 1:49; 11:2/Jn. 17:11/2 Cor. 7:1/1 Tim. 6:15-16/Heb. 12:10/Jam. 1:13/ 1 Pet. 1:15-16/1 Jn. 1:5; 2:20; 3:3/Rev. 4:8; 6:10; 15:4/etc.

c. *Demonstrations* of God's Holiness.

---

[7] Tony Evans, – *Our God is Awesome: Encountering the Greatness of Our God*, (Chicago: Moody Press, 1994), WORD*search* CROSS e-book, 77.

(1) His *Creation.*

- Angels (Ezk. 28:15/Jude 6).
- Universe (Gen. 1:25).
- Man (Gen. 1:31/Eccles. 7:29).

(2) His *Commandments* (Psa. 19:7-9/Rom. 7:12).

(3) His *Crucifixion.*

Arthur Pink in The Attributes of God makes this observation:

God's holiness is manifested at the cross. Wondrously and yet most solemnly does the atonement display God's infinite holiness and abhorrence of sin. How hateful sin must be to God for Him to punish it to its utmost deserts when it was imputed to His Son![8]

d. *Deductions* from God's Holiness.

(1) His *Transcendence* of everything (Ex. 15:11/1 Sam. 2:2/Isa. 44:6/1 Ki. 8:22/Hos. 11:9).

Marva Dawn shared this:

---

[8] Pink, Arthur W.. The Attributes of God (p. 42).

I remember an animated discussion with my high school freshman English teacher over the word *awful*. I insisted on using *awe-full* to describe something so exalted as to arouse reverence. She preferred that I stick with the word's common spelling and its usage to designate something dreadful.

We should have looked in the dictionary. My old *Webster's* lists as its first definition "inspiring awe; highly impressive." Not until its fourth entry does it supply the definition usually assumed in idiomatic English: "very bad, ugly, unpleasant."

But the teacher had the final word that day in class. Even at age 14 I felt that a vital perception was being lost—the sense that something, someone, was higher than we. I longed to verbalize awe-full-ness; my teacher made class awful.

Today teenagers apply the related word *awesome* to clothes, food, music, and cinematic effects. The word is so overused that when people sing Rich Mullins's "Awesome God," they seem to trivialize the Awe-full One and put the Trinity on the same level as toothpaste and togs.

As our culture has worked hard to establish equality among persons, we've somehow put God into that parity and gradually reduced our sense that this is a breathtakingly transcendent GOD we're talking about.[9]

Raymond Ortlund shared this:

As a boy, I enjoyed Saturday morning television—Sky King, The Lone Ranger, Roy Rogers. What annoyed me was the weekend warriors of the Air National Guard flying their F-80 Shooting Stars over the house and interfering with the TV signal. Whenever they broke the sound barrier, the window panes of our family room would rattle. But even the temple shakes at the voice of just one seraph. So we should not think of God's seraphim as chubby babies with wings, like the angels in the art of Peter Paul Rubens. They were more like jet fighters breaking the sound barrier. And as the

---

[9] *Marva J. Dawn,* Reaching Out Without Dumbing Down *(William B. Eerdmans, 1995), pp. 98-99*

smoke from the incense altar fills the temple with the felt presence of God, Isaiah is overwhelmed. God is always more than we bargain for.[10]

(2) His *Absence* from sin (Psa. 25:8/Mt. 5:48/1 Jn. 1:5).

R. C. Sproul in What is Reformed Theology gives this brief summary:

God's holiness refers to two distinct but related ideas. First the term holy calls attention to God's "otherness," the sense in which he is different from and higher than we are. It calls attention to his greatness and his transcendent glory. The second meaning of holiness has to do with God's purity.[11]

(3) His *Abhorrence* of sin (Psa. 5:5; 7:11/Prov. 3:32/Hab. 1:13).

We may say, well, it is just one little sin! But let us ask the question:

---

[10] Raymond C. Ortlund, Jr., *Preaching the Word – Isaiah: God Saves Sinners*, (Wheaton, IL: Crossway Books, 2005), WORD*search* CROSS e-book, 78.

[11] Sproul, R. C.. What is Reformed Theology?: Understanding the Basics (p. 45). Baker Publishing Group. Kindle Edition.

- How many sins did it take for Adam to fall?

- How many sins kept Moses from entering the Promised Land?

- How many sins did it take to kill Ananias and Sapphira?

Let's say that I committed only one tiny sin in my life everyday (I wish!). As of this writing I am 64 years old, I was born on July 16, 1953, it is March 07, 2018. That is 23,610 sins! And it only takes one sin to be separated from a holy God.

God hates any violation of his holy character, we have a perverted sense of what sin should be tolerated. A sort of situation ethics or a code of conduct based on a perverted standard.

In *Words We Live By,* Brian Burrell tells of an armed robber named Dennis Lee Curtis who was arrested in 1992 in Rapid City, South Dakota. Curtis apparently had scruples about his thievery. In his wallet the police found a sheet of paper on which was written the following code:

1. I will not kill anyone unless I have to.

2. I will take cash and food stamps—no checks.

3. I will rob only at night.

4. I will not wear a mask.

5. I will not rob mini-marts or 7-Eleven stores.

6. If I get chased by cops on foot, I will get away. If chased by vehicle, I will not put the lives of innocent civilians on the line.

7. I will rob only seven months out of the year.

8. I will enjoy robbing from the rich to give to the poor.

This thief had a sense of morality, but it was flawed. When he stood before the court, he was not judged by the standards he had set for himself but by the higher law of the state.

Likewise when we stand before God, we will not be judged by the code of morality we have written for ourselves but by God's perfect law.[12]

(4). His *Acceptance* demands perfection (Mt. 5:20, 48/Gal. 3:10b).

In his book *(Re)union*, Bruxy Cavey asks the question:

How much sin do you think it would be wise for God to let into heaven? What would be the acceptable level of sin for God to allow into the realm of eternal life? Should God allow 5 percent? Maybe 0.5 percent? Would 0.05 percent be okay?

The answer to that question has to be zero. When Olympic athletes are tested for performance-enhancing drugs, they fail the blood test if they have even a trace of these drugs. Their blood is either clean or not clean. The standard for passing is 0 percent of banned substances. They can't protest, "But I only have traces of the banned substances, so obviously I don't use

---

[12] Citation: Craig Brian Larson, Choice Contemporary Stories and Illustrations (Baker, 1998), p. 181; Brian Burrell, Words We Live By (S&S Trade, 1997)

them too much." The standard is perfection.

When someone wants to donate blood, the blood bank must ensure that the donor's blood is completely free from various things, like HIV. The person cannot protest, "But my blood is *mostly* HIV-free, and certainly I'm not doing as bad as some people who have full-blown AIDS, so what's the problem?" The standard has to be absolute purity, and for good reason.

The same is true for our relationship with God. God's standard for heaven must be sinless perfection, just as Adam and Eve were when they were first created. Just being a *comparatively* good person is not good enough. If God were to let us all into the eternal dimension with sin still a part of our spiritual makeup, we would pollute the realm of heaven, starting the whole mess of planet Earth all over again. So God bans sin from heaven. He quarantines the infection and the infected to a different realm. Hell is God's quarantine solution for people who prefer to hold on to their sin rather than accepting Christ's cleansing.[13]

A holy God and sinful man are not compatible. Think of it this way. Say God lived in the bottom of the ocean. Since I cannot breathe under water, I cannot get into God's realm. I would drown before I could get very far in my journey to Him. A very imperfect illustration, but perhaps you get what I am trying to say.

God is not only holy but demands holiness from others. I do not mind the fact that you fall short of the glory of God because I can identify. I have known a few people who really think they have reached perfection and frankly, I avoid them! Not God! You must have perfection to come into His holy presence.

Holy, Holy, Holy! God is Perfectly Holy.

[3] And one called out to another and said, "Holy, Holy, Holy, is the LORD of hosts, The whole earth is full of His glory." Isaiah 6:3

---

[13] Bruxy Cavey, (Re)union (Herald Press, 2017), pages 104-105.

There is a splendid moment in the movie *Jurassic Park,* when world-class paleontologist Allen Grant, who has devoted his life to the study of dinosaurs, suddenly comes face-to-face with real, live prehistoric creatures. He falls to the ground, dumbstruck. The reason is obvious. It is one thing to piece together an informed but nonetheless imperfect image of dinosaurs by picking through fossils and bones. But to encounter an actual dinosaur—well, there can be no comparison.

William Hendricks in an interview notes:

For many people, spirituality amounts to picking through the artifacts of faith that survive from long ago and far away. In that bygone era, humans saw God, heard His voice, and experienced his awesome, at times terrible, power. But that was then. Today, those kinds of gripping encounters with God—with a God who wasn't an illusion, but Someone who was real, Someone you could see, and touch, and feel—well, there could be no comparison.[14]

Such an encounter takes place when the Holy Spirit drives home to our hearts that God is holy.

2. Just as He is.

Thomas Jefferson warned us, "I tremble for my country when I reflect that God is just."[15]

We love to sing the song *Just as I Am,* but God is Just as He is also. He is Just! It is close to the idea of righteousness, in fact the same Hebrew word forms the basis for both the English words, "Justice" and "Righteousness."

a. It is *Intrinsical.*

Meaning that it is a part of who God is, He does not try to be just, rather He is just by His very nature. Gen. 18:25/Heb. 12:23).

Tozer notes:

We can define the word attribute as... simply whatever may be correctly

---

[14] William D. Hendricks, Exit Interviews (Chicago: Moody, 1993).
[15] Reagan, Ronald. QUOTABLE REAGAN: An A-Z Collector's Edition of Quotations (Kindle Location 1866). Quotable Wisdom Books. Kindle Edition.

ascribed to God [as it has been revealed to us by God]..."[16]

Louis Berkhof notes:

They may be defined as the perfections which are predicated of the Divine Being in Scripture, or are visibly exercised by Him in His works of creation, providence, and redemption.[17]

We must also note there is never a conflict with God in who He is: Erickson notes:

If we begin with the assumptions that God is an integrated being and the divine attributes are harmonious, we will define the attributes in the light of one another. Thus, justice is loving justice and love is love that is just... What we are saying is that love is not fully understood unless seen as including justice. Otherwise, it is mere sentimentality.[18]

---

[16] Tozer, A.W.. The Knowledge of the Holy (p. 12). Fig. Kindle Edition.
[17] Berkhof, Louis. Systematic Theology (Kindle Locations 822-824). E4 Group. Kindle Edition.
[18] Erickson, Millard J.. Christian Theology (p. 267). Baker Publishing Group. Kindle Edition.

It is so wonderful to know that God is just, not according to circumstances or outside influences but according to His nature.

On the fourteenth day of April, 1865, President Lincoln was assassinated. The following morning, placards were pasted up in New York, Brooklyn, and Jersey City, calling upon loyal citizens to meet around Wall Street Exchange at eleven o'clock. Thousands came, armed with revolvers and knives, ready to avenge the death of the martyred President. General James A. Garfield, the future President of the United States, stepped forward and beckoned to the excited throng. Lifting his right arm toward heaven, in a clear, distinct, steady, ponderous voice, that the multitude could hear, the speaker said:

Fellow citizens: Clouds and darkness are round about Him! His pavilion is dark waters and thick clouds of the skies! Justice and judgment are the habitation of His throne! Mercy and truth shall go before His face! Fellow citizens; God reigns, and the Government at Washington still lives!

The effect of contemplation of God's ultimate sovereign judgment was amazing. One man wrote:

As the boiling wave subsides and settles to the sea when some strong wind beats it down, so the tumult of the people sank and became still. As the rod draws the electricity from the air, and conducts it safely to the ground, so this man had drawn the fury from that frantic crowd, and guided it to more tranquil thoughts than vengeance.[19]

b. It is *Incomparable*. Job 4:17/Neh. 9:33

Man's justice, cannot be compared to God's because no man has all of the facts about any situation including things like motives.

For the first three weeks of the 2012 NFL season, replacement referees took the place on the playing field of the regular refs. The team owners had locked out the regular refs because they

---

[19] William M. Thayer, From Log-Cabin to White House: The Story of President Garfield's Life (London: Hodder and Stoughton, 1881), 337-9.

could not agree on a new contract. The consequence of using college referees to judge pro games was predictable. The replacement refs missed calls, took too long to make the right calls, called too many fouls, and in the process made coaches, players, and fans furious.

The anger came to a head in the third week of the season. An angry Bill Belichick, coach of the New England Patriots, grabbed one of the replacement refs, and was fined $50 thousand by the league. And on Monday Night Football the game between the Green Bay Packers and Seattle Seahawks was decided by a call on the last play of the game that was so clearly wrong the whole country was talking about it the next day. The media pointed out that because of the missed call, 150 million dollars changed hands in Las Vegas.

Confidence in the credibility of the game had been marred. Players didn't know what to expect on the field and worried about injuries. Newspapers routinely used the word "outrage" to describe the reaction from millions of fans. ESPN declared, "Let's cut to the chase—the replacement officials have lost control of the game." Even an NPR (National Public Radio) blog chimed in: "It's the talk of the nation today as fans beg for the league and its regular officials to settle their differences so that the 'real' refs can come back."

The truth is the only one who can rightly judge the universe is God Himself. The rest of us are like those replacement referees, we lack all the facts to judge correctly. But God, who is omniscient, does not.

c. It is *Impartial.* Rom. 2:11/Col. 3:25/1 Pet. 1:17

It means that everybody is going to get what they deserve based on God's infinite understanding of what we really are and what we have done. He never plays favorites! Joseph Stowell notes:

Our evangelical culture tends to take the awesome reality of a transcendent God who is worthy to be feared and downsize Him so He could fit into our "buddy system." The way we talk about Him, the way we pray, and, more strikingly, the way we live shows that we have somehow lost our sense of being appropriately awestruck in the presence of a holy and all-powerful God. It's been a long time since we've heard a good sermon on the "fear of God." If God were to show up visibly, many of us think we'd run up to Him and high-five Him for the good things He has done.[20]

God does not have his little buddies who He turns a blind eye to their sins because they are his pet students.

d. It is *incorruptible*. Dt. 32:4; 10:17/2 Chron. 19:7/Job 34:12/Zeph. 3:5.

I was watching Gunslingers the other day, and they had an episode on Deacon Jim Miller – The Pious Assassin. He was given that nickname because he regularly attended the Methodist Church, and he did not smoke or drink – but he ruthlessly killed about 12 men. He was a paid assassin. He was, by the way, born in Van Buren Arkansas. When he was 8 years old he murdered his grandparents but was not prosecuted

---

[20] Joseph M. Stowell in *Moody* (Nov./Dec. 1997). *Christianity Today*, Vol. 42, no. 2.

for the crime. He later left a church service, went and shot his brother-in-law, and rode back to the church service! He was arrested, but got off on a technicality. Later he became a deputy sheriff as a cover for his murders. He was arrested time and time again but always got off by either buying the jury, or threatening them, or it ending in a hung jury.

God is not like that! He cannot be bribed or threatened but will always administer fair justice.

By the way, Deacon Jim Miller was arrested for murdering former Deputy U.S. Marshal Allen Augustus "Gus" Bobbitt of Ada, Oklahoma. He was calmly sitting in jail knowing that he had bribed the jury and would soon be free. A mob, estimated from 30 to 40 in number, broke into the jail and dragged them to an abandoned livery stable behind the jail and hung them all.[21]

---

[21] wikipedia.org/wiki/JimMiller(outlaw).

God's justice always prevails in the end, both in time and eternity. Which brings me to my next point.

e. It means that judgment is *Inevitable*. Ac. 17:31/Rom. 2:4-6/Rev. 16:5-7.

The modern judge can only pronounce the sentence; he does not actually carry out the sentence. But God, not only passes out the sentence, but is His own executioner.

Hal Lindsey in Liberation of Planet Earth says it well:

God is absolutely just. It's impossible for Him to do anything that's unfair either to Himself or to man. He executes perfect justice in accordance with His attributes of righteousness. All that is unrighteous must be judged and separated from a relationship with Him (Rom. 1:18/Deut. 32:4/Isa. 45:21).

As Leon Morris has written: The doctrine of final judgment. . . stresses man's accountability and the certainty that justice will finally triumph over all the wrongs which are part and parcel of life here and now. The former gives a dignity to the humblest action, the latter brings calmness and assurance to those in the thick of the battle. This doctrine gives meaning to life. . . The Christian view of judgment means that history moves to a goal. . . Judgment protects the idea of the triumph of God and of good. It is unthinkable that the present conflict between good and evil should last throughout eternity. Judgment means that evil will be disposed of authoritatively, decisively, finally. Judgment means that in the end God's will will be perfectly done.[22]

A man in Chester, England fought with his estranged wife and killed her because she threatened to expose his homosexuality unless he gave her more money, something he said he could not afford to do. He hid her body on the edge of a peat bog. Twenty-two years later when he heard that some peat diggers unearthed a skull he assumed it was hers so he confessed. Tests showed that the skull was 1,600 years old, that of a woman who died before the Romans left Britain. The authorities

---

[22] The Biblical Doctrine of Judgment, p. 72.

have not been able to find any of the remains of his wife. Now he faces murder charges."[23]

Although this man imagined that he had covered up his crime, God's justice may be slow but it is sure.

f. It is often *Imperceptible.* Psa. 73:4/Lu. 18:7-8

Justice in this life doesn't always seem to prevail, many like O. J. Simpson have gotten away with murder. Or so it would seem, but in reality there is an accounting someday.

Then we also see how many seemingly godly people suffer while often the ungodly do not have a care in the world.

Randy Alcorn shares the following in his book If God is Good:

More people point to the problem of evil and suffering as their reason for not believing in God than any other—it is not merely *a* problem, it is *the* problem. A Barna poll asked, "If you could ask God only one question and you knew he

---

[23] Norwich Bulletin, Norwich, CT 01/08/84.

would give you an answer, what would you ask?" The most common response was, "Why is there pain and suffering in the world?"

Erickson noted, "God's justice must not be evaluated on a short-term basis. Within this life it will often be incomplete or imperfect, but there is a life beyond, in which God's justice will be complete."[24]

Before his appointment as a Supreme Court Justice, Horace Gray once presided over a case where a man was justly charged. Through a technicality, Gray was obligated to release him, but as he did so he addressed him, saying, "I believe you are guilty and would wish to condemn you severely, but through a petty technicality, I am obliged to discharge you. I know you are guilty, and so do you, and I wish you to remember that one day you will pass before a better and wiser Judge, when you will be dealt with according to justice and not according to law." [25]

---

[24] Erickson, Millard J.. Christian Theology (p. 260). Baker Publishing Group. Kindle Edition.

Richard Swinburne, writing in the *Oxford Companion to Philosophy*, says the problem of evil is "the most powerful objection to traditional theism." Ronald Nash writes, "Objections to theism come and go... But every philosopher I know believes that the most serious challenge to theism was, is, and will continue to be the problem of evil."

You will not get far in a conversation with someone who rejects the Christian faith before the problem of evil is raised. Pulled out like the ultimate trump card, it's supposed to silence believers and prove that the all-good and all-powerful God of the Bible doesn't exist.

What people fail to see is the problem of evil and suffering all began with man's sin! The problem God has, humanly speaking, is that He is just and must justly separate Himself from fallen mankind.

Con:

---

[25] L. Nye, Anecdotes on Bible Texts, The Epistles of Paul the Apostle to the Corinthians and the Galatians (London: Sunday School Union, 1882), 22.

The Wall Street Journal reported a story about how fake news stories and photos can have a powerful impact on shaping our minds and hearts.

The story quoted Randi Romo, a female photographer whose photograph at an immigration rally had been manipulated by a Russia-backed account. The fake photo conveyed an anti-immigration message while the original photo clearly conveyed a pro-immigration message. Ms. Romo had a powerful warning for all of us:

"We are living in the greatest era of information access. People will watch cat videos endlessly, but they won't take a minute to ascertain whether what they are being told is true or not."[26]

One fake new story has been out there for many years, it is that God's only attribute is love, and that He is too kind to judge anybody and that when all the dust settles He will embrace everyone with His saving love.

---

[26] Georgia Wells, "The Big Loophole That Helped Russia Exploit Facebook: Doctored Photos," The Wall Street Journal (2-22-18).

3. I Love to tell the *whole* Story.

"Jellyfish Lake, based on the Pacific island of Palau, was once connected to the Pacific Ocean. But when the sea level dropped, jellyfish became isolated in the algae rich lake and eventually lost their sting."[27]

I think we have a generation with a stingless jellyfish God mentality. Words like Holiness, righteousness, justice, and wrath have been phased out and replaced with a passive, permissive, and pathetic god. But the truth is God is Holy, Just, and wrathful and is unchangeably so.

Most love to tell the story of God's love and we should tell it, but that is not the whole story. That story includes the wrath of God. And very few love to tell that story today! God is not embarrassed by His wrath, it is a just expression of His displeasure with sin.

Arthur Pink in his book the Attributes of God says it well:

---

[27] Caters News Agency via Yahoo News, 2/28/12.

Now the wrath of God is as much a divine perfection as is His faithfulness, power, or mercy. It must be so, for there is no blemish whatever, not the slightest defect in the character of God; yet there would be if "wrath" were absent from Him!... How could He who is the Sum of all excellency look with equal satisfaction upon virtue and vice, wisdom and folly? How could He who is infinitely holy disregard sin and refuse to manifest His "severity" (Rom 11:22) toward it? How could He, who delights only in that which is pure and lovely, not loathe and hate that which is impure and vile? The very nature of God makes Hell as real a necessity, as imperatively and eternally requisite, as Heaven is.[28]

On July 8, 1741, Jonathan Edwards preached the most famous sermon "Sinners in the Hands of an Angry God." It is rare to hear such sermons anymore. Here is an excerpt from his message:

---

[28] Pink, Arthur W.. The Attributes of God (p. 83). . Kindle Edition.

Your wickedness makes you as it were heavy as lead, and to tend downwards with great weight and pressure towards hell; and if God should let you go, you would immediately sink and swiftly descend and plunge into the bottomless gulf, and your healthy constitution, and your own care and prudence, and best contrivance, and all your righteousness, would have no more influence to uphold you and keep you out of hell, than a spider's web would have to stop a falling rock. . . . There are the black clouds of God's wrath now hanging directly over your heads, full of the dreadful storm, and big with thunder; and were it not for the restraining hand of God, it would immediately burst forth upon you. The sovereign pleasure of God, for the present, stays his rough wind; otherwise it would come with fury, and your destruction would come like a whirlwind, and you would be like the chaff of the summer threshing floor.[29]

Why does this generation make so light of God's wrath, is it not because we

---

[29] Phillipsburg, N.J.: Presbyterian and Reformed Publishing, 1992], pp. 20-21).

make so light of man's sin? R. A. Torrey writes:

> Shallow views of sin and of God's holiness, and of the glory of Jesus Christ and His claims upon us, lie at the bottom of weak theories of the doom of the impenitent. When we see sin in all its hideousness and enormity, the holiness of God in all its perfection, and the glory of Jesus Christ in all its infinity, nothing but a doctrine that those who persist in the choice of sin, who love darkness rather than light, and who persist in the rejection of the Son of God, shall endure everlasting anguish, will satisfy the demands of our own moral intuitions. . . . The more closely men walk with God and the more devoted they become to His service, the more likely they are to believe this doctrine.[30]

When we no longer see that our sin separates us from a holy, just, and wrathful God we are living in a dangerous bubble of lies that is one day going to burst. Ted Koppel noted:

---

[30] (What the Bible Teaches [New York: Revell, 1898], pp. 311-313).

What is largely missing in American life today is a sense of context, of saying or doing anything that is intended or even expected to live beyond the moment. There is no culture in the world that is so obsessed as ours with immediacy. In our journalism, the trivial displaces the momentous because we tend to measure the importance of events by how recently they happened. We have become so obsessed with facts that we have lost all touch with truth.[31]

Now, God says if you violate my holiness and justice, you will inevitably experience my wrath. It doesn't matter who agrees or disagrees, it is an undeniable truth.

Dorothy Sayers, the mystery writer, was also a devoted Christian. Dorothy Sayers was attempting to explain the moral law of God. She pointed out that in our society there are two kinds of laws. There is the law of the stop sign, and there's the law of the fire. The law of the stop sign is a law that says the

---

[31] Ted Koppel in a speech to the International Radio and Television Society, quoted in *Harper's* (Jan. 1986). *Christianity Today*, Vol. 32, no. 8.

traffic is heavy on a certain street, and as a result the police department or the city council decides to erect a stop sign. They also decide that if you run that stop sign, it will cost you $25 or $30 or $35. If the traffic changes, they can up the ante. That is if too many people are running the stop sign, they can make the fine $50 or $75, or if they build a highway around the city, they can take the stop sign down, or reduce the penalty, making it only $10 if you go through. The police department or city council controls the law of the stop sign.

But then she said there is also the law of the fire. And the law of the fire says if you put your hand in the fire, you'll get burned. Now imagine that all of the legislatures of all the nations of the entire world gathered in one great assembly, and they voted unanimously that here on out that fire would no longer burn. The first man or woman who left that assembly and put his or her hand in the fire would discover that the law of the fire is different than the law of the stop sign. Bound up in the nature of fire itself is the penalty for abusing it. So, Dorothy Sayers says, the moral law of God is like the law of the fire. You never break God's laws; you just break yourself on them. God can't reduce the penalty, because the penalty for breaking the law is bound up in the law itself.[32]

See, Mt.3:7/Mk.3:5/Lk.3:7 ; 21:23; Jn.3:36/Ro.1:18 ; 2:5, 8; 3:5; 4:15; 5:9 ; 9:22 ; 12:19; 13:4,5/Eph.2:3 ; 4:31;5:6/ Col.3:6, 8/ 1 Th.1:10; 2:16; 5:9/1Ti. 2:8 ; Heb.3:11 ; 4:3 ; Jam. 1:19-20/Rev.6:16, 17; 11:18; 14:10; 16:19; 19:15.

A Doctrine is all that the Scriptures has to say about any given subject arranged logically. I try to put things in a way that is easy to remember. Here is a survey of Wrath:

- God's wrath is an *Outflow* of His violated Holiness and justice (Rom. 2:8; 3:5-6/Rev. 16:6-7). The flow of God's Holiness is violated which kicks His justice into action, which is the release of His wrath.

[32] Haddon Robinson, "Crafting Illustrations," PreachingToday.com

- Therefore God's wrath against the *Sinful* (Psa. 7:11; 21:8-9/Isa. 3:8; 13:9/Rom. 1:18/Eph. 5:6/Col. 3:6). The greatest sin is unbelief (Jn. 3:36).

- God's wrath is *Merciful* (Psa. 103:8/Isa. 48:9/Jon. 4:2/Nah. 1:3). Why slow? To give people an opportunity to repent. A Fortaste now (Jn. 3:36/Rom. 1:18), not fulfilled until a Future Day (Zeph. 2:2/Rom.2:5/Rev. 6:17; 11:18; 19:15).

- God's wrath is *Awful* (Psa. 78:49-51; 90:7/Jer. 7:20; 10:10/Lam. 2:20-22/Mt. 10:28/Rev. 6-19).

- A *Photo* of God's wrath: The Flood (Gen. 7:21-23); Tower of Babel (Gen. 11:8); Sodom and Gomorrah (Gen. 19:24-25); On the Egyptians in the Ten Plagues (Ex. 7:20; 8:6, 16, 24; 9:3, 9, 23; 10:13, 22; 12:29; 14:27); Great Tribulation Period (Rev. 6-19).

- God's wrath is *Final* – no appeals! (Mt. 18:8; 25:41/Jude 7/ 2 Thess. 1:9/Rev. 14:10-11; 19:3).

Flamingo Flats, a spicy sauce company located in St. Michaels, MD, wants to spice up your life. It claims as its motto, "Life is too short to eat boring food" and boasts such culinary condiments as "Sting and Linger," "Dave's Insanity Sauce," and "Hell in a Jar." According to CHILI PEPPER MAGAZINE, Flamingo's bestselling sauce at one time was "Religious Experience," which came in Original, Hot, and WRATH.[33]

But the "Religious Experience" is no longer available, I have a feeling the Wrath part was unacceptable to most folks. People today only want a religious experience with a God of love but the whole truth is that God is not only love but light as well.

Note: God never changes, He is eternally Holy, Just, and wrathful (Mal. 3:6/Heb. 1:10-12; 13:8/Jam. 1:17).

---

[33] Flamingo Flats and Chili Pepper Magazine.

God is infinitely, eternally holy, just, wrathful and much more, and will remain so. He is what we call immutable.

A. W. Tozer in his fine book The Knowledge of the Holy writes:

For a moral being to change it would be necessary that the change be in one of three directions. He must go from better to worse or from worse to better; or, granted that the moral quality remain stable, he must change within himself, as from miniature to mature or from one order of being to another. It should be clear that God can move in none of these directions. His perfections forever rule out any such possibility. God cannot change for the better. Since He is perfectly holy, He has never been less holy than He is now and can never be holier than He is and has always been. Neither can God change for the worse. Any deterioration within the unspeakably holy nature of God is impossible.[34]

---

[34] Tozer, A.W.. The Knowledge of the Holy (p. 49). Fig. Kindle Edition.

Again, we think if we declare that God is flexible that declaration makes it so.

In his book Jesus Mean and Wild, Mark Galli references his interview with Stephen Prothero in 1994. During that interview, Prothero said:

Christians traditionally, as they've shaped Jesus, have been worried about getting it wrong, including the Puritans. Americans today are not so worried. There isn't the sense that this is a life-and-death matter, that you don't want to mess with divinity. There's a freedom and even a playfulness that Americans have...The flexibility our Jesus exhibits is unprecedented. There's a Gumby-like quality to Jesus in the United States...that kind of chutzpah is something that was unknown even to Americans in the Colonial period.[35]

I would call it dangerous stupidity myself, and it does not change God in the least.

---

[35] Mark Galli, Jesus Mean and Wild (Baker, 2006), p. 16.

I read that they are trying to develop a stingless bee. One Canadian scientist warns:

Such a seemingly desirable little creature would immediately become the helpless prey of every kind of bug. The ant, wasp, moth, and other honey-consuming insects would overrun the hives, and the bear, the skunk and the human robber would feast unmolested on the treasure therein stored.

Our sick and twisted generation has sought to produce a stingless God! One, who at best, is helplessly shrugging his shoulders at our sin. But do not be deceived, God is a holy, righteous, just and wrathful God who for those who reject the Lord Jesus Christ's love, manifested in His death, burial, and resurrection, will one day feel His painful and eternal sting. That need not happen to you, and I pray it will not happen to you. If you put your hand into a fire you will get burned – every time. And if you violated God's holiness, God's justice will release His wrath. There is only one hope. I have heard about a fire proximity suit, it is designed to protect a firefighter from high temperatures. There is only one fire-proof suit when we think of the wrath of God – being in Christ! More about this later.

B. God's *Creation*.

Intro:

1. Keith Hunt in his book, "Is There Life in Outer Space?" writes:

Despite popular and influential science fiction books and films as *Star Wars, E.T., Star Trek, 2001, A Space Odyssey* and *Close Encounters of the Third Kind,* there really is no scientific evidence for intelligent extraterres-life. Hundreds of millions of tax dollars have been spent trying to find life in outer space... A few people are searching for signals from outer space that would imply an intelligent source. Radio telescopes, linked with computers, simultaneously search millions of radio frequencies for a nonrandom, nonnatural, extraterrestrial signals—any short sequence of information.

2. The truth is, there is life in Outer Space, and the Bible refers to these spirit beings as angels.

3. God's Creation.

Trans: We have looked at God's Perfection and now we see that God decided to create, and first on his list were angels.

1. The *Inception* of *spirit* beings. [This series is not a study of angels, so we do not want to get bogged down here]

a. They were *Created*.

- **Agent** who created them is God (Neh. 9:6/Psa. 148:2-5/Jn. 1:1-3/Col. 1:16/Heb. 1:7/etc.).

- **Act** of their creation. We do not know the exact time but it was *before* the creation of the physical universe (Job 38:4-7). The term "sons of God" in Job is a reference to angels in the Old Testament (Job 1:6; 2:1). Notice "all" indicating that at the time God created the universe all of the angels were in harmony, there was no sin at that time.

- **Assumptions.** They were created ***instantaneously* and *simultaneously.*** They are not a race but called a host; they are ***innumerable*** or too many to count (Heb. 12:22/Psa. 68:17/Jude 14/ Rev. 5:11/etc.); they are ***indestructible***, they never die (Lu. 20:36); are ***incapable*** of reproduction (Mt. 22:30); they were all ***initially*** created good and holy (Job 38:4-7), yet it is a creaturely holiness (Job 4:18; 15:15); they were created with ***incredible*** power (Psa. 103/2 Thess. 1:7/2 Pet. 2:10-11/Rev. 4:8, 11; 10:1-11/etc.); and are obviously ***inferior*** to God. They are limited by space while God is omnipresent (Dan. 9:21-23). They are limited in their power while God is Omnipotent (Job 1:12; 2:6/Dan, 10:10-14). They are limited in their understanding while God is omniscient (Mt. 24:36/1 Pet. 1:11-12). They were created

in the image of God meaning that they have personality – will or self-determination, intellect, emotion, moral reasoning power or conscience, and eternity of being.

b. Their *Characteristics.*

- They are *Persons*, as we have already pointed out, created ***in the image of God*** meaning that they have personality – will or self-determination (Jude 6), intellect Eph. 3:10/1 Pet. 1:12), emotion (Lu. 2:13; 15:10), moral reasoning power or conscience, and eternity of being (Lu. 20:36), they, like human beings, have a beginning but no end.

- The *Place* where they abide. There are three heavens (2 Cor. 12:2) and angels apparently can relate to all three places, while their abode is in the third heaven (Isa. 6:1-6/Mt. 18:10; 24:36/Mk. 12:25/Lu. 22:43/Gal. 1:8/2 Thess. 1:7).

- Their *Posture*. They are spirit beings (Heb. 1:14) thus they are invisible but real; immaterial and yet have some form (1 Cor. 15:38-40). They can become visible and take on physical form (Gen. 18:1-2, 16, 22; 19:1/Mk. 16:5/Ac. 1:10-11) and weird symbolic forms (Ezk. 1:4-14; 10:15, 20/ Isa. 6:1/Rev. 4:6-8). At times it appears that something can happen to human beings allowing them to penetrate into their dimension (Num. 22:3/2 Ki. 6:17).

c. Their *Classification*.

- *Descriptions* are many such as elect angels (1 Tim. 5:21); ministers (Heb. 1:14); host (Psa. 103:20-21); chariots (2 Ki. 6:16-17/Psa. 68:17); watchers (Dan. 4:13, 17/Isa. 62:6); sons of the Mighty (Psa. 29:1; 89:6); sons of God (Job 1:6; 2:1; 38:7); holy ones (Psa. 89:5-7/Job 5:1; 15:15/Dan. 4:13-17; 8:13); stars (Job 38:7/Rev. 13:4); principalities and powers(Eph. 1:21; 3:10; 6:12); etc.

- *Designations* include Cherub (Gen. 3:24/Ex. 25:18, 19/2 Sam. 22:11/Psa. 18:10/Ezk. 1:1, 28/etc.); Seraphim (Isa. 6:1-6); Living Creatures (Rev. 4:5-9); and Archangels (1 Thess. 4:15/Jude 9/Dan. 10:13). Three angels are named, Lucifer (Isa. 14:12); Michael (Dan. 10:13, 21; 12:1/Jude 9/Rev. 12:7); and Gabriel (Dan. 8:16; 9:21/Lu. 1:19, 26).

Trans: We cannot believe the Bible and reject the existence of angels. Angels are mentioned in thirty-four books of the Bible for a total of some 273 times (108 times in the Old Testament and 165 in the New Testament).

Charles Herbert Lightoller was tall, sun-bronzed, and handsome, possessing a deep, pleasant speaking voice. His mother died during his infancy, his father abandoned him, and he ran off to sea at the age of thirteen. By 1912, he was a respected seaman for the White Star Line and was assigned to the maiden voyage of the greatest ocean liner ever built, the *Titanic.* He was just drifting off to sleep on April 14th, when he felt a bump in the ship's forward motion.

Hopping from his bunk, he soon learned that the *Titanic* had struck an iceberg. As the horrors of that night unfolded, Lightoller finally found himself standing on the roof of the officer's quarters, the water lapping at his feet, as he helped any and all around him into lifeboats. Finally, there was nothing left for Lightoller to do but jump from the roof into the freezing waters of the North Atlantic. The shock of the 28-degree water against his sweating body stunned him. As he struggled to regain his bearing and swim away from the ship, he was suddenly sucked back and pinned against a ventilation grate at the base of a funnel that went all the way down to Boiler Room 6. He was stuck, drowning, and going down with the ship.

Suddenly Psa. 91:11 came clearly to his mind: For He shall give His angels charge over you, To keep you in all your ways.... At that very moment, a blast of hot air exploded from the belly of the ship, shooting Lightoller like a missile to the surface of the ocean. At length, he managed to grab a piece of rope attached to the side of an overturned lifeboat and float along with it until he pulled himself on top of the upside-down boat. He turned and watched the last moments of the Titanic. Her stern swung up in the air until the ship was in "an absolutely perpendicular position." Then she slowly sank down into the water, with only a small gulp as her stern disappeared beneath the waves. There were about thirty men atop the lifeboat, and together they recited the Lord's Prayer, then Lightoller took command of the boat and guided them to safety.

There are many testimonies of people who have experienced the ministry of angels.

The problem is that there are also demons, and many today call these demons – angels. They have rejected God and His Word, and, so, have a Satanic concept of angels.

One example is Geddes MacGregor, he was a professor of philosophy at the University of Southern California. His book *Angels: Ministers of Grace* advances the idea that angels are a super-race of evolved extraterrestrials. He bases his view on his belief in evolution. He also believes that life exists on other planets, and that extraterrestrial spirits communicate with us as angels.[36]

He does not know it, but he is trafficking with demons!

The main thing is we need to get our information from the Bible not the nut jobs of this world. Juliana Dukes, worked for the Pfizer U.S. Pharmaceutical Group. She found a stray and starving dog far out in the hills of New Mexico. She found the dog's owner by calling the number on his collar tag. The owners explained that the dog had run off two weeks earlier while they were vacationing in New Mexico. Juliana said she had learned a number of lessons from the experience. One was how important name tags were and most importantly that angels come from within us![37]

---

[36] Garrett, Angels and the New Age Spirituality, 100-101.

2. *Introduction* of *sin* into the universe.

a. The *Problem* of sin related to angels. It was angels, not Adam, that introduced sin into the universe.

(1) The Presupposition that Ezk. 28:11-19 and Isa. 14:12-23 refer to an angel named Lucifer, who because of his sin, is now, referred to as Satan.

- The *Reason* for this understanding is the change from "prince" of Tyre being changed to "king" of Tyre, this king is the one behind the earthly prince (Ezk. 28:12); while vv. 1-10 describe a human leader, vv. 11-19 go beyond a mere human being. It goes from a "man" (vv. 2, 9) to a cherub (vv. 14, 16); all of this fits well with what we know about Satan's sin (Ezk. 28:17 with 1 Tim. 3:6 and Isa. 14:13, 14).

- The *Recognition* by good Bible teachers. This not some wild speculation but is taught by such Bible teachers as Hal Lindsey, Josh

---

[37] Albuquerque Journal, 24 November 1996.

McDowell, Charles Ryrie, Richard DeHaan, Dwight Pentecost, Lewis Chafer, Donald Barnhouse, C. S. Lewis, Scofield, W. A. Criswell, just to name a few.

(2) The *Passages*:

(a) Ezk. 28:11-19.

Ezekiel prophesized in the sixth century B.C. He was taken captive by Nebuchadnezzar to Babylon where he prophesied to the Jews who were exiles in Babylon for some 22 years.

Ezekiel chaps 1-24 were written before Jerusalem fell to the Babylonians.

Ezekiel chaps 25-32 are prophecies against a number of foreign nations.

Ezekiel chaps 33-39 are prophecies about Israel's restoration.

Ezekiel chaps 40-48 are prophecies about the future Millennial kingdom.

So the passage we are focusing on speaks of the fall of Tyre. Obviously 28:1-10 is talking about the human leader of Tyre, Ethbaal III, who was the ruler over the Phoenician seacoast city of Tyre. He is called a "man" in vv. 2, 9. He was arrogant, but still a mere man!

But then the focus shifts to Satan, the supernatural one behind this human leader in 28:11-19. The description given in these verse go beyond any mere human leader. He is called a Cherub in vv. 14, 16. But Cherub is a class of angel created by God (28:13,15). Ezekiel saw a vision of "four living beings (1:5) which he identified as cherubim (10:5, 9).

- Lucifer's *Privileges*. His **Position** of great authority is seen in the fact that he is called "anointed" speaking of God's favor; a "Cherub" which is the highest order of angels; "who covers" or overshadows, having the idea of leading; and "I place you there" means it was God Himself that gave him this high position (Ezk. 28:14, 16). He apparently lead the other angels in worship of God. His **Place** was in the very presence of God as indicated by "in Eden, the garden of God"; "on the holy mountain of God"; "midst of fiery stones" (Ezk. 28:13, 14, 16). His **Perfection** as seen in the descriptions "seal of perfection"; "full of wisdom"; "perfect in beauty" "tumbrels and pipes"; and "perfect in all your ways from the day you were created." (Ezk. 28:12, 15).

This was a remarkable creature to say the least!

Billy Graham notes, "Lucifer before he sinned was the most brilliant and most beautiful of all created beings in heaven. He was probably the ruling prince of the universe under God...Prior to his rebellion, Lucifer, an angel of light, is described in scintillating terms."

- Lucifers **Pride**. "*unrighteousness was found in you*"; "*were internally filled with violence*"; "*you sinned*"; "*Your heart was lifted up*." This is where sin first began!
  His **Pink slip.** God responded by "casting" him out of his position (16, 17). He still has access to

God's presence (Job 1:6, 9; 2:1,7; Rev. 12:10).

His **Prophetic** future. In the future, in the middle of the Great Tribulation, he will be restricted to the earth where he continues his evil work (Rev. 12:7-13). When Christ returns to set up His earthly kingdom at that time Satan will be confined to the abyss (20:1-3). At the end of this thousand year reign, Satan will be loosed for a short time, then cast again permanently to the lake of fire (20:10).

(b) Isa. 14:12-19

Isaiah wrote in the eighth century before Christ. At that time, the enemy of Israel was the Assyrians. He predicted that the Babylonians would defeat Assyria and take Judah into captivity. But God would eventually judge Babylon as well.

Isaiah 14 is a taunt against Babylon and her king (vv. 4, 22). It is clear that the historic king of Babylon is the focus of 14:1-11. But beginning with verse 12, he pulls back the curtain and reveals who is behind this Babylonian king – it is Satan.

- His **Description.** O star of the morning, son of the dawn! "Lucifer" is the Latin form of "Day-Star," meaning "light-bearer" or "shining one."
  His **Downfall.** 12 "How you have fallen from heaven... You have been cut down to the earth, You who have weakened the nations! Perhaps our Lord referred to this in Luke 10:17-18?
  His **Desire.** 13 "But you said in your heart, *'I will* ascend to heaven; *I will* raise my throne above the stars of God, And *I will* sit on the mount of assembly In the recesses of the north. 14 *'I will* ascend above the heights of the clouds; *I will* make myself like the Most High.' Five times he is said to choose his will. The essence of all sin is choosing our will over God's. These "I will's" reveal his pride in which he wants to be the sole ruler of heaven, over both God and the

angels (1 Tim. 3:6).

His **Doom.** *15 Yet you shall be brought down to Sheol, To the lowest depths of the Pit. 16 "Those who see you will gaze at you, They will ponder over you, saying, 'Is this the man who made the earth tremble, Who shook kingdoms, 17 Who made the world like a wilderness And overthrew its cities, Who did not allow his prisoners to go home?' 18 "All the kings of the nations lie in glory, Each in his own tomb. 19 "But you have been cast out of your tomb Like a rejected branch, Clothed with the slain who are pierced with a sword, Who go down to the stones of the pit Like a trampled corpse.* He will ultimately be thrust down to Sheol (Rev. 20:3) and spend eternity in the lake of fire (Rev. 20:10).

So sin, is not the creation of God, nor did it begin with man, but sin entered the universe through this angelic being, Lucifer. Sin, can be defined as, any lack of measuring up to the standard of God, in nature, thought, word or deed.

(3) The *Persuasion* related to other angels.

- *Possible Theory* is that after Lucifer rebelled against God he persuaded some of the other angels to follow him in his rebellion against God. Why? Perhaps he thought he could get enough angels on his side to overpower God? Or maybe get them to go along with his scheme to replace God? We are not told exactly what happened.

- *Proof Texts* can be given to prove that some of the angels did join him and are today called demons (Job 4:18/Mt. 25:41/Rev. 12:1-6/etc.).

Again, when we leave the Bible out of the picture, Satan and his demons, come off as an angel of light and deceive people. They use much of the same language we do, but the meaning is not the same.

For example in the book *Ask Your Angels* it describes angel activity in three waves: In Bible times, the time of the first wave, angels appeared only to a select few, such as the prophets and patriarchs. The second wave came in the Dark Ages or the medieval period in which angels appeared only to outstanding Christians and significant leaders. The third wave is today, in which angels reveal themselves to ordinary people.

They give steps to have access to angels, which lead to angels honoring your request to reach a higher self. Now get this – the exercise, is called, G-R-A-C-E! It stands for Grounding; Releasing; Aligning; Conversing; and Enjoying the angel contact.[38]

Not exactly what any student of the Bible would describe grace as!

Why God *Permitted* this rebellion?

We need to understand the purpose of all creation is to glorify God (Psa. 19:1/Col. 1:16 notice "for Him").

---

[38] Understanding Christian Theology, Swindoll and Zuck editors, p. 549, Thomas Nelson Publishers.

Dwight Pentecost noted, "Creation was brought into existence not only for the benefit of the creatures who one day would walk upon the face of the earth, but for God's glory. This universe was created that it should bear testimony to, and reflect the glory of, an all-glorious God."

I believe the main purpose was so God could reveal one of His attributes that had been somewhat hidden – His grace.

Grace is for the guilty and mercy is for the miserable. The unfallen angels never experience grace and mercy because they did not need it. The fallen angels did not experience God's grace and mercy because it was not offered to them.

God created operation humanity, knowing man would fall, but unlike with the angels He, would save some among mankind, revealing His grace and mercy. This would be a testimony especially among the unfallen angels (Lu. 12:8-9; 15:10/1 Cor. 4:9; 11:10; Eph. 3:10/1 Tim. 5:21).

That is why the essence of what we are, is not, trophies of goodness but of grace. God is going to display us like a trophy! Of course, a trophy does not glorify the trophy, but the one who earned it.

⁶ and raised us up with Him, and seated us with Him in the heavenly *places* in Christ Jesus, ⁷ so that in the ages to come He might show the surpassing riches of His grace in kindness toward us in Christ Jesus. Ephesians 2:6-7

Listen to that verse in other translations:

⁷ So God can point to us in all future ages as examples of the incredible wealth of his grace and kindness toward us, as shown in all he has done for us who are united with Christ Jesus. Ephesians 2:7 (NLT)

⁷ Throughout the coming ages we will be the visible display of the infinite, limitless riches of his grace and kindness, which was showered upon us in Jesus Christ. For it was only through this wonderful grace that we believed in

him. Nothing we did could ever earn this salvation, for it was the gracious gift from God that brought us to Christ! So no one will ever be able to boast, for salvation is never a reward for good works or human striving. Ephesians 2:7 (PassionNTPsa)

During a British conference on comparative religions, experts from around the world debated what, if any, belief was unique to the Christian faith. They began eliminating possibilities. Incarnation? Other religions had different versions of gods appearing in human form. Resurrection? Again, other religions had accounts of return from death.

The debate went on for some time until C. S. Lewis wandered into the room. 'What's the rumpus about?' he asked, and heard in reply that his colleagues were discussing Christianity's unique contribution among world religions. Lewis responded, 'Oh, that's easy. It's GRACE.'[39]

---

[39] What's So Amazing about GRACE? (Zondervan, 1997), p.11.

Con: So there is not only life in Outer Space, but here among us and they are both friend and foe!

It is interesting that Guideposts, publishes a bimonthly magazine, *Angels on Earth*. Every issue is filled with accounts of people who believe they have been touched by an angel or a group of angels. These stories are from and about ordinary people who have had extraordinary experiences they attribute to angelic contact. You can subscribe to it for $ 16.99.[40]

The problem is if you play around in the angelic realm with being united with Christ, the only kind of angel you will experience is a fallen angel – a demon!

C. God's Demonstration of Grace through project humanity.

F. B. Meyers said it well, "Man was placed in the world like a king in a palace stored with all to please him... The sun to labor for him like a very Hercules; the moon to light his nights... elements of nature to be his slaves and

---

[40] www.guideposts.org/our-magazines/angels-on-earth-magazine.

messengers: flowers to scent his pathway; fruit to please his taste; birds to sing for him; beasts to toil for him and carry him; and man himself, amidst all the luxury, God's representative, His vice-regent. This is as God made him."[41]

1. *Creation*.

a. There was *Amity* between God and man.

The word Amity means, "a harmony, a peaceful and good relationship."

[26] Then God said, "Let Us make man in Our image, according to Our likeness; and let them rule over the fish of the sea and over the birds of the sky and over the cattle and over all the earth, and over every creeping thing that creeps on the earth." Genesis 1:26

[30] and to every beast of the earth and to every bird of the sky and to every thing that moves on the earth which has life, *I have given* every green plant for food"; and it was so. [31] God saw all that

---

[41] Palmer, Johnny. Genesis: Roots of the Nation volume 1 (Pastor Palmer's Pen) (Kindle Locations 1699-1702). Kindle Edition.

He had made, and behold, it was very good. And there was evening and there was morning, the sixth day. Genesis 1:30-31

God created man in what we call an innocent state. There was perfect harmony between God and His creation. How wonderful life was in the Garden of Eden.

Keep in mind the purpose of this study is an overview of basic truths not a detailed study on these things. We are not getting into:

- Intimacy with Almighty God

- The Ability to reproduce in the context of a loving family.

- Authority to rule.

- Abundancy of blessings like creating for them a perfect planet for life; an inexhaustible supply of food; perfect weather conditions; every conceivable need met; Perfect health; no sickness or death; etc.

- An environment free from Anxiety.

The blessings go on and on...For a detailed study get my book on Genesis vol. 1.

Mike Herman had collected baseball cards during his college years. But finances got tight and he had to set aside his little hobby.

Several years later, after being in a career, he was able to resume the hobby. He writes:

As I opened a fairly expensive pack the other day, I was amazed to find one of the rarest cards of the set sitting there in my hand. It had a real autograph on it. It was one of those serendipitous moments when I wasn't sure if this was really what I thought it was. The shock eventually wore off, and the realization kicked in that I had found something I would have paid hundreds of dollars for if I had not found it in that $5.00 pack of cards.[42]

---

[42] PreachingToday submitted by Mike Herman, Illinois, God's Gracious Surprises.

I wonder how Adam and Eve felt to all of a sudden exist! To meet their creator, to experience each other and the many blessings that God had bestowed upon them.

I had a similar experience on the 7th of May 1974, when I trusted Jesus Christ as my Savior! I, for the first time in my life, existed spiritually. I was met by God Himself! I entered into a world of forgiveness, righteousness, acceptance, adoption, love, faith, and hope. Wow!

Now for our present study, let us focus on the idea that Man was created in the image of God so that he may glorify God by having fellowship with God.

A needed caution:

Tozer gives a good warning, "When the Scripture states that man was made in the image of God, we dare not add to that statement an idea from our own head and make it mean, "in the exact image." To do so is... to break down the wall, infinitely high, that separates that-which-is-God from that which-is-not-God. To think of creatures and Creator as alike in essential being is to rob God of most of His attributes and reduce Him to the status of a creature."[43]

The greatest example of this is the Lord Jesus Christ.

[4] in whose case the god of this world has blinded the minds of the unbelieving so that they might not see the light of the gospel of the glory of **Christ, who is the image of God.** 2 Corinthians 4:4 Jesus Christ shares in God's being and is a perfect manifestation of that being.

[15] **He is the image of the invisible God**, the firstborn of all creation. Colossians 1:15

[3] And He is the radiance of His glory and the exact representation of His nature, and upholds all things by the word of His power. When He had made purification of sins, He sat down at the right hand of the Majesty on high, Hebrews 1:3

Jesus Christ is God/man, always glorified God through nonstop

---

[43] Tozer, A.W.. The Knowledge of the Holy (p. 7). Fig. Kindle Edition.

fellowship, He lived as a perfect man lived, using his mind to know God; His emotions to love God, and His will to obey God.

Man was created for the purpose of knowing, loving, and obeying God. That is part of what it means to be in the image of God.

26 Then God said, "Let Us make man in **Our image**, according to Our likeness; and let them rule over the fish of the sea and over the birds of the sky and over the cattle and over all the earth, and over every creeping thing that creeps on the earth." 27 God **created man in His own image, in the image of God** He created him; male and female He created them. Genesis 1:26-27

As one noted:

The word "image" or "likeness" emphasizes resemblance, the correspondence between one thing and another. The word translated "likeness" gives us the interesting picture of a coin that has been stamped in a die, so that what was in the die reappears in the coin. One who examines the coin can tell what was engraved in the die, because the coin bears the image of the die that pressed it. Now, when Scriptures assert that man is made in the likeness of God, it does not say that man is a little god. Rather, it says that by representation and manifestation, there is in man that which was in God, and that which was in God was manifested in Adam as he was created, and in Jesus Christ in His humanity.[44]

So how does man bear the image of God? There is much that could be said here, but for the sake of our study, we will keep it simple.

It speaks primarily of a God-ward personality, consisting of mind, emotion, and will. Animals have personalities but not God-ward, they are also conscious but not self-conscience. As Blanchard notes:

Blanchard, "Man is not a chemical fluke or an atomic accident. Nor is he an

---

[44] J. Dwight Pentecost. Designed to Be Like Him (Kindle Locations 226-229). Kindle Edition.

educated ape; he is as different from other animals; as animals are from vegetables; and vegetables from minerals. All other living creatures are conscious; man is self-conscious. If a giraffe could say, "I am a giraffe" it would cease to be a giraffe."

- Adam was given a mind so that he could primarily know God. He exercised this capacity when he named all of the Animals. God also named his wife (Gen. 2:23; 3:20).

In 1873, Hudson Taylor wrote a letter to a fellow-worker going through a difficult trial. He encouraged him with these words: The one thing we need is to know God better…Oh, to know Him! Well might Paul, who had caught a glimpse of His glory, count "all things" as dung and dross compared with this most precious knowledge! This makes the weak strong, the poor rich, the empty full; this makes suffering happiness, and turns tears into diamonds like the sunshine turns dew into pearls. This makes us fearless, invincible. If we know God, then when full of joy we can thank our Heavenly

Father, the Giver of all... Oh to know Him! How good, how great, how glorious— our God and Father, our God and Saviour, our God and Sanctifier— to know Him![45]

- Adam was given emotions so that he could primarily respond to God's love. He exercised this in relationship to Eve.

One follows the other, when we know Him, we cannot help but love Him. A group called The Teddy Bears, had a hit song in 1958 called "To Know Him is to Love Him"

Just to see him smile makes my life worthwhile
To know, know, know him is to love, love, love him

Phil Spector was fooling around with a guitar and piano. Inspired by the inscription on his father's tombstone, "To have known him is to have loved him," Phil Spector penned the words to the song "To Know Him Is to Love Him."

---

[45] Dr. and Mrs. Howard Taylor, Hudson Taylor and the China Inland Mission (London: China Inland Mission, 1918), 236-7.

So, in the summer of 1958, seventeen-year-old Phil Spector and his friends made the recording, which was sold to Dore Records. By that fall, it was the number 1 record on both the *Billboard* and *Cashbox* magazine charts.[46]

We might say the same about God: To know Him is to love Him.

- Adam was given a will so that he could primarily obey God. He has the opportunity to exercise this in relationship to the tree of the knowledge of good and evil.

In the eleventh century King Henry, Duke of Bavaria, grew weary of the pomp of court life and the cares of being a monarch. As he visited the Abbey of Verdun, he asked the prior there if he would be accepted into the monastery as a monk. The prior, Richard, told him that the first vow would be one of obedience. The monarch promised his willingness to follow his will in every detail. The prior said, "Then back to

---

[46] Tony Rufo, *The Complete Book of Pop Music Wit & Wisdom: What 200 Pop Songs Say About God*, (Carol Stream, IL: Tyndale House Publishers, 2006), WORD*search* CROSS e-book, 84.

your throne and do your duty in the station God assigned you."[47]

Adam had a will, it was given so that he might obey God. It is the same with us, He has given us assignments – what gifts we have; where we will use them; how effective they will be (1 Cor. 12:4-6). Our place is simply to rejoice in God's will for our lives (Eph. 2:10).

God made fellowship possible between the mind of Adam and the mind of God, the heart of Adam and the heart of God, and the will of Adam and the will of God. For Adam, fellowship was the exercise of these three capacities of his personality God-ward.[48]

The John Phillips Commentary series has this:

Man stands alone. *Physically,* he alone of all the creatures on the globe walks upright; *mentally,* he alone has the ability to communicate in a

---

[47] James Hastings, ed., The Expository Times, Vol. 16 (Edinburgh T. & T. Clark, 1905), 303.
[48] Dwight Pentecost. Designed to Be Like Him (Kindle Locations 267-268). Kindle Edition.

sophisticated manner; *spiritually,* he alone has the capacity to know the mind and will of God. Thus, God created Adam. Then God *crowned Adam* (1:28-31). He crowned him in three ways; first by bestowing upon him a *posterity*—"Be fruitful and multiply" (1:28a)... God crowned Adam with a *position* (1:28b) giving him dominion over the fish of the sea, over the fowl of the air, and over every living thing... Finally, God crowned Adam with a *possession* (1:29-31). He gave him paradise to enjoy.[49]

There was a time when man had a perfect fellowship with God in a perfect place. Charles Ryrie in Basic Theology:

How can we express Adam's original condition? Some use the word innocent, but Adam was more than innocent, which seems to connote only the absence of wrong. Adam's original holiness was positive; yet it was not equal with God's— it was creaturely.[50]

---

[49] John Phillips, The John Phillips Commentary Series – Exploring Genesis: An Expository Commentary, (Chicago, IL: Moody Press, 1980; repr., Grand Rapids, MI: Kregel Publications, 2001), WORDsearch CROSS e-book, 45.

[50] Ryrie, Charles C.. Basic Theology: A Popular Systematic Guide to

Maybe you have seen the TV drug store commercial featuring scenes of an idyllic town with hauntingly beautiful music and the soft-spoken announcer who says, "Beyond the reach of cell phones and super highways, there's a place called Perfect. In a town called Perfect the only crime is not having ice cream on your pie."

The scene switches to a dog coming up a white carpeted staircase. His muddy paw prints magically vanish behind him. The soft voice says, "Carpets never stain." In another scene two women in white hats sit in a manicured garden sipping tea while the waiter stands over them with an umbrella. The announcer says, "A town where everyone gives 110 percent, even when tipping."

Finally, after many such scenes the voice says, "Of course, we don't live anywhere near Perfect." One of the Walgreen's thousands of stores appears on the screen as we're told that's why

---

Understanding Biblical Truth (p. 219). Moody Publishers. Kindle Edition.

they exist, as a place to find everything needed for "the real world."[51]

It is true no one lives in a perfect world but it is important to realize at one time Adam and Eve did.

b. The *Ability* to choose.

God did not want robots that had no choice but to love Him. Tony Evans writes:

In order for man to function authentically as God's image-bearer with a moral will, the possibility of evil must exist. For God to have negated that possibility would be for Him to nullify the very thing He created— namely, beings with the ability to choose. And choice, of necessity, requires options. By allowing His creatures to have choice, God made evil and sin *possible*. But mankind made it *real* by making wrong choices.

2. One *Obligation*.

---

[51] The Town of Perfect, U.S.A - Walgreens Commercial.

God's has revealed to us His perfect character in His Law.

Adam was given only one law (Gen. 2:16-17).

Later we have the Mosaic Law and the Sermon on the Mount. God's law expresses His Holiness (Rom. 7:12).

Man is not left to wonder or speculate about what God is like and what He wants, it is spelled out in His Law. Again, Hal says it well:

The Law of God, which is summarized in the ten commandments and the Sermon on the Mount, expresses the overwhelming purity of God's holy character. All the laws that God has ever given to men tell us what we'd have to be like if we were to try and approach God on the basis of our own merit. But according to James and Paul, we could keep every single point of the law and yet stumble in just *one small area* and that would be enough to disqualify us from enjoying fellowship with God for even a moment. What a commentary on the magnitude of God's holiness.[52]

There was only one law in that garden.

16 The LORD God commanded the man, saying, "From any tree of the garden you may eat freely; 17 but from the tree of the knowledge of good and evil you shall not eat, for in the day that you eat from it you will surely die." Genesis 2:16-17

Obviously, the creation is obligated to obey his Creator.

So there we have the Situation – God's Creation, a perfect couple, in a perfect place, in perfect fellowship with God for His glory, with only one Obligation Proclamation, and man's Possession.
PS: Again if you want to look at this in more detail, get my three-volume book on Genesis.

All of this reveals just how good God has been, even after the Fall, and He is

---

[52] The Liberation of Planet Earth, by Hal Lindsey, p. 41-42. Zondervan Publishing House, 1974.

good to us every second of every day. Tony Evans notes:

"In His goodness, God not only created you, but He also created everything for you. In other words, God didn't create the plants, animals, or fish just to have them around. He created them for the benefit of mankind. The earth was created to give us a home to enjoy. Every day when you get up and see the sun shine and say, "What a beautiful day!" God sits back and says, "How do you think that happened? Today didn't just jump up here by itself. It's a beautiful day because I'm a good God." You eat that fried catfish and you say, "Umm, that sure was good." God says, "Hold it. If you read Genesis 1, you will find that I created the water and the dry land. I separated the dry land from the water. I created every fish in every body of water. So whenever you eat catfish, don't just say, 'It was good.' Say, 'God is good.'" Every time I pick up a piece of fried chicken, I am reminded that God is good. Every time you see a rose, God says, "I don't want you just talking about how pretty those roses are, or you miss the point. The point is I know what I'm doing when I make flowers because I am a good God." When it rains and you say, "It's a bad day," God says, "Hold it! Hold it!" Why? Because Acts 14: 17 says He gives the rain and makes the seasons change to bring satisfaction to the human race. No rain, no vegetation; no vegetation, no vegetables or fruit. So the next time you enjoy a vegetable or a piece of fruit, you ought to pause and have a time of prayer and thanksgiving because our good God causes it to rain."[53]

Chapter Two

II. THE SEPARATION.

A. We have already seen the Standard of Deity.

B. Sin Debt.

1. Inception of sin.

---

[53] Evans, Tony. Theology You Can Count On: Experiencing What the Bible Says About... God the Father, God the Son, God the Holy Spirit, Angels, Salvation... (Kindle Locations 1502-1503). Moody Publishers. Kindle Edition.

As we have already demonstrated this took place in the angelic realm.

2. Imputed sin.

Not only did Satan persuade some of the angels to follow him, but he was the one in the Garden who was working behind that serpent to tempt Eve.

a. The *Sin* – a violation of God's law (Gen. 2:16-17; 3:6).

Now God Himself becomes a barrier between God and man. Man violated God's holiness, therefore His justice responded with wrath. God still loved man but He could not compromise His holiness for the sake of His love. Only if there was a just way to deal with man's sin and satisfy God's offended holy Character could His love be experienced by man.

b. The *Separation*.

1. This is related to the fact that God is Holy.

When Adam sinned, a separation from a holy God took place. Thus, there is a wall, a barrier, a hindrance between God and man. That Hindrance is the very Perfection of God.

Man being sinful cannot remove that separation and come into God's presence (Isa. 64:6/Jer. 17:9).

They used to play a game in California; it was called jumping to Catalina. They had a pier down in Santa Monica where they would play this game. Guys would take a long run and a flying leap into the Pacific Ocean. Some would go farther than others, but they all had one thing in common. None could jump all the way to Catalina, some 26 miles away. Some seemingly can jump farther to God, but none can jump far enough to satisfy God's righteousness.

Of course, they tried:

- *Self-righteousness*. One inadequate way we try to deal with our sin is seeking to produce a righteousness based on our own works. We try to make up for what we have done by good deeds, especially religious deeds. But we can do nothing to make up for our sins by what we do. Judas betrayed Jesus, and, in Mt. 27:1-5, felt remorse or guilt. He launched operation self-righteousness. He went back to those and confessed he had betrayed innocent blood. But it was worthless because he was trying to do something to pay for the deed he had done by giving back the money. Adam and Eve also felt a sense of guilt immediately so they tried to hide from God. The progression: first there was sin, which immediately produced a sense of guilt; which produced estrangement from God, which brings a fear of judgment and rightly so. Their making of the fig leaves to cover themselves was an act of self-righteousness which God soundly rejected.

- *Self-justification*. We begin to say I am not responsible, it was not my fault. We blame society or someone else. Adam blamed Eve, it was that woman YOU gave me! In reality, Adam had no one to blame for his sin but his own choice!

- Today people try to deal with their guilt with *Self-deification*. They seek to deal with their guilt by saying there is no God, if there is no God then there is no standard to violate. In essence they seek to take the place of God, decreeing that their sin is really no sin at all.

Yet truth remains, there is a God, and a violation of His Person results in just separation from God unto His judgment.

2. This removed the intimacy.

- The Mind. Man's fallen mind no longer had the capacity or the desire to know God. A radical change took place in man's mind: It became **dark** (Rom. 1:21/Eph. 4:17). Dwight Pentecost noted:

By the use of this word "darkened" the apostle is emphasizing the fact that the mind of the natural man, of itself, has no power to receive light. It cannot receive divine revelations. Just as a fish born in the Mammoth Cave in Kentucky without the capacity of sight cannot respond to light-no matter how bright-focused upon it because it has no sensory perception, so the men born into this world cannot, of themselves, respond to light from God because the intellect has been darkened in respect to divine truth.[54]

It became **Depraved** (Gen. 6:5); **Distorted** (Rom. 1:22); **Denounces** God's law (Rom. 8:6-7); it has no capacity to **Discover** God's revelation, nor does it want to (1 Cor. 2:14/Eph. 4:17, "empty" of the things of God); is **Degenerate**, totally given over to evil (Rom. 1:28); it **Delights** only in sensual, earthly, natural things (Rom. 8:7/2 Cor. 4:4/Phil. 3:19/Col. 2:18); **Dictatorial**, it is filled with conceit and pride (Col. 2:18); **Defiled** (Tit. 1:15/1 Tim. 6:5); is characterized by **Death** (Rom. 8:6).

A side note: Even as believers we still have such a mind! As one noted:

Since the mind of man is marked and designated as a reprobate, carnal, empty, puffed up, fleshly, defiled,

---

[54] J. Dwight Pentecost. Designed to Be Like Him (Kindle Locations 389-392). Kindle Edition.

corrupt, earthly, blinded, and dead mind, do you begin to understand, child of God, why it is difficult for you to control your thoughts? Do not be deceived into thinking that your mind has been changed because you have been born into God's family. What we have seen from the Scripture is that which describes the mind you have, which you received by physical birth from Adam.[55]

As believers we can choose to allow that old mind to influence us.

- The emotion. The heart has become **Enhardened**, it is calloused and insensitive toward God (Rom. 2:5/Eph. 4:18); it is **Erring** (Heb. 3:10); **Evil unbelieving** heart (Heb. 3:12); led into **Error** by self-deception (Jer. 17:9/Jam. 1:26); it is **Egocentric**, in love with itself (2 Tim. 3:2).

It does not have a love for God, nor does it have a capacity to receive God's love.

---

[55] J. Dwight Pentecost. Designed to Be Like Him (Kindle Locations 445-448). Kindle Edition.

- The will. It is a **Slave** to sin (Rom. 6:16-20/Eph. 2:2). Fallen man is free in the same way a bird in a cage is free. The bird is free to move within that cage, but his life is bounded by that cage. Likewise fallen man is free to move in the element of sin (Gal. 5:16/Rom. 7:23, if this is true of believers, how much more with unbelievers who have no new nature and no indwelling Holy Spirit). It **Stubbornly** opposes God's will. The fallen will cannot obey God and does not want to obey God (Jn. 6:44, 65/Rom. 3:11). As one noted:

A man, in the deadness of his will toward God, may do things that morally or ethically are acceptable and approved by society. But he can never do anything that is pleasing to God because all that he does, he does in response to the commands issued by sin, which is his master. And God cannot and will not accept obedience to sin as acceptable to Himself.[56]

c. The Succession.

---

[56] J. Dwight Pentecost. Designed to Be Like Him (Kindle Locations 902-905). Kindle Edition.

Succession means a number of people or things sharing a specified characteristic and following one after the other.

- The Representation of Adam.

Adam was a representation of the human race, and when he sinned, plunged the entire human race into sin (Gen. 3:6/Rom. 5:12/1 Cor. 15:22).

6 When the woman saw that the tree was good for food, and that it was a delight to the eyes, and that the tree was desirable to make *one* wise, she took from its fruit and ate; and she gave also to her husband with her, and he ate. Genesis 3:6

This is interesting; Eve was deceived, even though what she did was sin, but not Adam, he yielded with his eyes wide open so to speak.

14 And *it was* not Adam *who* was deceived, but the woman being deceived, fell into transgression.
1 Timothy 2:14

Eve was deceived when she sinned, she is guilty but not as legally responsible for bringing sin into the universe. The one fully responsible for bringing sin into mankind was Adam. Sin starts in the heart, the moment she decided not to believe God she sinned, and then she actually did it. Adam was watching the whole thing – he knew exactly what he was doing. Eve was deceived not Adam.

While both men and woman are born sinners, the sin is passed on from Adam, through the man.

1. The Choice. Rom. 5:12a

^{12} Therefore, just as through one man – the context is clear that the one man was Adam, in the garden.

2. The Consequences. Rom. 5:12b

sin entered into the world, and death through sin, and so death spread to all men, because all sinned— [in Adam].

3. The Compelling proof that Adam's sin was imputed to the entire human race. Rom. 5:13-14

a. The Presence of sin. 13a

¹³ for until the Law sin was in the world – people were always sinners.

b. The Principle. 13b

but sin is not imputed when there is no law – Rom. 4:15.

c. The Proof. 5:14

¹⁴ Nevertheless death reigned from Adam until Moses, even over those who had not sinned in the likeness of the offense of Adam, who is a type of Him who was to come - The logic is there was only one law given from God until Moses, that was "You shall not eat of the fruit of the tree of good"...Yet with no law to break man died anyway. Why? Not because of personal acts of sin but because of being united with Adam.

D. James Kennedy notes:

For Adam and Eve, the condition was very simple: They were to simply obey one command from God— to not eat the fruit from the tree of the knowledge of good and evil. And yet Adam, who was the federal head of the human race, sinned and plunged both himself and all his posterity into guilt and corruption and death... All of Adam's descendants would be born with a sinful nature, they would grow up and express this sinful nature in all the different kinds of iniquity, they would die, and then finally they would be judged and condemned to hell. This would happen generation after generation.[57]

Lightner notes:

The term "imputation" means putting to someone's account what may or may not be his. It's an accounting term...What's is the relationship between Adam and the race of mankind? Does his sin affect the rest of the human race? The Bible's answer is "yes." Adam is viewed by God as the reprentative head as well as the natural head of the human race (Rom. 5:12)...What is being taught is that every member of the human family who has ever been born or will ever be born was related in some

---

[57] Kennedy, Dr D. James; Jerry Newcombe. Cross Purposes: Discovering the Great Love of God for You (p. 58). The Crown Publishing Group. Kindle Edition.

way to Adam. When Adam sinned, we sinned. He not only represented us, but we sinned in him. The potential of the entire human family was in him, so that what he did, all did in him and through him (1 Cor. 15:22).[58]

Millard J. Erickson is helpful:

The last clause in verse 12 tells us that we were involved in some way in Adam's sin; it was in some sense also our sin. But what is meant by this? On the one hand it may be understood in terms of federal headship – Adam acted on behalf of all persons...Our involvement in Adam's sin might better be understood in terms of natural headship, however...the entirety of our human nature, both physical and spiritual, material and immaterial, has been received from our parents and more distant ancestors by way of descent from the first pair of humans. On this basis we were actually present within Adam so that we all sinned in his act. There is no injustice then to our

---

[58] Sin, the Savior, and Salvation by Robert P. Lightner, Th.D, p. 33. Thomas Nelson Publishers.

condemnation and death as a result of original sin.[59]

In other words if we had been in that garden we would have done the same thing – only probably quicker!

A hired hand was out chopping wood and he kept repeating over and over "Oh Adam! Oh Adam!" His boss happened to walk by and asked him why he kept saying that. He said, "Well, because if it hadn't been for Adam I wouldn't have to work." So the boss said, "Tell you what, from now on you do not have to work at all, just come in and do what you want to. You can have the run of the place and you will still draw your pay."

This went on for a few days and the boss said he wanted to see him. He said, "Only one stipulation. You see this box on my desk. Don't you ever open it." He was goofing off but kept thinking about that box, so he went in and picked it up and finally opened it. Inside was a note: "Don't you curse Adam

---

[59] Erickson, Christian Theology (Grand Rapids, MI: Baker Book House, 1985) 2:637.

anymore, if you had been there you would have done the same thing!"

That is the point of Rom. 5:12, Adam was the Federal head of the human race. If we think that is unfair, just remember if we would have been there, we would have done the same thing.

Several years ago Coach Joe Paterno and his Penn State football team were playing for the national championship against Alabama in the Sugar Bowl. They probably would have won, but they had a touchdown called back because there was a twelfth man on the field. One man's mistake affected the entire team.[60]

Adam' sin affected the entire human race.

- The Reception of a sin debt. This should not be that hard for us to understand, we have a national debt that is over 18 trillion dollars! It will be even greater debt then that, when we pass it on to our grandchildren.

---

[60] Illustrations Unlimited, by James S. Hewitt. Forgiving and Forgetting p. 214. Tyndale Publishers.

Our overspending and irresponsibility is going to be passed on to the next generation. It is the same with the sin debt. The difference is that it is possible to pay off our national debt but not our sin debt.

Joe Louis was one of the greatest heavyweight champions of all time. He was champion from 1937 until he retired in 1949 defending his title twenty five times over a twelve-year span. The sad thing is, he owed the government a lot of money in back taxes, a debt that hung over his head until his death on April 12, 1981.

Few things are more discouraging then having a debt that we cannot possibly pay. And sadly we are all born with a debt, a sin debt which we are incapable of paying for.

Let's keep it simple, if you drive 65 mph, in a 25 mph zone and a police officer pulls you over you have to pay a fine or what we might call a speed debt.

We have violated God's law and have incurred a sin debt (Rom. 3:19-20/Col.

2:14). This is a debt that we cannot pay.

¹⁴ having canceled out the certificate of debt consisting of decrees against us, which was hostile to us...Colossians 2:14

Dwight Pentecost gives this background:

If a man was found guilty as indicted and was put in prison, it was the custom to nail that indictment over his prison cell so that any individual going through the prison could look at that indictment and know exactly why the prisoner was in prison. That indictment was a "handwriting of ordinances."[61]

Hal Lindsey notes:

Man owes God perfect obedience to His holy laws as summarized in the Ten Commandments and the Sermon on the Mount. By his failure to live up to this standard of perfection, man has become offensive to the very character of God, and the eternal court of justice has pronounced the death sentence upon

---

[61] J. Dwight Pentecost. Designed to Be Like Him (Kindle Location 1208). Kindle Edition.

man. A certificate of Debt was prepared against every person who would ever live, listing his failure to live in thought, word, and deed in accordance with the Law of God. This death sentence has become a DEBT OF SIN which has to be paid either by man or if possible, someone qualified to take his place (Col. 2:14).[62]

And we cannot even pay for one small tiny sin!

Irene Phillips opened a package of frozen peas and out came a frog! She said, "It was the most revolting thing I have ever seen. Even one of its legs was missing!" The spokesman for the supermarket responded by saying, "It wasn't such a big frog." That is the way many people view their sin – it's no big deal! But as we have seen it is not sin itself that makes it such a big deal but the one we have sinned again.

When I was a kid we played, "Hurt, don't it!" I would ask one of my friends if he wanted a hurt donut. He would

---

[62] The Liberation of Planet Earth, p. 46, Hal Lindsey.

look puzzled and say, "I guess so." Then I would wallop him in the arm as hard as I could and say, "It hurt don't it!" Now years later, I entered the United States Air Force. I played hurt donut with a few fellow Airmen. But imagine walking up to a four star General and playing that game! Same game, same question, same joke, but very different consequences. Sin is serious because it is against Almighty God.

3. Inherited sin.

The once populous and prosperous fishing village of Houtou Wan was on one of the Shengsi Islands of China's Yangtze River. Several decades ago, its residents were relocated, leaving all its structures to nature. Well, nature took little time to reclaim the town for its own. Today the town has been swallowed up by vegetation.

The sin nature is like that, it swallows up everything that is good and decent and leaves nothing but an on-growing slime of sin.[63]

---

[63] Causey, David. A Fourth Portion of Insightful Illustrations:

So we are all born with a sin nature (Psa. 51:5/Jer. 17:9/Eph. 2:3/1 Jn. 1:8).

We are not sinners because we sin, we sin because we are sinners. When a Frenchman, Daneil Hugon, was convicted of murder he argued that his actions were due to an extra Y Chromosome. Well, we are all born with an S Chromosome, if you will, a sin nature.

We are born with a sin nature but that is no excuse for our sin. But we do have a propensity to sin from birth. There is only one man who ever became a sinner because he sinned and that was Adam.

David Causey notes:

Our fallen, sinful nature is the real source of evil in our society. Though, for millennia, we have sought to identify society's evil in certain individuals, in different ethnic groups, in institutions, in economics, in the lack of education, or in forms of government – the

Illuminated Paths to Guide Us through Life's Labyrinth (Kindle Locations 5311-5313). Kindle Edition.

presence of evil is located in every human heart. Our sinful nature is what sabotages all our efforts to achieve peace in the world. It undermines every marriage. Our sinful nature is like a hook lodged in our soul that always drags us downward and causes us to rebel against our Creator, Lawgiver, and Judge.[64]

That is why we are sinners no matter what we do, everything we do is tainted by sin. There is only one man who ever became a sinner because he sinned and that was Adam.

Spurgeon notes:

"Every sin that he commits helps to fill up the measure of his iniquity and there is nothing that he can do without sin being mixed with it. Solomon says that "the plowing of the wicked is sin" (Prov. 21:4 kjv). That is to say even his common actions, in performing the ordinary avocations of his daily life, bring sin upon him."[65]

---

[64] Causey, David. A Fourth Portion of Insightful Illustrations: Illuminated Paths to Guide Us through Life's Labyrinth (Kindle Locations 10628-10629). Kindle Edition.

Even when a lost man offers a sacrifice and tries to do good, it is still an abomination to the Lord (Prov. 15:8).

We are born with a sin nature with a propensity to sin from birth.

Hal Lindsey notes:

The Bible teaches that when Adam and Eve disobeyed God in the Garden of Eden, they didn't just lose their sense of fellowship with God and become unlike Him in their character; they actually had something added to them – a sin nature. Since that awful day of infamy, all men have been born with the same sinful nature, and that is the source of our sins. I know it's hard to believe that a tiny, innocent cooing sweetly in our arms has in it a sin nature that will soon begin committing sins, but that's what the Bible teaches from start to finish[66]

Wayne Grudem notes:

---

[65] Spurgeon, Charles. The Complete Spurgeon Sermons on Genesis (The Complete Spurgeon Series Book 1) (Kindle Location 8665). 19Baskets, Inc.. Kindle Edition.
[66] Liberation of Planet Earth, p. 49.

A similar idea is affirmed in Psalm 58:3, "The wicked go astray from the womb, they err from their birth, speaking lies." Therefore, our nature includes a disposition to sin so that Paul can affirm that before we were Christians "we were by nature children of wrath, like the rest of mankind" (Eph. 2: 3). Anyone who has raised children can give experiential testimony to the fact that we are all born with a tendency to sin. Children do not have to be taught how to do wrong; they discover that by themselves.[67]

Our problem is that man does not realize his real problem. Robert McGee notes:

Understanding this, the term sin in these passages refers to a sin nature. The sin nature mechanism is in operation to motivate man to sin. The sin nature is not just some theoretical concept. It exists as surely as your heart exists. Treat it as some vague idea and you will be at a great disadvantage in combating it.[68]

[67] Grudem, Wayne A.; Grudem, Wayne A.. Systematic Theology: An Introduction to Biblical Doctrine (Kindle Locations 13537-13539). Zondervan. Kindle Edition.

4. Individual sins.

We all know, only too well, what it is like, to commit acts of sin. The truth is there is not a day in our lives when we do not sin in word, thought, or deed (1 Ki. 8:46/Eccles. 7:20/Rom. 3:23/1 Jn. 1:10). I cannot imagine how much I have sinned during my lifetime. This reminded me of an investigation related to an elevator accident. A blond was put on the stand who had a multitude of inconsistencies in her testimony. The insurance company's lawyer, irritated, said, "I suppose when the elevator began to fall, all of your sins flashed before you?" She said, "Oh no, we only dropped eight stories!" If all of our sins flashed before us, we would probably drop several trillion stories before all of our sins would have time to flash across our minds.

Trans: So our Sin Debt is a problem that separates us from God. There is imputed sin, inherited sin and individual sin.

---

[68] McGee, Robert. The Search for Significance: Seeing Your True Worth Through God's Eyes (Kindle Locations 2298-2300). Thomas Nelson. Kindle Edition.

Con:

1. So we have a debt that we cannot possibly pay. How bad is it, well let's put it this way, as of this writing our national debt is $20,957,314,831,621! Just imagine if you as an individual had to pay that debt off by the end of this day.

2. That is nothing compared to our sin debt, and if it is not paid off by the end of our lives we will spend eternity in a place called hell.

3. The good news is that the Lord Jesus has paid it off in full as we will see later.

Joseph Hart was described as "a loose backslider, an audacious apostle, and a bold-faced rebel." Then he came under conviction. At times he was afraid to sleep, fearing he would "awake in hell." He went from church to church to find peace, but as he said, "Everything served only to condemn me." Finally, at the age of forty-five, he wandered into a Moravian chapel in London and heard words of hope. On returning home he knelt in prayer. Three years later, he became a minister and began writing hymns to touch the hearts of others who had experienced similar spiritual struggles. One such hymn was "Come Ye Sinners, Poor and Needy.

Come, ye sinners, poor and needy,
Weak and wounded, sick and sore;
Jesus ready stands to save you,
Full of pity, love, and power;
He is able, He is able,
He is willing; doubt no more.

Now, ye needy, come and welcome;
God's free bounty glorify;
True belief and true repentance,
Every grace that brings you nigh;
Without money, without money,
Come to Jesus Christ and buy.

Let not conscience make you linger,
Nor of fitness fondly dream;
All the fitness He requireth
Is to feel your need of Him:
This He gives you, this He gives you;
'Tis the Spirit's glimmering beam.
Come, ye weary, heavy laden,
Bruised and mangled by the Fall;
If you tarry till you're better,
You will never come at all;

Not the righteous, not the righteous;
Sinners Jesus came to call.
JOSEPH HART (1712– 1768)[69]

C. Satanic Dominion.

Back in September 2015, CBS reported the story of a prisoner who was to testify against a suspect in a murder trial. But prison guards mistakenly placed the witness in the same cell as the murder suspect, the man he was supposed to testify against – not the place you want to be. A fight immediately broke out and it took guards several minutes to pry them apart. Both the defendant and the witness for the prosecution were treated for injuries.[70]

The truth is that we are not only in a cage of sin, but the one in there with us is our arch enemy Satan!

1. Power of Attorney.

---

[69] Petersen, William J.; Petersen, Ardythe. The Complete Book of Hymns (pp. 330-331). Tyndale House Publishers. Kindle Edition.

[70] Causey, David. A Fourth Portion of Insightful Illustrations: Illuminated Paths to Guide Us through Life's Labyrinth (Kindle Location 8971). Kindle Edition.

a. Ownership belongs to God.

Gen. 14:19, 22/Ex. 19:5/Psa. 24:1-2; 50:10-12; 89:11/ 1 Cor. 10:26.

The late Bishop Edwin Hughes once delivered a rousing sermon on "God's Ownership" that put a rich parishioner's nose out-of-joint. The wealthy man took the Bishop off for lunch, and then walked him through his elaborate gardens, woodlands, and farm. "Now are you going to tell me," he demanded when the tour was completed, "that all this land does not belong to me?" Bishop Hughes smiled and suggested, "Ask me that same question a hundred years from now."[71]

God, not man, not Satan, not you nor I, but God the Creator and sustainer, owns this universe!

Tony Evans notes, "Satan may temporarily control a lot of this world's assets and use them against believers, but he even does that within the limits of God's permission. Ultimately, it all belongs to God.[72]

---
[71] Bennett Cerf, *Leadership*, Vol. 1, no. 2.

We must understand that "there is no authority except from God" (Rom. 13:1). He remains the sovereign Lord of the universe!

b. Lordship over the earth was given by God to man.

[26] Then God said, "Let Us make man in Our image, according to Our likeness; and let them rule over the fish of the sea and over the birds of the sky and over the cattle and over all the earth, and over every creeping thing that creeps on the earth." Genesis 1:26

[28] God blessed them; and God said to them, "Be fruitful and multiply, and fill the earth, and subdue it; and rule over the fish of the sea and over the birds of the sky and over every living thing that moves on the earth." Genesis 1:28

See, Psa. 8:6-8; 115:16

We might say that man was given power of attorney over the earth. Webster's defines power of attorney as

---

[72] Evans, Tony. Theology You Can Count On: Experiencing What the Bible Says About... God the Father, God the Son, God the Holy Spirit, Angels, Salvation.

"a written authority, authorizing a person to act as the agent of the person granting it."

J. Vernon McGee notes:

"And have dominion" is God's instruction to man. Adam was not just a gardener to cut the grass. Man was created to rule this earth. I think that Adam could control the weather just as we control the air-conditioning in our homes. He ruled this earth. This is what we see in the Lord Jesus. When He was here on this earth, He had control over nature. He could say to a storm, "Be still." He could feed a multitude with five loaves and two fishes. It is my opinion that Adam could have done all of that until his fall.[73]

You can see this dominion in the way the last Adam exercised dominion:

- Over the fish (Mt. 17:24-27/Lu. 5:1-11/Jn. 21:1-11).

- Over the animals (Mt. 21:4-11).

---

[73] Vernon McGee, Thru The Bible with J. Vernon McGee, (Nashville, TN: Thomas Nelson, 1983), WORDsearch CROSS e-book, Under: "Chapter 1".

- Over nature (Mt. 14:26-32/Jn. 2:1-11).

Martin Luther noted, "I am fully convinced that before Adam's sin his eyes were so sharp and clear that they surpassed those of the eagle. He was stronger than the lions and the bears, whose strength is very great; and he handled them the way we handle puppies."

2. Persuasive Adversary.

a. The Temptation.

As we have already observed Satan had to tempt them through a serpent which they had total dominion over. Satan was not allowed to overpower them.

b. The Turning over of their dominion to Satan.

6 When the woman saw that the tree was good for food, and that it was a delight to the eyes, and that the tree was desirable to make *one* wise, she took from its fruit and ate; and she gave also to her husband with her, and he ate. Genesis 3:6

From that moment, they turned dominion over to Satan. Things drastically changed:

- That they turned Dominion over to Satan was never disputed by our Lord (Lu. 4:5-8).

Hal Lindsey noted:

"In capitulating to Satan's temptation they unwittingly turned over their God-given power and authority to Satan's control. He became the legal controller of all who would ever be born from Adam's seed. He also took control of the planet itself...But you may be saying couldn't He have taken control of the power away from Satan once he'd gotten it from Adam? No, He couldn't. You see, God is so just in His nature that He couldn't even be unjust to Satan. A legal transference of property and power had taken place, and a legal means of reversing it would have to be found."

Dwight Pentecost:

"Adam had to release his hold on the scepter that God had given to him when

He said, "Have dominion over the earth." For Adam could not hold the scepter and the forbidden fruit in his hand at the same time…And [Satan] was there to snatch up the scepter that Adam dropped."

Henry Morris noted, "apparently Adam lost his God-given dominion over the earth. Satan became the god of this world."

A most revealing verse related to this Satanic dominion is found in 1 Jn. 5:19:

[19] We know that we are of God, and that the whole world lies in *the power of the evil one.* 1 John 5:19

Lewis Sperry Chaffer gives us this detailed description:

First: the word "in" is the same as is used everywhere of the believer when he is said to be in Christ, and in the case of the believer it signifies an organic union to Christ - as a branch is in the vine, so the believer is in Christ. Though the word, when used of the unregenerate, probably cannot mean the same degree of organic life-relationship as exists between Christ and the believer, yet it does denote a deep relationship; and Satan is the light, inspiration, and power, of all those whom he energizes.

The second revelation in the passage is found in the word "lieth" - "The whole world lieth in the evil one." It might as well be translated "lieth asleep;" for its condition is not only a fixed position in the evil one, but is also a condition of unconsciousness. The saved ones are said to be in the Father's hand where no created thing can pluck them out (Jn. 10: 29), and underneath are the everlasting arms: so the great mass of unsaved humanity is in the arms of Satan; and by his subtlety they are all unconscious of their position and relation.[74]

The Bible is very clear that Adam turned over his rule to Satan (Jn. 12:31; 14:30; 16:11/2 Cor. 4:4/Eph. 2:2; 6:12/2 Tim. 2:26).

---

[74] Chafer, Lewis Sperry. The Biblical Doctrine of Satan (Annotated) (Kindle Locations 555-560). Exegetica Publishing. Kindle Edition.

Note: Some in their ignorance try to teach that Christians today can reclaim that dominion over the earth, that if we are super concerned about the environment we can transform this planet, but that is not according to the Word of God! It is interesting that after the flood the phrase "subdue the earth" is not part of the covenant given to Noah (Gen. 9:1). The Curse on the planet is still in effect (Gen. 3:17) and will not be removed until the future millennial kingdom (Rom. 8:20-22/Zech. 14:11). The first Adam's sin was the cause of God putting a curse on the earth in the first place (Gen. 3:17-19) and it will only be removed during the Millennial Kingdom because of the obedience of the Last Adam (Heb. 2:5-9).

Satan is a cruel master! See Mt. 9:32-33; 12:22; 17:15-18/Mk. 5:4-5; 9:22/Lu. 8:27-29, 37-42/Rev. 9:14-19/etc.

January 2017, a video was published by numerous news agencies of a great white shark that was lured to the bars of a diving cage – to give the diver a "close up view" of the shark. But as the great white lunged after a chunk of tuna being suspended in front of the cage, his head became stuck between the bars. Since sharks cannot swim backward, the great white could only release himself by forcing his way into the cage. For the next 30 terrifying seconds, observers from above watched the cage – now occupied with a diver and a great white shark – bounce about violently.[75]

- Humanity is now in the kingdom of Darkness (Ac. 26:18/Col. 1:13). We are talking about spiritual darkness. It blinds people to the gospel until or unless the Holy Spirit works (2 Cor. 4:3-4). Charles Spurgeon noted:

DARKNESS is used in Scripture to express a great many things. Sometimes it represents sorrow. "A night of weeping" is a common expression among us. We speak, too, of "walking in darkness, and seeing no light." We commonly say to one

---

[75] Causey, David. A Fourth Portion of Insightful Illustrations: Illuminated Paths to Guide Us through Life's Labyrinth (Kindle Locations 8976-8977). Kindle Edition.

another, that our minds are in a dark and gloomy state when we are surrounded by the fogs and mists of sorrow... Darkness, too, frequently represents Satan, and the mysterious spiritual influence which he exerts upon the human mind. He is called *"the prince of darkness."* Darkness seems to be his element... Satan—sin—thick darkness, a darkness which may be felt, the Egyptian darkness in which we are naturally born, and out of which we are not delivered, except by the supernatural power of God... Darkness hides things. No matter how glorious yonder landscape may be as you stand upon the mountain's brow; if the sun has gone down, and if night has spread its wings over the whole, you can see nothing. It may be very well for the guide to tell you that yonder is a silver lake, and there the Black Forest, and that far away are the brows of mountains covered with their eternal snows, but you can see nothing; night has effectually blotted it all out. Now, the power of sin is just like that. It hides from the human mind what that mind ought to see. The man is lost, but he does not know it; he cannot see the rocks that are just ahead. The man has soon to stand before the bar of God and receive his sentence, but he does not know it; I mean his heart does not know it. He trifles on, caring for none of these things.

- Humanity is Described as having a relationship with Satan as a Father and his children (Mt. 13:38/Jn. 8:38, 44/Ac. 13:10/Eph. 2:2-3; 5:6/Col. 3:6).

There is an old story about a scorpion who, being a very poor swimmer, asked a turtle to carry him on its back across the river. The turtle replied, "Are you mad? You'll sting me while I'm swimming and I'll drown."

The scorpion objected, "My dear turtle, if I were to sting you, you would drown and I'd go down with you. Now where is the logic in that?"

Turtle gave it some thought and said, "You're right, hop on." The scorpion climbed aboard and halfway across the river gave the turtle a mighty sting. As they both sank to the bottom, the turtle, sighed as he asked, "Do you mind if I ask you something? You said there is no logic in your stinging me. Why did you do it?"

The scorpion explained, "It has nothing to do with logic, it's just my nature to sting."

Satan's nature is evil and to hurt, and fallen man is just like that, he has a nature that is evil and causes only harm. It is true like father like son! If you doubt that take a look at the history of mankind.

- Humanity is Doomed to share in Satan and his demons destiny (Mt. 25:41).

So Satanic Dominion is a horrible thing, mankind is born under Satanic Dominion, living in gloomy Darkness, Described as in a family relationship with the devil, Doomed to a destiny of eternal judgment.

In November 2016, a Phoenix, Arizona mom placed her son's parakeet cage outside for the two birds, Petey and

Snowy, "to get some fresh air." But while the mom was attending other business, a hawk swooped down, wiggled his way into the cage and proceeded to attack the two parakeets. By the time mom returned, nothing was left of Petey but a few feathers. Snowy, however, had somehow managed to evade the hawk – still trapped in the cage with her.[76]

Mankind is trapped in a cage with one who only wants to steal, kill, and destroy (Jn. 10:10)!

D. Spiritual Death.

In medicine there is a condition known as *mya-sthe-nia grav-is*, in which the muscles of the body cannot respond to the signals being sent to them by the brain. In a normal patient, the brain signals the muscles to contract by sending electrical impulses along the nerves to the muscles where they are received by a special apparatus known as the motor-end-plate. The motor-end-

---

[76] Causey, David. A Fourth Portion of Insightful Illustrations: Illuminated Paths to Guide Us through Life's Labyrinth (Kindle Locations 8972-8974). Kindle Edition.

plate receives the signal and passes it along to the muscle. In those afflicted by this disease the end-plates are missing. Consequently, although the brain sends the signal, it is never received by the muscle. Because it is not received, the muscle does not respond and eventually shrivels up.

That is an analogy of what has happened in the human personality because of the death of the spirit. In the human system, the spirit was meant to play the part of the motor-end-plates. It was meant to receive signals sent to it from God. When man sinned, however, the motor-end-plate died. Although the signals are still there, although God is still speaking, the signal is not received and the spiritual life withers.[77]

a. Basic Concept.

(1) Definition of Death is separation.

Ryrie notes, "Death always indicates a separation of some kind, so spiritual

---

[77] James M. Boice, Foundations of the Christian Faith: A Comprehensive & Readable Theology, (Downers Grove, IL: InterVarsity Press, 1986), WORDsearch CROSS e-book, 203.

death means a separation from the life of God in this present life (Eph. 2:1–3)."[78]

John Stott calls it "the most dreadful of all sin's consequences," writing, "Man's highest destiny is to know God and to be in personal relationship with God. Man's chief claim to nobility is that he was made in the image of God and is therefore capable of knowing Him. But this God whom we are meant to know and whom we ought to know is a moral Being," and we are sinners. Consequently, "our sins blot out God's face from us as effectively as the clouds of the sun.... We have no communication with God. We are 'dead through trespasses and sins' (Eph. 2:1) which we have committed."[79]

Tony Evans writes, "Probably the hardest thing for unbelievers to grasp is that outside of Jesus Christ, they are dead. Not just a little bit ill or even

---

[78] Ryrie, Charles C.. Basic Theology: A Popular Systematic Guide to Understanding Biblical Truth (p. 253). Moody Publishers. Kindle Edition.
[79] John R. W. Stott, *Basic Christianity* (Grand Rapids: Eerdmans, 1958), 72, 75.

barely alive, but as dead now as they will be throughout eternity apart from God's saving grace. This is the true condition of lost people. They are the living dead because death in Scripture is separation, never mere cessation of existence. We will never stop existing, for our souls and spirits are immortal... But the Bible's overriding concern is with spiritual death, in which the unsaved already exist, and which will become irrevocable when they die and are separated from God forever.[80]

Imagine being created by God and for God but being allergic to God! Where you cannot come into His holy presence.

Johanna Watkins suffers from a rare genetic disease which makes her deathly allergic to just about everything, including her own husband Scott. After three years of marriage Johanna began to have severe allergic reactions to certain foods, then certain smells, and finally certain people. Her allergic

---

[80] Evans, Tony. Theology You Can Count On: Experiencing What the Bible Says About... God the Father, God the Son, God the Holy Spirit, Angels, Salvation... (Kindle Locations 23565-23566). Moody Publishers. Kindle Edition.

disorder, called Mast Cell Activation Syndrome (MCAS), is a rare genetic disorder that causes her body to develop life-threatening anaphylactic reactions to virtually everything. Her face swells, her throat and airways tighten and close, and she gets terrible rashes. Because of this disorder Johanna must live in total isolation from everyone except her brother and sister – the only people her body doesn't react to. She can only communicate with her husband - who cooks and cares for her – via Skype.[81]

Spiritually dead people are allergic to God! They cannot come into His holy presence without judgment.

Adam went from an intimate love relationship with God to complete separation because of His own willful sin.

(2) Description of death.

(a) Spiritual death.

---

[81] Causey, David. A Fourth Portion of Insightful Illustrations: Illuminated Paths to Guide Us through Life's Labyrinth (Kindle Locations 5122-5125). Kindle Edition.

¹⁷ but from the tree of the knowledge of good and evil you shall not eat, for in the day that you eat from it you will surely die." Genesis 2:17

Spiritual death is the separation of the soul/spirit from God making man incapable of responding to the spiritual realm (Jn. 4:24/1 Cor. 2:14/Eph. 2:1, 5; 4:18-19/Col. 2:13/1 Tim. 5:6/ 1 Jn. 5:12

Erickson notes, "Spiritual death is both connected with physical death and distinguished from it. It is the separation of the entire person from God. God, as a perfectly holy being, cannot look upon sin or tolerate its presence. Thus, sin is a barrier to the relationship between God and humans, bringing them under God's judgment and condemnation.[82]

Robert McGee notes:

The Westminster Shorter Catechism says, "The chief end of man is to glorify God and enjoy Him forever." Man,

---

[82] Erickson, Millard J.. Christian Theology (pp. 559-560). Baker Publishing Group. Kindle Edition.

however, rejected God's purpose and chose to go his own way. Because of that rebellion, he experienced spiritual death, separation from God. Cut off from God, man had to find a new source of worth, so he turned to his performance and the approval of others.[83]

The truth is we are born dead and spend our life pretending to be alive. I could not help but think of something I read. On April 12, 2013, news agencies reported the story of Zeng Jia, a woman in China who pretended to be dead and staged her own funeral. She wanted to see how people really felt about her. As she lay silent in an open casket, she soaked in all the praise and admiration which mourners lavished upon her. Near the end of the ceremony she "awoke" to the relief of some and the anger and irritation of others.[84]

She pretended to be dead but was physically alive, but in the spiritual

---

[83] McGee, Robert. The Search for Significance: Seeing Your True Worth Through God's Eyes (Kindle Locations 2715-2716). Thomas Nelson. Kindle Edition.

[84] Causey, David. A Fourth Portion of Insightful Illustrations: Illuminated Paths to Guide Us through Life's Labyrinth (Kindle Locations 6271-6274). Kindle Edition.

realm, it is just the opposite. We pretend to be alive but are in reality spiritually dead. How many religious people, cults, and others claim to know God apart from a personal life-changing encounter with the Lord Jesus Christ, but are in fact separated from Him. There is a lot of fake news today but a whole lot more of fake life!

(b) Physical death.

5 So all the days that Adam lived were nine hundred and thirty years, and he died. Genesis 5:5

Physical death is the separation of the soul/spirit from the body (Ja. 2:26).

Physical death is actually proof that man is spiritually dead. Adam would not have died physically if he had not died spiritually that day he disobeyed God.

(c) Eternal death.

Grudem notes:

The punishment of death began to be carried out on the day that Adam and Eve sinned, but it was carried out slowly over time, as their bodies grew old and they eventually died. The promise of spiritual death was put into effect immediately, since they were cut off from fellowship with God. The death of eternal condemnation was rightfully theirs, but the hints of redemption in the text (see Gen. 3: 15, 21) suggest that this penalty was ultimately overcome by the redemption that Christ purchased.[85]

Evangelical Dictionary of Theology notes:

The "second death" (Rev. 20: 14; 21: 8), does not mean that the soul or personality lapses into nonbeing, but rather that it is ultimately and finally deprived of that presence of God and fellowship with him, which is the chief end of humankind and the essential condition of worthwhile existence. To be bereft of it is to perish, to be reduced to utter insignificance, to sink into abysmal futility. An automobile is said to be wrecked, ruined, destroyed, not only

---

[85] Grudem, Wayne A.; Grudem, Wayne A.. Systematic Theology: An Introduction to Biblical Doctrine (p. 524). Zondervan. Kindle Edition.

when its constituent parts have been melted or scattered away, but also when they have been so damaged and distorted that the car has become completely unserviceable.[86]

b. Intrinsic Cause.

(1) As we have seen the Source is Adam.

He died Immediately in his spirit...
He died gradually in his soul...
He died eventually in his body...

(2) The Course.

As we have previously seen his sin effected the entire human race (Rom. 5:12/1 Cor. 15:22/etc.).

Trans: It is both sad and sickening to watch a Fallen, spiritually dead society try to pretend it is alive! It reminds me of California's drought of 2015 when the state enforced measures to conserve water. Swimming pools remained empty, public fountains were turned off,

---

[86] Walter A. Elwell. Evangelical Dictionary of Theology (Baker Reference Library) (p. 64). Baker Publishing Group. Kindle Edition.

showering and bathing were curtailed, restaurants would only give water to drink upon request, and lawns were turning brown everywhere. State sponsored commercials attempted to turn popular opinion against green lawns, advising them to "Get down with brown." But these proved ineffectual. Only dead grass is brown, green is alive. Under these circumstances an obscure business erupted across Southern California – lawn painting. Landscaping businesses with names like Xtreme Green Grass, Lawn Lift, and Lawn Paint Pros sprung up everywhere to transform the looks of dying lawns from blotchy shades of brown to a lush green. They did it by spray painting dried up lawns with a vegetable-based green dye. Of course, the dye wouldn't last. Every couple of months the dye had to be reapplied to give the appearance of a living lush lawn.[87]

That's mankind without Christ, they spray paint with religion and synthetic

---

[87] Causey, David. A Fourth Portion of Insightful Illustrations: Illuminated Paths to Guide Us through Life's Labyrinth (Kindle Locations 4397-4398). Kindle Edition.

fun to give the appearance of life – but sooner or later reality sets in. Death is death! Therefore, we have an insurmountable barrier between God and man, the Standard of Deity; the Sin Debt; Satanic Dominion; and Spiritual Death.

Hal Lindsey notes:
"So here we have the complete picture of the universal barrier which separates man from God. Man can't tear the barrier down and he can't climb over it by his own efforts. In fact, he can't even climb over with God's help. The barriers must come down, and God alone can do that. You will meet people every day who say they have no need for God and don't feel any of the barriers we've looked at...I may visit the doctor, and he could say to me, "Hal, you have a severe illness which proper treatment can completely cure." "But, Doc, I don't *feel* sick!"...God says we have a problem. That problem is called sin."[88]

Our problem is the Standard of Deity; our Sin Debt; our Satanic Dominion;

---
[88] The Liberation of Planet Earth, Hal Lindsey, p. 66.

and our Spiritual Death – producing a barrier that no one but God Himself could ever remove.

Chapter Three

THE SOLUTION BY GOD

Intro:

1. In Eighteenth Century Europe fine writing paper remained a precious commodity because the raw material from which it was made– rags and linen – were in short supply. Then, in 1719, the French scientist, Rene-Antoine Reaumur, observed wasps making a fine paper from the wood fibers they had consumed and digested. This ultimately led to the wide-spread use of wood pulp to manufacture paper.

2. I suppose because man is created in the image of God, he is able to come up with many solutions to life's many problems. But none of them compares with the solution that God uses to solve man's sin problem.

3. Solution through the Deliverer.

I. REPRESENTATION.

Just as the first Adam was a representation of all those born the first time, so the last Adam was a representation of all who would be born-again.

As the first Adam built the barriers, the last Adam would tear them down.

As the first Adam failed by yielding to temptation, the last Adam succeeded in saying no to temptation (Mt. 4:1-11).

See, 1 Cor. 15:21-22/Rom. 5:17-19.

Hal Lindsey notes:

On several occasions in the New Testament, Jesus is referred to as the "second Adam." It's because as a man He perfectly fulfilled all the dreams and aspirations that God had originally had for the first Adam...The first man got mankind into all its trouble, but God sent another Man into the world and He undid it. In order to qualify as a true human being who could undo sin's damage, Jesus did not use His divine power while He was on earth (Phil. 2:6-

7). Jesus' whole life was lived in total dependence upon the Father who worked through Him by the Holy Spirit who indwelt Him. That's the exact way that God intended for all men to live.[89]

We see this in the temptation by Satan in trying to get the Lord Jesus to depend upon His deity, which would have disqualified him as the second Adam. He said, "Turn those stones to bread" that would not have been a temptation to us because we could not do it! Nor would it be a temptation to our Lord in His humanity. It would take an act of God to turn stones into bread. Had Jesus done that by depending upon His deity it would have been like Adam taking of that tree of the knowledge of good and evil. Our Lord as a perfect man remained totally dependent upon His Father.

See John 5:19, 30; 7:16; 8:28.

The Son of God became the God/man. He had to be man in order to die (Heb. 2:9, 14; 9:12-15) and God in order to

---

[89] The Liberation of Planet Earth, Hal Lindsey, p. 81-82. Zondervan Publishing House.

make that death effective (Mk. 2:7). He was from God (Jn. 6:38; 16:27-28; 17:5); and was God (Mt. 8:2-3; 9:1-8, 18; 14:33/ Mk. 2:5-12; 14:61-62/Jn. 1:1; 10:30; 20:26-29/etc).

The inventor of Velcro got his idea from the "gripping power" of cockleburs that clung to his clothing and his dog's fur after a walk in the woods. He reduplicated the very hooks of the burs he observed in a magnifying glass.

But God reveals a greater genius when he revealed how a second Adam could undo all that the first Adam did.

II. INCARNATION.

A. No Beginning!

He began before He was born! The Son of God's preexistent, He existed eternally as the Second Person of the Trinity. His physical birth was not His origin (Jn. 10:36; 17:5, 24).

The term Son of God has nothing to do with His birth but His eternal relationship with God the Father.

- The Son of God Existed at the time of creation and had a part in that creation (Col. 1:13-17/Heb. 1:2).

- The Son of God is Explained as being in the Father's bosom (Jn. 1:18/1 Jn. 1:1-2).

- The Son of God Entered as being sent by the Father (Isa. 9:6/Jn. 3:16; 20:21/Rom. 8:32/Gal. 4:4/1 Jn. 4:10,14).

- The Son of God Exited this world and returned to the Father (Jn. 16:28; 17:5, 24).

John Walvoord notes:

The scriptural view of the Sonship of Christ as recognized in many of the great creeds of the church is that Christ was always the Son of God by eternal generation and that He took upon Himself humanity through generation of the Holy Spirit; the human birth was not in order to become a Son of God but because He was the Son of God.[90]

---

[90] John F. Walvoord, Jesus Christ Our Lord (Chicago:Moody Press, 1969, p. 42.

Understanding Christian Theology:

Some Bible teachers have suggested that Jesus *became* the Son of God in His incarnation. In other words, He was not God's Son in eternity past before He became incarnate. This view has several weaknesses. First, it ignores clear statements in the Scriptures about Jesus' existence as the Son of God before the Incarnation. Galatians 4:4, for example, states that the Incarnation occurred "when the time had fully come," implying that the "Actor" was waiting in the wings for the appropriate moment of His appearance. The verse continues, "God sent his Son." The verb translated "sent" is coupled with a preposition that more literally could be translated "sent out from," again implying that He was the Son of God before He was incarnated. The same exact form of that verb is used in verse 6, which says, "God sent the Spirit of his Son"; the Spirit obviously came from heaven. Other Scriptures also speak of God sending His Son (1 Jn. 4:9-10, 14), using a compound verb that literally could be translated "sent away from," implying preexistence with God the

Father. And dozens of times the Gospel of John records that God "sent" His Son from heaven. Not one verse in the Bible states that Jesus ever became God's Son. He always was His Son, from all eternity.

Jesus' own references to His relationship with God the Father prior to the Incarnation are also significant. In His high priestly prayer Jesus requested, "And now, Father, glorify me in Your presence with the glory I had with you before the world began" (Jn. 17:5). Later He prayed concerning the disciples, "They knew with certainty that I came from you, and they believed that you sent me" (Jn. 17:8).

Another affirmation of Jesus' eternal Sonship is His participation in creation. The writer to the Hebrews stated that through His Son, God "made the universe" (Heb. 1:2). The Son, whom the Father "loves" (Col. 1:13), "is the image of the invisible God, the firstborn over all creation. For by him all things were created...all things were created by him and for him (1:15-16).

The teaching that Jesus' Sonship began at the Incarnation ignores and destroys the eternal relationship among the three Persons of the Trinity, whereas the Bible clearly teaches the eternal distinctions in the Trinity as Father, Son, and Holy Spirit.[91]

See Rom. 1:3-4; 9:5/Phil. 2:5-11.

To deny the deity of Christ is cultic and contradicts the clear teaching of the Word of God. Oswald Sanders makes it clear:

If Jesus is not God, then there is no Christianity, and we who worship Him are nothing more than idolaters. Conversely, if He is God, those who say He was merely a good man, or even the best of men, are blasphemers. More serious still, if He is not God, then He is a blasphemer in the fullest sense of the word. If He is not God, He is not even good… The deity of Christ is the key doctrine of Scripture. Reject it, and the Bible becomes a confused jumble of words devoid of any unifying theme. Accept it, and the Bible becomes an

---

[91] Understanding Christian Theology, Swindoll, Zuck, p. 321. Nelson Publishing.

intelligible and ordered revelation of God in the person of Jesus Christ. Christ is the center of Christianity, and the conception we form of Christianity is therefore the conception we have of Him.[92]

This is not based on human reasoning but divine revelation, Louis Berkhof gives a good presentation of the evidence:

We find that Scripture (1) explicitly asserts the deity of the Son in such passages as John 1: 1; 20: 28; Romans 9: 5; Philippians 2: 6; Titus 2: 13; John 5: 20; (2) applies divine names to Him, Isaiah 9: 6; 40: 3; Jeremiah 23: 5, 6; Joel 2: 32 (comp. Acts 2: 21); 1 Timothy 3: 16; (3) ascribes to Him divine attributes, such as eternal existence, Isaiah 9: 6; John 1: 1, 2; Revelation 1: 8; 22: 13, omnipresence, Matthew 18: 20; 28: 20; John 3: 13, omniscience, John 2: 24, 25; 21: 17; Revelation 2: 23, omnipotence. Isaiah 9: 6; Philippians 3: 21; Revelation 1: 8,

---

[92] Sanders, J. Oswald. The Incomparable Christ (Moody Classics) (p. 95). Moody Publishers. Kindle Edition.

immutability, Hebrews 1: 10-12; 13: 8, and in general every attribute belonging to the Father, Colossians 2: 9; (4) speaks of Him as doing divine works, as creation, John 1: 3, 10; Colossians 1: 16; Hebrews 1: 2, 10, providence, Luke 10: 22; John 3: 35; 17: 2; Ephesians 1: 22; Colossians 1: 17; Hebrews 1: 3, the forgiveness of sins, Matthew 9: 2-7; Mark 2: 7-10; Colossians 3: 13, resurrection and judgment, Matthew 25: 31, 32; John 5: 19-29; Acts 10: 42; 17: 31; Philippians 3: 21; 2 Timothy 4: 1, the final dissolution and renewal of all things, Hebrews 1: 10-12; Philippians 3: 21; Revelation 21: 5, and (5) accords Him divine honour, John 5: 22, 23; 14: 1; 1 Corinthians 15: 19; 2 Corinthians 13: 13; Hebrews 1: 6; Matthew 28: 19.[93]

Orville and Wilbur Wright developed the steering system for their airplane, the "Wright Flyer," from watching seagulls flex and alter the shape of their wings. They called the system "wing warping."

---

[93] Berkhof, Louis. Systematic Theology (Kindle Locations 1964-1980). E4 Group. Kindle Edition.

Old Orville and Wilbur demonstrated insight but what is that compared to the insight of God's plan of salvation for man!

B. A Birth.

The Son of God became the God/Man. He was fully God and fully man in one person (Jn. 1:1,14).

He had to bypass the sin nature passed on by the man, for if He had had a sin nature He would have needed a savior Himself! This was accomplished by the virgin birth (Gen. 3:15; 12:3/Gal. 3:16/Mt. 1:18/Lu. 1:26-38/Jn. 1:14/1 Tim. 3:16/1 Jn. 4:2). The miracle was not in the birth but the conception. The Lord Jesus was born like anybody else.

While watching a cat take swipes at a chicken and coming up with just a paw full of feathers, Eli Whitney got the inspiration for the "Cotton Gin." By replicating the "cat claws" on a tumbler.

Eli Whitney's solution was wonderful, but it pales into insignificance when we think of God's wise solution of becoming

God/man. Who but God could think of such a plan!

C. A Blameless life.

He was born under the Law (Gal. 4:4) and obeyed it perfectly in word, thought, and deed (Heb. 4:15) thus fulfilled the law (Mt. 5:17/Rom. 10:17). And He lived this blameless life, as God intended man to live, by total dependency upon God.

Hal Lindsey notes:

"Jesus' whole life was lived in total dependence upon the Father who worked through Him by the Holy Spirit who indwelt Him. That's the exact way that God intended for all men to live. If Jesus had ever withstood one temptation or performed one miracle using His own divine power, He would not have been behaving as a true man and He would have disqualified Himself from being the Savior of men (Jn. 5:19,30).[94]

---

[94] The Liberation of Planet Earth p. 82.

Now we must hasten to say His perfect life was not enough to save anybody, He had to die for our sins. But without that perfect life He would not have been qualified to die for our sins.

A veteran logger, Joseph Buford Cox, got his idea for the C-shaped blades of the modern chain saw from observing beetle larva chomp away at wood with its C-shaped jaws.

Again, that turned out to be a very useful idea, but think and marvel at God's idea of a Second Adam succeeding where the first one failed.

III. SUBSTITUTION.

Intro:

1. Bishop John Taylor Smith, former Chaplain General of the British Army, was once preaching in a large cathedral using John 3: 7 as his text, "Ye must be born again." In order to drive it home, he said, "My dear people, do not substitute anything for the new birth. You may be a member of a church, even the great church of which I am a member, the historic Church of England,

but church membership is not new birth, and 'except a man be born again he cannot see the kingdom of God.'" The rector was sitting at his left. Pointing to him, he said, "You might be a clergyman like my friend the rector here and not be born again, and 'except a man be born again he cannot see the kingdom of God.'" Then he pointed directly at the archdeacon in his stall and said, "You might even be an archdeacon like my friend in his stall and not be born again and 'except a man be born again he cannot see the kingdom of God.' You might even be a bishop, like myself, and not be born again and 'except a man be born again he cannot see the kingdom of God.'"

A day or so later he received a letter from the archdeacon, in which he wrote: My dear Bishop: You have found me out. I have been a clergyman for over thirty years, but I had never known anything of the joy that Christians speak of. I never could understand it. Mine has been hard, legal service. I did not know what was the matter with me, but when you pointed directly to me and said,

"You might even be an archdeacon and not be born again," I realized in a moment what the trouble was. I had never known anything of the new birth." He went on to say that he was wretched and miserable, had been unable to sleep all night, and begged for a conference, if the bishop could spare the time to talk with him. The next day they got together over the Word of God and after some hours, were both on their knees, the archdeacon taking his place before God as a poor, lost sinner and telling the Lord Jesus he would trust Him as his Saviour. From that time on everything was different.[95]

2. There is no substitute for being born-again, and there is no being born-again without the substitutionary death of the Lord Jesus Christ.

3. The Substitutionary death of Christ alone can bring Satisfaction of God's offended holy character.

---

[95] H. A. Ironside, Illustrations of Bible Truth (Chicago: Moody Press, 1945), 47-8.

Trans: The concept is simple to understand as Billy Graham shared in this illustration:

Billy Graham told the true story of driving too fast through a small town, a police officer pulled him over and directed him to the local justice of the peace. The judge asked how he pleaded and Graham said, "Guilty your honor." He then said that will be $15 dollars, Billy reached for his wallet to get out the money. Then the judge recognized him and said, "Say, aren't you Billy Graham, the evangelist?" Billy said, "Yes sir, I am" regretfully as he hopefully tucked his wallet back into his pocket.

The judge smiled and said, "That'll be $15 dollars. But I tell you what I am going to do, I'm going to pay this fine for you." The judge reached for his wallet took out $15 dollars and gave it to the clerk, saying, "You have been a blessing to our family."

That is an example of substitution, we are guilty of breaking God's law, but by contrast, we have not been a blessing but rebels who have caused much havoc. Yet God has chosen to justly pay for our sin debt.

A. Definition.

Charles Ryrie notes:

Substitutionary or vicarious atonement simply means that Christ suffered as a substitute for us, that is, instead of us, resulting in the advantage to us of paying for our sins. Man could atone for his sins personally only if he could suffer eternally the penalty that sin incurred. Man, of course, could never do this, so in His love and compassion, God stepped into a hopeless situation and provided a Vicar in Jesus Christ who did provide an eternal satisfaction for sin.[96]

The Lord Jesus became our substitute and only the Lord Jesus Christ, the God/man, could qualify to be such a substitute.

I thought of rope! Yes, rope. Without it, we would never have built the pyramids, crossed the oceans or scaled Mount

---

[96] Ryrie, Charles C.. Basic Theology: A Popular Systematic Guide to Understanding Biblical Truth (p. 329). Moody Publishers. Kindle Edition.

Everest. It has saved countless lives, pulled thousands from the angry seas and stopped the fall of many a mountain climber.

Rope had been around for a long time. And throughout its history - from the early Egyptians, through the Industrial Age, down to the present – rope has taken on the same basic pattern: fibers are twisted (clockwise) into yarns, yarns are twisted (counterclockwise) into strands, and strands (clockwise again) into rope. The best modern synthetic material is nylon, polypropylene, or Dacron. Far inferior - more easily obtainable material has also been used for rope. But a rope is only as good as the fibers that go into it.

The example of an English manufacturer of rope graphically illustrates this idea. The man lived in the early days of the Industrial age. His arduous work and attention to detail earned him the reputation for producing the finest and strongest rope in the world. But the man began to pay more attention to profit than to quality. He sought out cheaper materials for fibers and substituted the inferior for the superior. He amassed a fortune in the process and managed to keep his reputation unstained. Then one day, as fate would have it, while sailing the Atlantic to America, a tempest-driven wave washed the man overboard. The sailors scrambled to rescue him. They tossed him a rope which he managed to grasp. But as the sailors pulled him through the buffeting waves the rope suddenly snapped. The man drifted hopelessly away from the ship to his destiny. Upon inspection the seamen observed that the rope was not only new – it was the famous rope made by the very man they had sought to rescue. He had died a victim of his own inferior rope.[97]

There is no substitute for Jesus Christ! Man has foolishly tried to substitute His death with works, human goodness, religion, self-righteousness, the list seems endless. But if we reject His death for our sins, at our death the rope

---

[97] Causey, David. Insightful Illustrations: Making Sense of Life's Ups and Downs: STORIES, PARABLES, AND ANALOGIES THAT HELP PIECE TOGETHER LIFE'S PUZZLE (Kindle Locations 3776-3777). Unknown. Kindle Edition.

will snap and we will break hell wide open!

⁶ Yes, remember your Creator now while you are young—before the silver cord of life snaps and the gold bowl is broken; before the pitcher is broken at the fountain and the wheel is broken at the cistern; Ecclesiastes 12:6 (TLB)

B. Dissension.

Some object to this concept:

1. It makes God unjust since He condemns His sinless son in our place.

The answer is that the son voluntarily took our place (Jn. 10:17-18). Also, in one sense God the Father Himself was actually involved since the Lord Jesus is God/Man and there is one God.

2. It makes the innocent suffer for the guilty.

The answer is that is absolutely true! Since it was clearly God's purpose the objection is foolish since all of God's plans and purposes are always infinitely wise and just (1 Pet. 3:18).

3. A person cannot be responsible for sin unless he personally commits sin.

The obvious answer is – since when! Every time we drop bombs anywhere, innocent people die. A simple off-side penalty by one player penalizes the entire team. It is not odd nor wrong for our Lord to die for our sins on the cross.

The truth is that God willingly became God/Man in order to die in our place. He was not like King Erra-Imitti:

In the early second millennium BC (1847 BC), King Erra-Imitti of Mesopotamia, chose his gardener, Enlil-Bani, to be king for a day. But this was no kind gesture. The King chose him to be his substitute during the Mesopotamian celebration of the New Year – the day on which the king was supposed to be sacrificed to the gods. The Mesopotamians believed that on the New Year, the gods would decide each person's fate for the coming year. To please them, the Mesopotamians would offer their king as a sacrifice. King Erra-Imitti had no intention of becoming such a sacrifice, so he selected his gardener to take his place. But something went amiss. As the poor gardener-king nervously sat on the throne before his celebrating "subjects," with his gallows in full view, a servant dashed into the court, announcing that King ErraImitti had suddenly died. Immediately, the humble gardener was proclaimed king and he went on to successfully reign for the next 24 years, from 1847-1823 BC.

We have to keep in mind the whole story, our Lord actually died on the cross, but then rose from the dead and will return to reign right here on planet earth.

C. Demonstration.

1. The Old Testament.

Actually, the concept of an innocent substitute dying in behalf of another is well established in the animal sacrifices, which all pointed to Christ [Book of Hebrews].

- One lamb for one *Person.* This was established right after Adam and Eve sinned (Gen. 3:21). We see this principle with Cain and Abel (Gen. 4:4/Job/ etc.).

- One lamb in the *Passover.* The Passover demonstrates the principle of one lamb for a family when they were told to put the blood on the doorposts which caused the death angel to pass over that family (Ex. 12:3-14).

- One lamb for *People* of Israel. That is seen in the Day of Atonement, where a lamb is brought into the Holy of Holies by the High Priest to atone for Israel's sin for that year.

- One lamb for the *Planet*. That is exactly what the Lord Jesus did on that cross. He died in our place! Jn. 1:29; 18:14/Heb. 10:5-10.

In his book (2017) *(Re)union*, Bruxy Cavey writes:

The Victoria Cross is Canada's highest military honor, similar to the Medal of Honor in the United States. These medals are awarded for personal acts of valor above and beyond the call of duty. Of the thousands awarded to date, more citations have been bestowed for falling on grenades to save comrades than any other single act.

The first Victoria Cross of World War II was awarded to Company Sergeant-Major John Robert Osborn. The sergeant-major and his men were cut off from their battalion and under heavy attack. When the enemy came close enough, the Canadian soldiers were subjected to a concentrated barrage of grenades. Several times Osborn protected his men by picking up live grenades and throwing them back, but eventually one fell in just the wrong position to pick up in time. With only a split second to decide, Osborn shouted a warning and threw himself on top of the grenade. It exploded, killing him instantly. The rest of his company survived that battle because of Osborn's selfless other-centeredness.[98]

The Lord Jesus died on the cross not for His friends but for vile sinful enemies, in our place, so we might be saved.

---

[98] Bruxy Cavey, (Re)union (Herald Press, 2017), pages 87-88.

⁶ For while we were still helpless, at the right time Christ died for the ungodly. ⁷ For one will hardly die for a righteous man; though perhaps for the good man someone would dare even to die. ⁸ But God demonstrates His own love toward us, in that while we were yet sinners, Christ died for us.
Romans 5:6-8

We were helpless to save ourselves, totally without God, sinners, and enemies of God. Notice we were not righteous, a righteous man does what is right. He loans you $10 dollars and you have to pay him back $10 dollars; a good man will give you $10 dollars and you don't have to pay him back. But a sinner may knock you on the head, and steal all your money from your wallet. The Lord Jesus did not die for us when we were righteous or good but sinners!

2. The New Testament.

- *Anti* – for, a preposition which means "in place of" (Mk. 10:45). In Understanding Christian theology:

"The Greek preposition translated "for" denotes substitution. The stronger of these is *anti,* "in place of." We see this in the word "Antichrist," who, as a counterfeit, will present himself in place of or instead of Christ. The meaning "in place of" is seen in Matthew 2:22 ("Archelaus was reigning over Judea *instead of* his father Herod")...and Matthew 20:28 ("Just as the Son of Man did not come to be served, but to serve, and to give His life a ransom *for* many").[99]

- *Huper* – a preposition which means "on behalf of" (2 Cor. 5:21/1 Pet. 3:18). Again from Understanding Christian Theology:

The other preposition is *hyper,* whose basic idea is "on behalf of" or "for the benefit of."...In 2 Cor. 5:14-15 Paul plays on the double sense of *hyper.* Christ's death is first "in our place" but it is then "on our behalf" or "for our sake."...The meaning of "in place of" can be seen in Hebrews 2:9 (Jesus tasted

---

[99] Understanding Christian Theology, Charles R. Swindoll, and Roy B. Zuck General Editors, p. 832. Thomas Nelson Publishers.

"death for [hyper] everyone." In 2 Cor. 5:21 ("For He made Him who knew no sin to be sin *for* us, that we might become the righteousness of God in Him") and 1 Timothy 2:5-6 ("Christ Jesus…gave Himself a ransom *for* all"). Hyper may carry either meaning "on behalf of" or "in place of" or perhaps both.

The only sin that Jesus ever knew was ours; and the only righteousness we will ever know is His.

Years ago in the war between France and Germany, a summons went out to Germans residing in England to take their place with the troops at Paris. At that time, a man was walking along the streets of London, when he met a German friend. Surprised to see him there, he asked why he was not in France.

"His answer was "Oh, I am dead! His friend replied, "Dead! What do you mean?"

He explained, "My name was called among others and I thought I should have to leave England; but I had no wish to do so and I set to work to find some way by which I might escape. The command was stringent, so that it was impossible to evade it, but at length I found a substitute, willing for a sum of money to take my place. I gladly paid the sum, and am thankful that I was free to remain in England. My substitute, however, had not had many days with the German army when a French shell burst close to where he was standing and he was killed. He was there for me, his death was counted as mine, so in the eyes of the law, I am dead, and the German nation has no further claim upon me."[100]

Of course, we did not provide the substitute, God did, and it cost us nothing. He died our death!

Con:

1. So we have one of the most wonderful words in Substitution – it is the only basis for God's Satisfaction of His holy character.

---

[100] All the Doctrines of the Bible, Herbert Lockyer, p. 183, Zondervan Press.

2. The problem is many have feel-good substitutions that won't work.

James Schlatter was a chemist with the pharmaceutical company G. D. Searle. In 1965 he was feverishly working on an anti-ulcer drug aspartame. But fate had a different path for Schlatter's anti-ulcer drug. One day after handling the drug with his bare hands, he licked his fingers to grab a piece of paper. A powerfully sweet taste remained on his tongue! His anti-ulcer drug was super-sweet – and it had no bitter aftertaste! Could it serve a better purpose as a no calorie sugar substitute? He made his discovery known to the heads of G. D. Searle and, after further testing, they decided to market the drug as a sugar substitute instead of an anti-ulcer drug. Aspartame never made it as an ulcer-fighting drug. But it did go on to sweeten hundreds of foods and millions of lives. Today the drug is marketed under the brand name NutraSweet and is used to sweeten about 1,200 different food products.

We have many sugary substitutes today – good works, church membership, fame and fortune, money, and the list seems endless. But the only one who can be your substitute is the Lord Jesus Christ.

IV. SATISFACTION.

Intro:

1. Africannews.com recently reported on a Ugandan man, the late Charles Obong, who decreed in his will that $55,000 should be buried with him in his coffin. What was Mr. Obong's reasoning? The 52-year-old public official wanted the money with him so he could use it to appease God on judgment day.

2. The only one who can appease and satisfy the offended character of God is God Himself.

3. We have come to Satisfaction, as we saw, it is based on Substitution, the substitutionary death of the Lord Jesus Christ.

A. God's Wrath.

This is important because without God's wrath there would be no need to satisfy His offended character. That is why, the Devil, tries so hard to get people to believe that God is *only* love and thus bypass the concept that God is light as well. But the Bible is our authority.

1. God's wrath is used 585 times in the Old Testament.

2. God's wrath is also used in the New Testament as well (Jn. 3:36/Rom. 1:18; 9:22/Eph. 5:6/Col. 3:6/ 2 Thess. 1:8-9).

Tony Evans:

God's wrath is not an easy subject to talk about. But it's as integral to His nature as any of His other perfections. If I failed to teach about it, I would be doing my readers a great disservice. Any discussion of God's character that does not include His characteristic called wrath is an incomplete study. Worse yet, it may even be an errant study of God, because one of the inescapable truths about our great God is that He is a God of wrath. In fact, the Bible has more to say about God's wrath than it does about His love.[101]

Henry Morris writes:

The wrath of God is a conception which cannot be eradicated from the [Bible] without irreparable loss. It is not the monopoly of one or two writers, but pervades the entire corpus so that there is no important section of which it can be said, "Here the wrath of God is unknown!" The ubiquity of the concept must be stressed, because of the tendency in some circles today to over look it or explain it away. Sin is not just a mere peccadillo which a kindly, benevolent God will regard as no consequence. On the contrary, the God of the Old Testament is One who loves righteousness (Psa. 33:5; 48:10, etc.), and whose attitude to unrighteousness can be described as hatred...Modern men find a difficulty with this aspect of the [Biblical] teaching, in part at least because they have so well learned that

---

[101] Evans, Tony. Theology You Can Count On: Experiencing What the Bible Says About... God the Father, God the Son, God the Holy Spirit, Angels, Salvation... (Kindle Locations 3182-3187). Moody Publishers. Kindle Edition.

God is love. But it is important to notice that this was a truth known and valued by men of Old Testament times, and they apparently did not find it insuperably difficult to combine ideas that God loved them and that He hated all that is evil and would punish it severely.[102]

Can you imagine how it felt to live in the shadow of an executioner – especially one as terrifying as the Halifax Gibbet? The Halifax Gibbet, heights of Halifax, England, is considered to be the first guillotine. From 1541 to 1650, the Lord of the Manor in Halifax used it execute anyone who stole goods in the value of a mere 13 ½ pence or was found in possession of such stolen goods or confessed to stealing them. Guards would bind the poor thief hand and foot, place his neck beneath the blade of this monster that towered fifteen feet high, drop the crossbeam, and cut off his head. But the Lord of the Manor was not the least secretive about using the Gibbet. He placed it conspicuously in the

---

[102] Leon Morris, The Apostolic Preaching of the Cross, 3d ed. (Grand Rapids: Eerdmans, 1965). 174.

center of the city, so that everyone would live in its shadow - always reminded of the penalty for stealing.

The truth is that Fallen humanity lives under the shadow of God's wrath, and all it takes is being born in Adam, one sin, to offend God's holy character and cause His just wrath to be upon us.

B. God-ward *Remedy*...Propitiation.

1. First, the *Direction* of propitiation.

It is Satisfaction that is Godward.

Propitiation is something God does for Himself.

None say it better than Watchman Nee:

"God overlooks what we have done, because He sees the blood. The blood is therefore not primarily for us but for God. If I want to understand the value of the blood, I must accept God's valuation of it... in Exodus 12: 13 the shedding of the blood of the Passover lamb in Egypt for Israel's redemption... The blood was put on the lintel and on the doorposts... God said, "When I see the blood, I will pass over you." Here we have another illustration of the fact that the blood was not meant to be presented to man but to God, for the blood was put on the lintel and on the doorposts where those feasting inside the house would not see it."

He also points out:

"On the Day of Atonement the blood was taken from the sin offering and brought into the Most Holy Place and there sprinkled before the Lord seven times... the Lord commanded that no man should enter the tabernacle itself except the high priest. It was he alone who took the blood and, going into the Most Holy Place, sprinkled it there to make atonement before the Lord. Why? Because the high priest was a type of the Lord Jesus in His redemptive work (Heb. 9: 11– 12)... Moreover, connected with his going in there was but one act, namely, the presenting of the blood to God as something He had accepted, something in which He could find satisfaction. It was a transaction between the high priest and God in the sanctuary, away from the eyes of the men who were to benefit by it...The blood is first for God to see. We then have to accept God's valuation of the blood is first for God to see. We then have to accept God's valuation of it. In doing so we shall find our salvation. If instead we try to come to a valuation by way of our feelings, we get nothing; we remain in darkness. No, it is a matter of faith in God's Word. We have to believe that the blood is precious to God because He says it is so (1 Pet. 1: 18-19)... The blood has satisfied God; it must satisfy us also."[103]

The mountains west of Camp Zama, Japan, are magnificent. From the hilltops of Zama you can see Mount Oyama. It rises to 4,107 feet above sea level.

There is, however, one downside to Mount Oyama, it blocks our view of something much greater - Mount Fuji. Mount Fuji is far bigger than Mount Oyama. In fact, at 12,388 feet tall, Mount Oyama, which is only 1/ 3 the

---

[103] Nee, Watchman. The Normal Christian Life. CLC Publications. Kindle Edition.

size, is much closer and blocks my view of Mount Fuji.

Mount Oyama is like our sin, it is a huge mountain but it is nothing compared to Mount Calvary, which is like Mount Fuji. The problem is we allow our sins to block the view of the blood! God never does this, and if we believe God we can by our eyes of faith see Mt. Calvary is bigger than our mountain of sin. See Rom. 5:20, keep in mind that our sin is finite while God's grace is infinite.

2. Next, a working Definition of propitiation.

Propitiation is "turn away wrath by the satisfaction of violated justice."

Robert McGee notes:

Propitiation means that the wrath of someone who has been unjustly wronged has been satisfied. It is an act that soothes hostility and satisfies the need for vengeance. Providing His only begotten Son as the propitiation for our sin was the greatest possible demonstration of God's love for man. To understand God's wondrous provision of propitiation, it is helpful to remember what He has endured from mankind. From Adam and Eve's sin in the Garden of Eden to the obvious depravity we see in our world today, human history is the story of greed, hatred, lust, and pride—evidence of man's wanton rebellion against the God of love and peace. If not done with a desire to glorify Him, even our good deeds are like filthy garments to God (Isa. 64:6). Our sin deserves the righteous wrath of God.[104]

God was under no obligation to do this! When the angels rebelled every single one of them will end up in the lake of fire. God could have turned this very planet into hell, after Adam sinned, if He wanted to.

Michael Douglas in a movie Falling Down, portrays a man who has lost his family and job. He goes off the deep end striking out at those whom He believes are the cause of the world's injustices. In the end he takes his own life. The problem was that man was,

---

[104] McGee, Robert. The Search for Significance: Seeing Your True Worth Through God's Eyes (Kindle Locations 1563-1567). Thomas Nelson. Kindle Edition.

himself, just as unjust as the world he lashed out against.

But God really is just, and could have released His eternal wrath against all humanity but in His love, found a just way, to save all who would believe.

C. God's World.

God's world is a holy world and thus He must find a way to justly deal with man's sin.

Hermon Hoeksema gives us the concept:

First, is it not possible for God to excuse the sinner? God cannot excuse the sinner, or sin, because God is righteous. If God is to pardon sin, there must be a basis upon which that pardon can rest… Propitiation is that which appeases. Propitiation presupposes sin and that God is wrathful because of that sin. There is something that appeases this wrath of God. God's wrath is not some passing passion. God's wrath is the constant expression of his holy and righteous will with respect to the sinner. Therefore, God's wrath cannot be appeased except by the bearing of that wrath. God's wrath must be poured out. God cannot deny himself. His wrath is as constant as God is. It must be poured out. A propitiatory sacrifice is a sacrifice in which one is intentionally, from the principle of love, set forth to receive the wrath of God. If one loves God, loves God's wrath, loves to have God pour out that wrath upon him, and is able to bear that wrath to the full, this is propitiation. This the sinner cannot perform. It is impossible for the sinner to bring propitiation. It is impossible for the sinner to bear that wrath of God to the end. There is no end... God set forth Christ to be a propitiation. This indicates, for one thing, that God propitiates himself. We don't. We don't appease God. God provides for himself a sacrifice... He justifies the ungodly. He does this. God justifies the ungodly. To justify the ungodly without propitiation is unrighteous... Christ is the propitiation for sin. He bears indeed the sins of his people [and of the world, 1 Jn. 2:2]. Because Christ is indeed a propitiation, the cross is the demonstration of the righteousness of God as he justifies the ungodly.[105]

²⁵ whom God displayed publicly as a propitiation in His blood through faith. *This was* to demonstrate His righteousness…Romans 3:25

D. God's Word.

He did this to satisfy His Holy Character but God wants people to know this. When God saved those who believed in the Old Testament, it looked as if He did it without any righteous basis for it. God wants to make sure people tie the animal sacrifices to Christ's death.

²⁵ whom God displayed publicly as a propitiation in His blood through faith. *This was* to demonstrate His righteousness, because in the forbearance of God He passed over the sins previously committed; ²⁶ for the demonstration, *I say,* of His righteousness at the present time, so that He would be just and the justifier of

---

[105] Hoeksema, Herman. Righteous by Faith Alone: A Devotional Commentary on Romans (Kindle Locations 2040-2041). Reformed Free Publishing Association. Kindle Edition.

the one who has faith in Jesus.
Romans 3:25-26

That word *propitiation* is hilastērion in the Greek [hih lahss TAY ree ahn]. The only other place this term occurs in the NT is Heb 9: 5, which says:

⁵ and above it *were* the cherubim of glory overshadowing the mercy seat; but of these things we cannot now speak in detail. Hebrews 9:5

In the Greek OT, the word is used for the lid of the ark of the covenant (traditionally called "the mercy seat"; see Ex 25: 17-22; Lv 16: 2,13-15).

Another related word, hilasmos, atoning sacrifice, occurs twice in the NT (1 Jn 2: 2; 4: 10). This word family refers to the turning away of God's wrath against sin by means of a sacrifice. The main ideas of this word group are mercy and satisfactory sacrifice for sin. The innermost part of the tabernacle was the place where mercy was found, but only through the proper sacrifice. Similarly, Jesus's death is the only place one can find mercy. God's wrath against sin was turned away by Christ's atoning sacrifice... On the Day of Atonement, the high priest would sprinkle blood over the ark to atone for the nation. By this rite sins were deemed expiated or wiped away. Moreover God's wrath was averted or propitiated. But human sins could not literally be atoned for by the death of animals (Heb. 10:4). Thus Jesus came to accomplish what no priest slaying an animal could ever hope to accomplish: full satisfaction of God's requirements for atonement. God presented his Son as an atoning sacrifice. By means of Jesus's blood— his sacrificial death— God's holy wrath against sin was appeased, and the sins of those who place their faith in Christ are taken away.[106]

We know all these things only because God's Word has revealed them. As one notes:

It is established, then, that God cannot excuse sin. Would it not be possible for God to establish a basis of justification

---

[106] Staff, Holman Bible . CSB Study Bible (Kindle Locations 244845-244855). Holman Bible Publishers. Kindle Edition.

for his people? Suppose that God had provided a basis of justification that satisfied his own conscience, but that he had not published it. Then sin would have been propitiated, and the basis for righteousness would have been established, but we would not know anything about it. But now All the world must say that God is righteous.

So, we come to the bottom line as Charles Ryrie observes:

Because Christ had died, God is satisfied. Therefore, we should not ask anyone to try to *do* anything to satisfy Him. This would mean trying to appease someone who is already appeased, which is totally unnecessary. Therefore our message to men today should not suggest in any way that they can please God by doing something, but only that they should be satisfied with the sacrifice of Christ which completely satisfied the wrath of God.

Edward Roy ran a lowly business—Jiffy Johns of Pompano Beach, Florida. Five hundred portable toilets for rent. Band concerts, construction sites, church picnics, outdoor gatherings of any size could rent his product. But there was one big problem – what to do with all of that sewage! If he paid someone to haul it off it would have eaten up all his profits. In his search for a solution, he found a solar-heating process that turned sewage into fertilizer. Then came a masterstroke of marketing: instead of trying to sell the technology directly to local Florida communities, his company expanded and began to operate three $3 million plants itself. Under this new arrangement, the company would treat sewage for a fee and convert it into fertilizer, which was, in turn, sold for a substantial profit.[107]

His solution was to turn waste into wealth! God has done something similar. Good took our sinful sewage, without compromising His Holiness, and satisfied His offended character.

As we have seen, propitiation which is based on Christ's substitutionary death,

---

[107] Swindoll, Charles R.. The Tale of the Tardy Oxcart (Swindoll Leadership Library) (p. 60). Thomas Nelson. Kindle Edition.

removes the barrier of the Standard of Deity (Rom. 3:24-26/5:8-9).

Let's briefly look at this:

1. Exclusion of righteousness by the Law. See, Rom. 3:21-23.

a. Righteousness is not received by keeping the Law. 21a See Rom. 4:13-15.

21 But now apart from the Law *the* righteousness of God has been manifested…

b. Recognized by O.T. revelation.

being witnessed by the Law and the Prophets – this concept was nothing new!

c. Requirement fulfilled by Christ.

22 even *the* righteousness of God through faith in Jesus Christ for all those who believe; for there is no distinction; 23 for all have sinned and fall short of the glory of God,

2. Explanation of how to get righteous. Rom. 3:24-26

a. Justification. 24

²⁴ being justified as a gift by His grace through the redemption which is in Christ Jesus – later.

b. Propitiation. 25

²⁵ whom God displayed publicly as a propitiation in His blood through faith. *This was* to demonstrate His righteousness, because in the forbearance of God He passed over the sins previously committed; ²⁶ for the demonstration, *I say,* of His righteousness at the present time, so that He would be just and the justifier of...

c. Obligation.

the one who has faith in Jesus - later

3. Expectation of imputed righteousness. Rom. 3:27-31

a. Eliminates Pride. 27-28

²⁷ Where then is boasting? It is excluded. By what kind of law? Of works? No, but by a law of faith. ²⁸ For we maintain that a man is justified by faith apart from works of the Law.

b. Equalizes all People. 29-30

²⁹ Or is God *the God* of Jews only? Is He not *the God* of Gentiles also? Yes, of Gentiles also, ³⁰ since indeed God who will justify the circumcised by faith and the uncircumcised through faith is one – not only of Jew and Gentiles but of Black and White, or Republican and Democrat, etc.

c. Establishes the Purpose of the Law.

³¹ Do we then nullify the Law through faith? May it never be! On the contrary, we establish the Law.

To understand the purpose of the Law we need to go to Rom. 7:7-25

- The law *Expresses* God's Standard (Rom. 7:1, 12/Psa. 19:7; 119:142).

⁷ What shall we say then? Is the Law sin? May it never be!

- The law *Exposes* Sin (Rom. 3:20).

On the contrary, I would not have come to know sin except through the Law; for I would not have known about coveting if the Law had not said, "YOU SHALL NOT COVET."

- The law *Excites* the Sin nature (Rom. 5:20).

⁸ But sin, taking opportunity through the commandment, produced in me coveting of every kind; for apart from the Law sin *is* dead. ⁹ I was once alive apart from the Law; but when the commandment came, sin became alive and I died; ¹⁰ and this commandment, which was to result in life, proved to result in death for me; ¹¹ for sin, taking an opportunity through the commandment, deceived me and

through it killed me. ¹² So then, the Law is holy, and the commandment is holy and righteous and good. ¹³ Therefore did that which is good become *a cause of* death for me? May it never be! Rather it was sin, in order that it might be shown to be sin by effecting my death through that which is good, so that through the commandment sin would become utterly sinful.

- The law *Exhausts* all self-effort (to either save or sanctify).

¹⁴ For we know that the Law is spiritual, but I am of flesh, sold into bondage to sin. ¹⁵ For what I am doing, I do not understand; for I am not practicing what I *would* like to *do,* but I am doing the very thing I hate. ¹⁶ But if I do the very thing I do not want *to do,* I agree with the Law, *confessing* that the Law is good. ¹⁷ So now, no longer am I the one doing it, but sin which dwells in me. ¹⁸ For I know that nothing good dwells in me, that is, in my flesh; for the willing is present in me, but the doing of the good *is* not. ¹⁹ For the good that I want, I do not do, but I practice the

very evil that I do not want. [20] But if I am doing the very thing I do not want, I am no longer the one doing it, but sin which dwells in me. [21] I find then the principle that evil is present in me, the one who wants to do good. [22] For I joyfully concur with the law of God in the inner man, [23] but I see a different law in the members of my body, waging war against the law of my mind and making me a prisoner of the law of sin which is in my members. [24] Wretched man that I am! Who will set me free from the body of this death?

- The law brings us to Exercise faith in the Savior (afterwards, our sanctifier) (Gal. 3:24).

[25] Thanks be to God through Jesus Christ our Lord!

The ultimate purpose of the law was then to bring us to Christ.

We will get to justification, but for now, we are focusing our attention on propitiation.

Leon Morris comments:

Redemption is substitutionary, for it means that Christ paid the price that we could not pay, paid it in our stead, and we go free. Justification interprets our salvation judicially, and as the New Testament sees it Christ took our legal liability, took it in our stead. Reconciliation means the making of people to be at one by the taking away of the cause of hostility. In this case, the cause is sin, and Christ removed that cause for us. We could not deal with sin. He could and did, and did it in such a way that it is reckoned to us. Propitiation points us to the removal of the divine wrath, and Christ has done this by bearing the wrath for us. It was our sin which drew it down; it was He who bore it…. Was there a price to be paid? He paid it. Was there a victory to be won? He won it. Was there a penalty to be borne? He bore it. Was there a judgment to be faced? He faced it.[108]

Con:

---

[108] The Cross in the New Testament [Grand Rapids: Eerdmans, 1965], 405.

1. Solution through a Deliverer.

We have seen the Situation; the Separation, and now the Solution in: A Representation; Incarnation; Substitution; and now Satisfaction.

2. God through the Lord Jesus will turn sinful waste into spiritual wealth to all who will receive it and now has satisfied His offended holy character removing the most difficult barrier between God and man. It is not removed when we believe but is now an accomplished fact!

3. My wife has problems with her sciatic nerve and we have read that walking is good for her. So I bought her a cane with a light on it. If we walk around our property, we begin walking right under a street light, it is so bright that her little light on her cane appears not to even be on! She, while under that bright light, ignores her little cane light as she is totally satisfied with the big light.

As we walk through this life, we have a choice, we can trust God's light, which is totally satisfied with Christ's death or we can focus on our little light, still trying to satisfy God's offended character with what we do. Take your choice: His light or yours; His blood or your behavior; that God is satisfied through Christ or trying to satisfy Him through something you do.

Chapter Four

THE SALVATION OF MAN.

Intro:

1. In the 1951 science fiction movie, *The Day the Earth Stood Still*, space traveler Klaatu, lands his spaceship in Washington, DC. He is hunted down, shot, and imprisoned. But moments before he is finally taken, he warns Helen Benson, about his avenging robot – eight-foot-tall Gort. He warns her that. "If anything happens to him, Gort will wreak revenge on the city. Therefore, she must intercept him and repeat this command: "Klaatu Barada Nikto!" Helen responds, "But he's a robot. Without you, what could he do?" Klaatu gravely responds, "There's no limit to what he could do. He could destroy the earth."

2. That is just science fiction, but the reality is when it comes to the true and living God, there is no limit to what He can do! After man rebelled against Him He could have destroyed the earth, but instead He chose to do something so mindboggling that it stuns the imagination – to Pardon all sins and Impute righteousness to all who would receive it!

3. We now come to the Salvation – first step justification.

Trans: We have looked at The Situation: God's Perfection; Creation; and Demonstration of grace. The Separation: Standard of Deity; Sin Debt; Satanic Dominion; and Spiritual Death. We looked at God's Solution: Representation; Incarnation; Substitution; and Satisfaction. Now we come to the Salvation.

I. JUSTIFICATION.

A. Pardon. *Just-as-if-I'd-never-sinned!* Forgiveness is Subtraction.

Now technically pardon is not the same as justification, but we are doing a simple overview, a back to the basics. But keep in mind everything we look at is Biblically sound.

1. *Meaning* of forgiveness.

The Greek word means "to send away." To forgive means to remove the accusations against the sinner, after God has been satisfied concerning his sins, by His own work.

One notes:

The literal meaning of forgiveness is "to dismiss." "Dismiss from what?" we ask. Evidently it means dismiss from the only record that exists, that is, from the mind of God... God does not forget the fact of sin, but he dismisses it from his mind as sin. As a result of this forgiveness, God does not impute that sin to the sinner. Sin is debt. Sin causes us to be behind in our obligation... He gives us a clean sheet, so that there is no sin counted against us. God does not impute or reckon sin against us. This is a marvel! Would it not be a marvel if you should put your hand in the fire, and it did not burn you? This is the marvel of forgiveness…[And keep in mind] Without forgiveness, the door of hell is inevitably open. Without forgiveness, the doors of heaven are inevitably shut. Forgiveness is the key that shuts the door to everlasting damnation. Forgiveness opens the door to heaven, to everlasting glory, and to fellowship with God.[109]

I bought a cheap, used suit, from eBay, when it arrived it had a big round stain on it! And even after I had it dry cleaned, the stain remained. In fact, I showed it to several of you. Then I decided to have it dry cleaned, but this time told the woman, about the stain and sure enough, she got it out!

When we acknowledge our sin-stain and receive the Lord Jesus as our Savior, He *removes* the sin-stain from us, *sends it away*!

2. *Measure* of forgiveness.

---

[109] Hoeksema, Herman. Righteous by Faith Alone: A Devotional Commentary on Romans (Kindle Locations 2364-2365). Reformed Free Publishing Association. Kindle Edition.

a. It includes *All.*

Not only all our sins, but the self that produces those sins!

As one noted:

So we see that objectively the blood deals with our sins. The Lord Jesus has borne them on the cross for us as our Substitute and has thereby obtained for us forgiveness... But we must now go a step further in the plan of God to understand how He deals with the sin principle in us. The blood can wash away my sins, but it cannot wash away my "old man." It needs the cross to crucify me. The blood deals with the sins, but the cross must deal with the sinner... Our sins are dealt with by the blood, but we ourselves are dealt with by the cross. The blood procures our pardon for what we have done; the cross procures our deliverance from what we are.[110]

Our focus for now is on our sins...

---

[110] Nee, Watchman. The Normal Christian Life (p. 26). CLC Publications. Kindle Edition.

(1) It is *Biblical.* Col. 2:13/Heb. 10:14

¹³ When you were dead in your transgressions and the uncircumcision of your flesh, He made you alive together with Him, having forgiven us **all** our transgressions. Colossians 2:13

How much is all to an omniscient God? Every single one of them!

I read about a legal decision from a case in Pennsylvania, where the word "all" was defined as "All includes everything and excludes nothing."

Our Lord cried out on the cross, "It is finished", literally Paid in Full! The Complete Bible Library notes:

A similar use in classical Greek is to "complete" or "perform" obligations, especially taxes or tribute. The concept of perform is used to signify the execution of a dangerous feat. *Teleō* also refers to the carrying out of religious duties and the performing of prayers. It is often translated "to pay debts." A final use of the word in classical Greek is "to complete" in the sense of bringing to an end. Aristotle used the word to denote the bringing to an end the years of a person's life (*Liddell-Scott*). Josephus used *teleō* meaning to "fulfill" a promise and also to pay a tribute to masters (*Bauer*).[111]

Hal Lindsey writes:

Just before Jesus gave up His earthly life and commended His Spirit to the Father. He shouted a word which is the Magna Carta of all true believers. That victorious cry was "Tetelestai!" Let that word burn like a firebrand into your mind, because that's the *exact same word* that a Roman judge would write across a released criminal's Certificate of Debt to show that all his penalty had been paid for and he was free at last. The word used in this way means "paid in full" and is translated in many Bibles as "It is finished." In the mind of God, "Paid in Full" has been written across the Certificate of Debt of every man who will ever live because His debt to God has been fully paid by Jesus.

---

[111] Thoralf Gilbrant, ed., "4903. τελέω," in *The Complete Biblical Library Greek-English Dictionary – Sigma-Omega*, (Springfield, MO: Complete Biblical Library, 1991), WORD*search* CROSS e-book, Under: "4903.

But if a man would be so foolish as to insist on staying imprisoned by his sins, even though their debt has been paid...Then when he comes to the end of his life, he will have to pay the penalty of death and [eternal] separation from God.[112]

(2) It is also *Logical.*

Christ died in 33 A.D....I was born in 1953....born-again in 1974...one day I will die, let's say 2050.

When the Lord Jesus died in 33 A.D., how many of my sins were future sins? All of them! God being omniscient saw every single one of them. Therefore the Lord Jesus had to die for every single one of them. If there was one sin that He did not pay for, that one sin would have kept Him from accepting me in the first place. Sometimes people say that if you commit a certain sin you will lose your salvation, but again, that so called sin, was known to God before it was ever committed. He must forgive us of

---

[112] Liberation of Planet Earth, Hal Lindsey, p. 102.

all our sins or He cannot save us to begin with.

Trans: Hal Lindsey noted, "Many people have a concept of a cross that only looks to the rear of their lives, but never looks ahead. That's only half of a cross and that's really no cross at all. When God says He forgives us *all* sins, that's a cross with two arms, one stretched back into our past and one reaching into our entire future. Anything less than an all-inclusive forgiveness on the timeline of history falls pathetically short of God's infinite provision for sin."

Horatio Spafford penned this blessing in 1873:

My sin—oh, the bliss of this glorious thought!—
My sin, not in part but the whole,
Is nailed to the cross, and I bear it no more,
Praise the Lord, praise the Lord, O my soul!
It is well, with my soul,
It is well, it is well with my soul.

   b. It includes an inability to *Recall*.

He not only forgives, but he also forgets!

¹⁷ "AND THEIR SINS AND THEIR LAWLESS DEEDS I WILL REMEMBER NO MORE." Hebrews 8:12; 10:17

Charles Spurgeon writes:

This is a wonder of wonders, that God should say he will do what in some sense he cannot do. God's pardon of sin is so complete that he himself describes it as not remembering our iniquity. The Lord cannot in strict accuracy of speech forget anything. But he wishes us to know that his pardon is so true and deep that it amounts to an absolute oblivion, a total forgetting of all the wrongdoing of the pardoned ones.[113]

In his book, *Lee: The Last Years,* Charles Bracelen Flood reports that after the Civil War, Robert E. Lee visited a Kentucky lady who took him to the remains of a grand old tree in front of her house. There she bitterly cried that its limbs and trunk had been destroyed

---

[113] CSB Bibles by Holman; Begg, Alistair. CSB Spurgeon Study Bible (Kindle Locations 98731-98734). B&H Publishing Group. Kindle Edition.

by Federal Artillery fire. She looked to Lee for a word condemning the North or at least sympathizing with her loss. After a brief silence, Lee said, "Cut it down, my dear Madam, and forget it."[114]

That's what God has done! Because He paid for our sins He can forget about them. They are gone!

I have had a program on my computer for years, it is an LP Recorder and I have used it often. But it stopped working. So I decided I would uninstall it and then reinstalling it thinking that might somehow fix the problem. Problem was, after I unistalled it – it was gone! I emailed them and they were not the least bit sympathetic! I tried everything I could to get it back. But that program was gone! I was working on this sermon and it was as if the Lord said, "Hey, that is what I have done with all your sins! They are uninstalled and neither you, the devil or anyone else can bring them back!

3. *Means* of forgiveness.

---

[114] Craig Brian Larson, ed., *750 Engaging Illustrations*, (Grand Rapids, MI: Baker Books, 2008), WORD*search* CROSS e-book, 180-181.

The means is not Divine generosity or leniency or human tears, but the blood of Jesus Christ. A life has been given in our place providing a just basis for forgiveness (Heb 9:21-22).

It is not like a presidential pardon we hear so much about today, where the president can forgive anybody for any or no reason. In fact, President Trump even talked about having the power to pardon himself!

Someone may ask, "If God is gracious and merciful, couldn't He just forgive. Sort of live and let live? Here's the problem:

Someone always eats the cost of sin. Let's say your neighbor crashes his car through your fence. When you discover the shambles, you forgive him: "Don't worry about the fence! All is forgiven." But forgiving your neighbor doesn't do away with the bill or dissolve the damage; it means you eat the cost.

During the U.S. housing crisis, shoddy banking practices, fat-cat executives, and corporate corruption threw a sledgehammer into the global economy. Now, imagine a new man is installed in the aftermath as the new CEO of one of the massive corporations guilty for the crisis. The old CEO is out the door; a new boss is in town. This new guy is personally innocent: he wasn't behind the wheel when the ship got steered into the rocks. But there's still a huge debt. Bank of America alone owed people $17 billion.

Someone has to pay the costs. Here's what actually happened: in the aftermath of the housing crisis, the banks were deemed "too big to fail," and the government forgave the debt, covering the most expensive bailout of human history. Though the banking industry had caused massive damage, the debt was forgiven. But the debt didn't go away. Someone else covered it—in this case, the American people. Someone always eats the cost.

At the Cross, God was eating the cost of our sin. God justly forgave the sin debt—by personally covering the cost. The truth is the Government did not give the most expensive bail out in history - the most expensive bailout was when the Lord Jesus took the compounded wrath of God in our place. Thus providing the most outrageous debt-forgiveness plan the world has or ever will know.[115]

The means of our forgiveness is the substitutionary death of Christ (Eph. 1:7/Col. 1:14/1 Pet. 2:24; 3:18/etc.).

It is not our faith that forgives, but, the object of our faith, the Lord Jesus Christ.

It is not our repentance that brings forgiveness but forgiveness brings about repentance. The Ragamuffin Gospel:

The saved sinner is prostrate in adoration, lost in wonder and praise. He knows repentance is not what we do in order to earn forgiveness; it is what we do because we have been forgiven. It serves as an expression of gratitude rather than an effort to earn forgiveness. Thus the sequence of forgiveness and then repentance, rather

---

[115] *Joshua Ryan Butler, The Pursuing God (Thomas Nelson, 2016), page 100.*

than repentance and then forgiveness, is crucial for understanding the gospel of grace.[116]

D. James Kennedy points out the problem:

The cross is such good news. So why doesn't everyone embrace it? I'm convinced that the single biggest reason is our pride. Pride was the downfall of the devil and all his demons. So it is also the downfall of much of humankind. After looking at the incredible, marvelous, amazing grace of God, we can only marvel that God would provide such rich forgiveness for undeserving worms as we are in our unregenerate state… The problem is, so many people in this country assume they're saved because they've never believed they were lost. But one thing is absolutely sure: You cannot be saved unless you're lost. The Bible tells us that "God resists the proud, but gives grace to the humble" (James 4: 6). Humbling ourselves before God and

---

[116] Manning, Brennan. The Ragamuffin Gospel: Good News for the Bedraggled, Beat-Up, and Burnt Out (p. 75). The Crown Publishing Group. Kindle Edition.

acknowledging our sin and our lostness is what prepares us to receive His grace. We're wrong if we think, I am a good person, I am righteous and holy and just, and I am going to accept God's grace. No, His grace is for the wicked; God "justifies the ungodly" (Romans 4: 5). This is a most astonishing thing, but we have to humble ourselves and say, "O Christ, I am that lost sinner, that ungodly one for whom You came and for whom You died."[117]

If you think that you are part of the means that God used to forgive you of your sin – you are still lost in your sin!

4. *Imageries* of forgiveness.

- As far as the east is from the west (Psa. 103:12).

Jerry Bridges notes, "If you start west and continue in that direction you will always be going west. North and south meet at the North Pole, but east and west never meet… He is saying they

---

[117] Kennedy, Dr D. James; Jerry Newcombe. Cross Purposes: Discovering the Great Love of God for You. The Crown Publishing Group. Kindle Edition.

have been removed an infinite distance from us... He is saying His forgiveness is total, complete, and unconditional. He is saying He is not keeping score with regard to our sins... Because of Christ's death in our place, God's justice is now completely satisfied. God can now, without violating His justice or His moral law, forgive us freely, completely and absolutely. He can now extend His grace to us; He can show favor to those who, in themselves, deserve only wrath."[118]

- Vanish like a cloud (Isa. 44:22).

22 I've blotted out your sins; they are gone like morning mist at noon! Oh, return to me, for I have paid the price to set you free." Isaiah 44:22 (TLB)

- Blotted out (Isa. 43:25/Ac. 3:19).

25 "I, even I, am the one who wipes out your transgressions for My own sake, And I will not remember your sins. Isaiah 43:25

---

[118] Bridges, Jerry. Transforming Grace: Living Confidently in God's Unfailing Love (p. 44). NavPress. Kindle Edition.

- Cast into the depth of the sea (Mic. 7:19).

- Cast behind His back (Isa. 38:17).

- Disappear and not be found (Jer. 50:20).

5. *Message* of forgiveness.

a. The sin debt is Paid.

This barrier has been removed!

Giles Hembrough earns a modest salary working as a railway signal tester for the Amey Railroad in Bristol, England. A recent increase in his wages pushed him into a higher tax bracket. So naturally he was curious as to know how much tax he'd be required to pay at the end of the year. Well, when he opened and read the "dreaded letter" from Her Majesty's Revenue and Customs (HMRC), Mr. Hembrough received the shock of his life. According to "Her Majesty" Giles Hembrough owed her $ 18.7 trillion – and he had until April 5, 2017 to pay it! Now to get a handle on that figure, that's more than $ 1.3 trillion above the net worth of the

United States. That's enough money to purchase 46 billion iPhones or 94 million Lamborghini sports cars. Giles got out his calculator and tried to figure out how long it would take him to pay off the tax bill if he dedicated every cent of his paycheck to it: 369 million years! Of course, the amount was so ludicrous that Giles assumed it was a mistake from the start. "If the bill had been for $ 10,000 or so, then I'd have been worried. But for $ 18.7 trillion? That had to be a mistake." His hunch was right. When he called HMRC, a customer service rep commented, "It looks like someone has fallen asleep on the key board."[119] Our debt was higher than that, and it was no mistake, but it has been completely paid by the Lord Jesus Christ.

b. It silences the Devils accusations against God's *People.*

¹⁰ Then I heard a loud voice saying in heaven, "Now salvation, and strength, and the kingdom of our God, and the

---

[119] Information from: http:// www.mirror.co.uk/ news/ weird-news/ railway-worker-charged-14trillion-tax-8603513.]

power of His Christ have come, for the accuser of our brethren, who accused them before our God day and night, has been cast down. Revelation 12:10

No one can ever condemn the believer for one single sin!

[31] What then shall we say to these things? If God *is* for us, who *is* against us? [32] He who did not spare His own Son, but delivered Him over for us all, how will He not also with Him freely give us all things? [33] Who will bring a charge against God's elect? God is the one who justifies; [34] who is the one who condemns? Christ Jesus is He who died, yes, rather who was raised, who is at the right hand of God, who also intercedes for us. [35] Who will separate us from the love of Christ? Will tribulation, or distress, or persecution, or famine, or nakedness, or peril, or sword? Romans 8:31-35

Hoeksema writes:

"Who can be against us?" the suggestion of powers that are against us... There is the power of the devil and his host. There is the power of the world in an evil sense: the power of temptation; the power of the lust of the flesh, the lust of the eyes, and the pride of life. There is the power also of persecution, of reproach, of affliction... We cannot avoid them. There is in this world the power of sin and corruption. Even our nature is part of this world. The power of sin is within us. Other powers may be against us, but God is for us... The one answer here is God. That he is God means, first, that he is the supreme and final Judge. He passes sentence. He executes the verdict. From his verdict there is no appeal. If this Judge is for us, he justified us; otherwise, he could not be for us... But might it not be possible that we lose the favor of God? Scripture answers that God is unchangeable. Nothing can separate us from his love. Therefore, if we can really say that God is for us, we have no need of anything else.[120]

Watchman Nee notes:

---

[120] Hoeksema, Herman. Righteous by Faith Alone: A Devotional Commentary on Romans (Kindle Locations 5336-5337). Reformed Free Publishing Association. Kindle Edition.

Since God, seeing all our sins in the light, can forgive them on the basis of the blood, what ground of accusation has Satan? Satan may accuse us before Him, but "If God is for us, who is against us?" (Rom. 8: 31). God points him to the blood of His dear Son. It is the sufficient answer against which Satan has no appeal. "Who shall lay anything to the charge of God's elect? It is God that justifieth; who is he that condemneth? It is Christ Jesus that died, yea rather, that was raised from the dead, who is at the right hand of God, who also maketh intercession for us" (Rom. 8: 33– 34). Thus, God answers his every challenge… We have not recognized that it is God alone that can answer the accuser, and that in the precious blood He has already done so… Never should we try to answer Satan with our good conduct but always with the blood. Yes, we are sinful; but— praise God!— the blood cleanses us from every sin.[121]

---

[121] Nee, Watchman. The Normal Christian Life (p. 18). CLC Publications. Kindle Edition.

Martin Luther experienced in a dream a visitation of Satan himself. He said, "The devil had a scroll and as he unrolled it I saw all of my sins written down. He began to accuse me and I sank into depression." Then Martin suddenly had a verse come to his mind. He then demanded that the devil unroll the scroll all the way – and the bottom was 1 Jn. 1:7, "The blood of Christ cleanses from all sin!"

c. It *Purges* our conscience.

[22] let us draw near with a true heart in full assurance of faith, having our hearts sprinkled from an evil conscience and our bodies washed with pure water. Hebrews 10:22

Watchman Nee says it well:

The writer does not tell us that the blood of the Lord Jesus cleanses our hearts, and then stop there in his statement. We are wrong to connect the heart with the blood in quite that way… The heart, God says, is "desperately sick" (Jer. 17: 9, NASB), and He must do something more fundamental than cleanse it: He must give us a new one... "Having our hearts sprinkled from an evil conscience." What then is the meaning of this? It means that there was something intervening between myself and God, as a result of which I had an evil conscience whenever I sought to approach Him. It was constantly reminding me of the barrier that stood between myself and Him. But now, through the operation of the precious blood, something new has been effected before God which has removed that barrier... my conscience is at once cleared and my sense of guilt removed, and I have no more an evil conscience toward God. Every one of us knows what a precious thing it is to have a conscience void of offense in our dealings with God. A heart of faith and a conscience clear of any and every accusation are both equally essential to us, since they are interdependent. As soon as we find our conscience is uneasy, our faith leaks away, and immediately we know we cannot face God. In order therefore to keep going on with God, we must know the up-to-date value of the blood. It never loses its efficacy as our ground of access if we will but lay hold upon it... I come to God on the basis of the finished work of the Lord Jesus. I approach God through His merit alone and never on the basis of my attainment— never, for example, on the ground that I have been extra kind or patient today, or that I have done something for the Lord this morning. I have to come by way of the blood every time... A clear conscience is never based upon our attainment; it can only be based on the work of the Lord Jesus in the shedding of His blood.[122]

14 how much more shall the blood of Christ, who through the eternal Spirit offered Himself without spot to God, cleanse your conscience from dead works to serve the living God? Hebrews 9:14

A dead work is anything we do to try and gain God's acceptance apart from the blood of Christ!

Con:

---

[122] Nee, Watchman. The Normal Christian Life (p. 11, 12. 13). CLC Publications. Kindle Edition.

1. Have you received Christ as your Savior? Then you are forgiven! Now get preoccupied with the Savior not your sin.

2. Sen. Mark Hatfield recounts the following history:

James Garfield was a lay preacher and principal of his denominational college. They say he was ambidextrous and could simultaneously write Greek, with one hand and Latin with the other.

In 1880, he was elected president of the United States, but after only six months in office, he was shot in the back with a revolver. He never lost consciousness. At the hospital, the doctor probed the wound with his little finger to seek the bullet. He couldn't find it, so he tried a silver-tipped probe. Still he couldn't locate the bullet. They took Garfield back to Washington, D.C. Despite the summer heat, they tried to keep him comfortable. He was growing very weak. Teams of doctors tried to locate the bullet, probing the wound over and over.

In desperation they asked Alexander Graham Bell, who was working on a little device called the telephone, to see if he could locate the metal inside the president's body. He came, he sought, and he too failed. The president hung on through July, through August, but in September he finally died—not from the wound, but from infection.

The repeated probing, which the physicians thought would help the man, eventually killed him.

So it is with us who dwell too long on our sin and refuse to realize that God has already removed it.

B. Imputation of Righteousness. *Just-as-if-I'd-done-everything-right!* This aspect is an Addition.

Pilots of supersonic aircraft must always guard against the effects of multiple G-forces. G-forces (the force of gravity multiplied) increase for a pilot when his jet aircraft suddenly accelerates, lifts up from a dive, or turns steeply. They can cause a fatal loss of consciousness. This happens when G-forces drive blood from the brain to the lower half of the body. Blood deprivation of the brain can cause a "black out" or loss of consciousness, which is fatal. So they have invented the G-Suit. It is a tight-fitted pair of pants with sewn-in bladders that inflate with gas or liquid. When powerful G-forces trigger a sensor, the G-suit counters by squeezing the lower extremities and abdomen – preventing loss of blood from the brain. The greater the G-forces that cause a loss of consciousness – and death - the greater the G-suit reacts with pressure to keep the pilot conscious – and alive.

Fallen man cannot live in the presence of, what we might call a God-force, God's absolute Holiness. The good news is that God has provided those who trust the Lord Jesus Christ as their Savior not only Pardon but a God-suit! Clothing the believer in the very righteousness of Christ. Have you ever wished that you had lived a perfect life in word, thought, deed, and nature? Bad news is it is too late for that, but the good news is the Lord Jesus lived such a life and places that on your account when you trust Him as your Savior!

Imputation means "to attribute, or ascribe to another, a crime, an act, guilt or innocence, sin or righteousness."

An illustration is found in Philemon 18:

¹⁸ But if he has wronged you or owes anything, put that on my account. Philemon 1:18

There are two imputations:

- our sins imputed to Christ (Isa. 53:5,6,11/2 Cor. 5:21/1 Pet. 2:24/etc.); and

- Christ righteousness imputed to us (Rom. 3:21-22; 4:1-6; 9:30; 10:3/1 Cor. 1:30/2 Cor. 5:21/Phil. 3:9). This second imputation is what we are now looking at.

If you go over to Scotland, or anywhere there are many sheep, sooner or later you're going to see a very unusual sight. You'll see a little lamb with an extra fleece tied around its back. What has happened is that its mother has died. If you take the orphaned lamb and try to introduce it to another mother, the new mother will butt it away. She won't recognize the lamb's scent and will know the new baby is not one of her own lambs. Therefore, the shepherd will skin the dead lamb and make its fleece into a covering for the orphaned lamb, then he'll take the orphaned lamb to the mother whose baby just died. Now, when she sniffs the orphaned lamb, she will smell the fleece of her own lamb. Instead of butting the lamb away, she will accept it as one of her own.

In a similar way, we have become acceptable to God by being clothed with Christ.[123]

When God accepts the believer He is really accepting Himself! It is not that He merely gives us righteousness but that He Himself is our righteousness.

¹ Then he showed me Joshua the high priest standing before the Angel of the LORD, and Satan standing at his right hand to oppose him. ² And the LORD

---

[123] From Peter Grant's sermon, "In What Way Is Jesus Christ Different?"; submitted by Van Morris, Mount Washington, Kentucky.

said to Satan, "The LORD rebuke you, Satan! The LORD who has chosen Jerusalem rebuke you! *Is* this not a brand plucked from the fire?" ³ Now Joshua was clothed with filthy garments, and was standing before the Angel. ⁴ Then He answered and spoke to those who stood before Him, saying, "Take away the filthy garments from him." And to him He said, "See, I have removed your iniquity from you, and I will clothe you with rich robes." ⁵ And I said, "Let them put a clean turban on his head." So they put a clean turban on his head, and they put the clothes on him. And the Angel of the LORD stood by. Zechariah 3:1-5

1. Let's look at a few *Definitions*.

   a. *Secular* definition.

It is the justifying of an innocent man. It is a person, who was thought to be guilty, but later proven to be not guilty. We hear about these things all the time, someone is put into prison for a crime they did not commit and then later, through DNA or something else, they are proven innocent.

I have watched the movie *The Hurricane*, it was about Rubin "Hurricane" Carter a middleweight boxer who was wrongly convicted of murder and later freed after spending almost 20 years in prison. A few years ago, he died at the age of 76 last month. He was, in the secular sense, justified.

b. *Cultural* definition: In Paul's day it was used, to justify the outrageous acts of high officials, like a king. We might call it self-justification.

We see it often in politics these days, it looks like the FBI tried to sway things to elect Hillary and get rid of Trump. After a clear bias was proven beyond doubt they justified their findings by saying those with a clear bias against Trump did not affect the process. Right!

c. *Biblical* definition: the one who is justified, is neither proven innocent, or able, to excuse their guilt. It is the act of God, by a Divine declaration, by which He declares righteous, by way of imputation, the believing sinner who is guilty and under condemnation.

Swindoll puts it this way:

What is justification? It is the sovereign act of God whereby He declares righteous believing sinners while we are still in a sinning state. Being justified does not mean that we will never again sin. False teachers might question our justification, saying, "You're not righteous. Look at how you failed last week." But the doctrine of justification is the declaration of righteousness, the imputing of Christ's righteousness to our account. At the moment of our conversion, the Lord Jesus Christ enters our lives, and God declares us righteous. [124]

Jerry Vines:

Justification— The Greek noun for justification is derived from the Greek verb dikaioō, meaning "to acquit" or "to declare righteous" (used by Paul in Rom. 4: 2, 5, 25; 5: 1). It is a legal term used of a favorable verdict in a trial. The word, depicts a courtroom setting, with God presiding as the

---

[124] Swindoll, Charles R.. The Swindoll Study Bible NLT (Kindle Locations 119295-119297). Tyndale House Publishers, Inc.. Kindle Edition.

Judge, determining the faithfulness of each person to the Law. In the first section of Romans, Paul makes it clear that no one can withstand God's judgment (3: 9– 9– 20). The Law was not given to justify sinners but to expose their sin. To remedy this deplorable situation, God sent His Son to die for our sins, in our place. When we believe in Jesus, God imputes His righteousness to us, and we are declared righteous before God. In this way, God demonstrates that He is both a righteous Judge and the One who declares us righteous, our Justifier (3: 26).[125]

Trans: This is why so few refuse to be saved, in order to be righteous in God's eyes, you have to be guilty in yours. Righteousness is a gift and totally eliminates any pride or boasting on our behalf of the person believing, and that, is hard for fallen man to accept.

---

[125] HarperCollins Christian Publishing. The NKJV, Vines Expository Bible, Ebook: A Guided Journey Through the Scriptures with Pastor Jerry Vines (Kindle Locations 88575-88580). Thomas Nelson. Kindle Edition.

²¹ But now apart from the Law *the* righteousness of God has been manifested, being witnessed by the Law and the Prophets, ²² even *the* righteousness of God through faith in Jesus Christ for all those who believe; for there is no distinction; ²³ for all have sinned and fall short of the glory of God, ²⁴ being justified as a gift by His grace through the redemption which is in Christ Jesus; ²⁵ whom God displayed publicly as a propitiation in His blood through faith. *This was* to demonstrate His righteousness, because in the forbearance of God He passed over the sins previously committed; ²⁶ for the demonstration, *I say,* of His righteousness at the present time, so that He would be just and the justifier of the one who has faith in Jesus. ²⁷ Where then is boasting? It is excluded. By what kind of law? Of works? No, but by a law of faith. ²⁸ For we maintain that a man is justified by faith apart from works of the Law. Romans 3:21-28

Barclay, "We must never be self-righteous in goodness. How harmful is the so-called Christian who harps on about his goodness. How little does he realize that the man who is furthest from God is the man who thanks God he is not like others."

2. Furthermore, the *Declaration*.

a. It is *Judicial not Experiential*.

In justification, we are declared righteous, *not* made righteous, in our actual experience.

James Kennedy, "It is not anything done by us or wrought in us. Justification does NOT change our hearts, our souls, our lives one whit. It is something which is external to us. It is something which is declared about us by God. It is NOT God acting as a doctor or a surgeon in which He comes in and changes our hearts. Indeed God does change us, but that is regeneration and sanctification. Justification is a declaration about us; the declarative act of a Judge about a sinner. In this declaration, God declares us to be righteous."

One observes:

You understand that this word imputed implies that I am not righteous in myself. Otherwise, imputation would not be necessary. He to whom righteousness is imputed is not righteous. If he is not righteous, he is unrighteous. There is no third possibility. We are either righteous or unrighteous. When God imputes righteousness unto me, I am a sinner, I am corrupt, I am unrighteous. Otherwise righteousness would not have to be imputed. Faith is imputed to us for righteousness. Why? Not because God imputes something that is not. Not because faith is righteousness. Not because of the fruits of faith. Not because by faith we become better men and women before God...I believe that when the apostle Paul wrote [in 2 Tim. 4:7, 8], "I have fought a good fight, I have finished my course, I have kept the faith: Henceforth there is laid up for me a crown of righteousness," he was not more righteous than he was when he was on the way to Damascus. Faith is imputed for righteousness because it lays hold on the only perfect righteousness that exists, namely, Christ Jesus.

When you think about it, we will be no more righteous when we get to heaven, then we are right now!

There is no better example of this, that justification is not related to our experience, than Lot, who God's Word says was righteous:

7 and *if* He rescued righteous Lot, oppressed by the sensual conduct of unprincipled men 8 (for by what he saw and heard *that* righteous man, while living among them, felt *his* righteous soul tormented day after day by *their* lawless deeds), 9 *then* the Lord knows how to rescue the godly from temptation, and to keep the unrighteous under punishment for the day of judgment, 2 Peter 2:7-9

Yet in his daily experience, he was anything but righteous!

- He Compromised with the world, he did not have to live in Sodom (Gen. 19:1-3)

- He Condoned sin, by offering his daughter to homosexuals (Gen. 19:4-11).

- He did not have one Convert, not even among his own family (19:12-29).

- He Consented to get drunk (19:32).

- He Cohabited with his own daughters (19:33-38)

Yet in spite of all of that he was righteous in the eyes of God, because Christ's righteousness was imputed to him!

Chuck Swindoll, "You're telling me, Chuck, that by simply believing in Jesus Christ I can have eternal life with God, my sins forgiven, [righteousness put on my account], a destiny secure in heaven, all of this and much more without my working for that?" Yes, that is precisely what Scripture teaches. It is called grace."

Courson, "Lot Righteous? A guy who calls perverted people his brothers? A guy who offers his daughters to a homosexual mob? A guy who lingers when angels tell him to leave? Lot righteous? Yes, for that is what Peter calls him [under the inspiration of the Holy Spirit]. How could Lot possibly be considered righteous? Because righteousness is imputed solely on the basis of simple faith. I am righteous and so are you if you have confessed with your mouth that Jesus is who He claimed to be, and believed in your heart that God raised Him from the dead."[126]

Keep in mind that Old Testament saints were also justified and regenerated as Romans four reveals. They were not all indwelt, and Spirit baptism did not take place until the Day of Pentecost.

Was Lot grieved to the bone? He was but that was not related to justification but regeneration. Because of regeneration a believer can sin, but he or she will be miserable. If you can sin and enjoy it you are not a true believer.

---

[126] Palmer, Johnny. Genesis: Roots of the Nation Vol. 2 (Pastor Palmer's Pen Book 1) (Kindle Location 2061). Kindle Edition.

⁷ and *if* He rescued righteous Lot, oppressed by the sensual conduct of unprincipled men ⁸ (for by what he saw and heard *that* righteous man, while living among them, felt *his* righteous soul tormented day after day by *their* lawless deeds), 2 Peter 2:7-8

Justification is a judicial declaration not experiential.

b. It is *Additional not just Subtractional*.

As wonderful as Pardon is, it is not enough, it is a subtraction of our sins, but we need an addition of righteousness to be acceptable to God. Hal Lindsey notes:

"You see, even in light of the fact that Christ has taken all my sins away, that only leaves me in a *neutral* status with God. Just having no sin will never make me acceptable in God's sight. In order to be acceptable to God, I need more than just subtraction of my sins. I need the addition of Christ's righteousness."[127]

---

[127] The Liberation of Planet Earth, Hal Lindsey, p. 148.

²¹ For He made Him who knew no sin *to be* sin for us, that we might become the righteousness of God in Him.
2 Corinthians 5:21

c. It is *Scriptural not Pharisaical.*

The Pharisees way, was to try to earn righteousness, by fasting, prayer, synagogue attendance, and good works. They thought that if they became righteous in their behavior, God would declare them righteous in His sight. They had it backward! Their righteousness by behavior fell short of God's perfection. Why? Because we are all sinners by birth and behavior.

⁶ We are all infected and impure with sin. When we put on our prized robes of righteousness, we find they are but filthy rags. Like autumn leaves we fade, wither and fall. And our sins, like the wind, sweep us away. Isaiah 64:6 (TLB)

Elyse Fitzpatrick, writes in, *Give Them Grace*:

"The primary reason the majority of kids from Christian homes stray from the faith, is that, they never really had it to begin with...This is illustrated by a conversation I recently had with a young woman in her early twenties who had been raised in a Christian home and had attended church for most of her life. After assuring me that she was, indeed, saved, I asked her, "What does it mean to be a Christian?"

She replied, "It means that you ask Jesus into your heart."

"Yes, all right, but what does that mean?"

"It means that you ask Jesus to forgive you."

"Okay, but what do you ask him to forgive you for?"

"Bad things? I guess you ask him to forgive you for bad things, the sins you do."

"Why would Jesus forgive you?"

She fidgeted. "Um, because you ask him?"

[I asked], "What do you think God wants you to know?"

She beamed. "He wants me to know that I should love myself and that there's nothing I can't do if I think I can."

"And what does God want from you?" I asked.

"He wants me to do good stuff....You know, be nice to others and don't hang around with bad people."

Then Elyse noted, "[Apparently], we've transformed the holy, terrifying, magnificent, and loving God of the Bible into Santa and his elves. Instead of transmitting the gloriously liberating and life-changing truths of the gospel, we have taught our children that what God wants from them is morality. We have told them that *being good* (at least outwardly) is the be-all and end-all of their faith. This isn't the gospel; we're not handing down Christianity."

Self-righteousness is not the same as imputed righteousness. The first is based on what man can do, and the later based on was has already been done through the Lord Jesus Christ.

3. The *Doctrinal* Framework.

a. God *Initiates* it.

It is all by grace! God must initiate it because we are to fallen too even want God, or merit anything from Him, even if we wanted Him. But fallen man never seeks God without the Holy Spirit drawing them.

[10] as it is written, "THERE IS NONE RIGHTEOUS, NOT EVEN ONE; [11] THERE IS NONE WHO UNDERSTANDS, THERE IS NONE WHO SEEKS FOR GOD; [12] ALL HAVE TURNED ASIDE, TOGETHER THEY HAVE BECOME USELESS; THERE IS NONE WHO DOES GOOD, THERE IS NOT EVEN ONE." Romans 3:10-12 (NASB)

I never tire of quoting Dr. Gerstner:

Christ has done everything necessary for his salvation. Nothing now stands between the sinner and God but the sinner's good works. Nothing can keep him from Christ but his delusion that he does not need Him – that he has good works of his own that can satisfy God. If men will only be convinced that they have no righteousness that is not as filthy rags; if men will see that there is none that does good, no, not one; if men will see that all are shut up under sin – then there will be nothing to prevent their everlasting salvation. All they need is need. All they must have is nothing. All that is required is acknowledged guilt. But, alas, sinners cannot part from their virtues. They have none that are not imaginary, but they are real to them. So grace becomes unreal. The real grace of God they spurn in order to hold on to the illusory virtues of their own. Their eyes fixed on a mirage, they will not drink real water. They die of thirst in the midst of an ocean of Grace."

Tim Keller, "When a Christian sees prostitutes, alcoholics, prisoners, drug addicts, unwed mothers, the homeless, refugees, he knows that he is looking in a mirror. Perhaps the Christian spent all of his life as a respectable middle-class person. No matter. He thinks, Spiritually I was just like these people, though physically and socially I never was where they are now. They are outcasts. (Spiritually speaking) I was an outcast."

We are not only, saved by grace through faith in Christ, but the Bible says we are to live as we got in, by grace through faith.

⁶ Therefore as you have received Christ Jesus the Lord, *so* walk in Him, Colossians 2:6

Chandler notes, "The litmus test of whether or not you understand the gospel is what you do when you fail. Do you run from God and go try to clean yourself up a bit before you come back into the throne room, or do you approach the throne of grace with confidence? If you don't approach the throne of grace with confidence, you don't understand the gospel. You are most offensive to God when you come to him with all of your efforts, when you're still trying to earn what's freely given."

This might explain why so many turn down the gospel – it is too good to be true! I ordered a Bible once from eBay to give away. As I was paging through it I saw a hundred dollar bill! No way! It was too good to be true. Must be a counterfeit. I set it aside for several months. Then I decided to check it out – I found out that a real 100 Bill has a **100** at the right bottom and when you shift the bill it shifts from green to black. My 100-dollar bill did that!

It said to take your finger nail and scratch the surface, it should feel a little bumpy because it has raised printing. Again, mine had that!

It said that borders, printing, should not be blurry – while I do not have the best sight, it did not look blurry to me.

It said if you hold it up to the light, you can see an image of Ben Franklin, they called it a watermark. My Bill had that!

It said the left side would have a security tread and mine did.

It said something about the numbers which I could not figure out what it was talking about.

But as far as I can tell, this 100 bill which I found in a Bible, was too good to be true – but it is! By the way, I finally took it down to our bank and asked the teller if it was real or counterfeit. After studying it for a bit, she assured me it was the real deal. It was too good to be true, but it was – so is the gospel of grace!

To be forgiven of all our sins – past, present, and future; to be declared as righteous as Christ! Too good to be true but it is!

I have been told all of my life that if something is too good to be true it probably is – that why people turn down the gospel or add all kinds of stuff to it – to say that God offers a gift of pardon and imputed righteousness is so stunningly good, people just shake their head and say, "That just can't be!" But it is!

b. God supplies the *Instruments* [means].

As we have already established the Blood of Christ. The basis of Justification is the Substitutionary death of Jesus Christ, which has Propitiated God the Father (Lu. 18:9-14).

That Greek word for the English word translated "merciful" in Lu. 18: 13, is *hilastheti* which means "to be propitious."

As Hal points out:

"When the tax-collector prayed to God and asked Him to be "propitious" toward him, he was actually saying, "I know you're not satisfied with me. I'm nothing but a no-good sinner who only deserves Your righteous wrath. But please receive me in the light of the atoning blood of sacrifice on the mercy seat which has satisfied your judgment against me." He may not have used those words, but when he asked God to be propitious toward him, that's exactly what he meant...To be humble means to have a true estimation of yourself and where you stand with God. To recognize there's nothing you can do to gain acceptance in God's sight, but to merely allow Him to make you acceptable."

And it is, not only the blood that saves us initially, but it delivers us continually, each and every day of our lives.

Watchman Nee, "I approach God through His merit alone, and never on the basis of my attainment; never, for example, on the ground that I have been extra kind or patient today, or that I have done something for the Lord this morning. I have to come by way of the Blood every time...A clear conscience is never based upon our attainment; it can only be based on the work of the Lord Jesus in the shedding of His Blood...Do you come to Him on the uncertain ground of your feeling, the feeling that you may have achieved something for God today? Or is your approach based on something far more secure, namely, the fact that the Blood has been shed, and that God looks on that Blood and is satisfied? The Blood has never changed and never will. Your approach to God is therefore always in boldness; and that boldness is yours through the Blood and never through your personal attainment...Whether you have had a good day or a bad day, whether you have consciously sinned or not, your basis of approach is always the same – the Blood of Christ...My initial approach to God is by the Blood, and every time I come before Him it is the same. Right to the end it will always and only be on the ground of the precious Blood."

c. It is *Impossible!*

¹³ For the promise that he would be the heir of the world *was* not to Abraham or to his seed through the law, but through the righteousness of faith. ¹⁴ For if those who are of the law *are* heirs, faith is made void and the promise made of no effect, ¹⁵ because the law brings about wrath; for where there is no law *there is* no transgression. ¹⁶ Therefore *it is* of faith that *it might be* according to grace, so that the promise might be sure to all the seed, not only to those who are of the law, but also to those who are of the faith of Abraham, who is the father of us all ¹⁷ (as it is written, *"I have made you a father of many nations"*) in the presence of Him whom he believed--God, who gives life to the dead and calls those things which do not exist as though they did; ¹⁸ who,

contrary to hope, in hope believed, so that he became the father of many nations, according to what was spoken, *"So shall your descendants be."* [19] And not being weak in faith, he did not consider his own body, already dead (since he was about a hundred years old), and the deadness of Sarah's womb. [20] He did not waver at the promise of God through unbelief, but was strengthened in faith, giving glory to God, [21] and being fully convinced that what He had promised He was also able to perform. [22] And therefore *"it was accounted to him for righteousness."* [23] Now it was not written for his sake alone that it was imputed to him, [24] but also for us. It shall be imputed to us who believe in Him who raised up Jesus our Lord from the dead, [25] who was delivered up because of our offenses, and was raised because of our justification. Romans 4:13-25

What is it in the context that God calls that which does not exist as though it did? Imputed righteousness!

Herman Hoeksema notes:

The text says that God is, first, the one who calls the things that are not as though they were... If we are to call a thing, the thing must be there first, but God calls the things that are not as though they were. He calls the things out of himself. He calls them because He wills them... The idea is, first, that this is characteristic of God, that God always works this way. God never calls the things that are. He always calls the things that are not... Second, the text tells us that God quickeneth the dead... What did Abraham believe? He believed the promise of God...Why did Abraham believe the promise? Because he believed God who quickeneth the dead and calls the things that are not as though they were... Abraham's faith was this: the things he believed were contrary to all experience.

So it is with the Christian. The things we believe are contrary to all that we see and to all that we experience... this faith of the Christian is just as impossible as was the faith of Abraham. All within us testifies that we are not righteous... this promise seemed to be impossible of realization. Abraham had to hope against hope for the realization of that promise. All things testified against the possibility of the realization of this promise. At the time the promise was given to him, Abraham was dead as far as the possibility of having seed is concerned. Abraham was one hundred years old. Sarah had been barren. She was now beyond the age of having a child. According to all things that are seen and experienced, the realization of the promise was impossible... Righteousness, therefore, is not concerned with what I think of myself. Nor do I ask what you think of me...The gospel must be declared by God because it is only on the basis of God's declaration that we can believe impossible things. I believe in such impossible things as the forgiveness of sins. That the God who is unchangeably righteous forgives sin is impossible. Yet on the basis of God's declaration, faith is imputed for righteousness because it lays hold on the only perfect righteousness that exists, namely, Christ Jesus...Impossible is possible...In every sense of the word, salvation is impossible because righteousness is unattainable… What does the Christian believe? Of what is he certain? In general, he is certain of this: God justifies the ungodly. It is absolutely necessary that God justifies the ungodly if there is to be salvation. Yet this is impossible from every point of view… Everything in my experience testifies against this statement. My conscience testifies against the fact that I am justified. All the world testifies against me. The devil testifies against me. All my experience testifies against the fact that I am justified… Saving faith is that I am certain, against all this testimony, that I am justified. God comes to us and says, "I justify the ungodly."… we are ungodly. And God destroys the ungodly. But now God holds before us the promise of eternal life. Our last word must be ungodly. And God's last word is, "I justify the ungodly."[128]

What does all of this mean?

a. *Serenity.*

---

[128] Hoeksema, Herman. Righteous by Faith Alone: A Devotional Commentary on Romans (Kindle Location 2315). Reformed Free Publishing Association. Kindle Edition.

[1] Therefore, having been justified by faith, we have peace with God through our Lord Jesus Christ. Romans 5:1

In 1899, Dwight L. Moody went to speak to the Penitentiary in Canon City, Colorado on Thanksgiving Day. The governor of the state wrote him, enclosing a pardon for a woman imprisoned there. The woman was unaware of this and Mr. Moody was greatly pleased to be the bearer of the message. At the close of the address, Mr. Moody produced the document, saying, "I have a pardon in my hands for one of the prisoners before me." Calling her name, he said, "Will you come forward and accept the Governor's Thanksgiving gift?" The woman hesitated a moment, then arose, gave a shriek, and, crossing her arms over her breast, fell sobbing and laughing across the lap of the woman next her. Again she arose, staggered a short distance, and again fell at the feet of the matron of the prison, burying her head in the matron's lap. The excitement was so intense that Mr. Moody would not do more than make a very brief application of the scene to illustrate God's offer of pardon and peace.

Later Moody made these comments:

Strange that men prize more highly the pardon of a fellow-man than the forgiveness of their God![129]

Are we really that excited about the peace that is afforded through Pardon and the imputation of Christ's righteousness? If not we should be!

b. *Certainty*. Rom. 8:1, 31-39

Since it all originates with God and is sustained by God, we can be sure that God will never reject us – in fact, for God to reject the Christian, is the same as rejecting Christ! It is God's own righteousness that is upon the believer! In our experience, we are often a royal mess, but God does not see us, in ourselves, but in Christ.

While I do not like the word luck, I read a story some years ago that I found amusing. Philip Griffin tells of seeing a

---

[129] 234William R. Moody, The Life of Dwight L. Moody by his Son (New York: Fleming H Revell, 1900), 32-35.

lost dog sign. There was a big cash reward for whoever found a lost dog, and a description of the dog:

"He's only got three legs, he's blind in the left eye, he's missing a right ear, his tail has been broken off, he was neutered accidentally by a fence—ouch!—he's almost deaf, and he answers by the name 'Lucky.'"

That dog isn't lucky! He is a mess but He is surely blessed by having an owner who loves him and refuses to let him go. That is what salvation is all about!

c. *Purity.*

The reason for this is NOT imputed righteousness but, as we will later see, regeneration. This makes us a new creature, giving us a nature that always seeks to live righteously (1 Jn. 3:9). It gives us the desire, and the indwelling Holy Spirit gives us the power (Gal. 5:16). Justification always leads to sanctification and ultimately glorification.

It is important that we embrace the fact that we are already righteous in God's eyes, with Christ's righteousness.

[7] For as he thinks within himself, so he is..." Prov. 23:7

If you think you are nothing more than a rotten sinner, then you will act like a rotten sinner. It's like hypnotizing a person to actually think he is a dog – soon he will start barking! But with imputed righteousness, we really are righteous!

On May 1, 2009 at the 135th running of the Kentucky Derby a horse named *Mine* entered the race at 50-1 odds. *Mine* had not fared well in his two previous races. The jockey that rode him was Calvin Borel. Right at the beginning of the race *Mine* struggled, Calvin got squeezed between the other horses and quickly dropped into last place. At the first quarter-mile stage, *Mine* was still running dead last.

At one point, he was so far behind the other horses that NBC's announcer, Tom Durkin, at first missed seeing him. But at the three-eighths pole, *Mine* started gaining on the other horses. After passing Atomic Rain, the horse took off. He ended up winning the mile race by 6 and ¾ lengths. The victory stunned the horse racing world. The owner of the horse commented, "[The victory] wasn't something that was on our radar."

But Calvin Borel, the jockey said he wasn't surprised at all that *Mine* won. He said, "I rode him like a good horse." He rode him like a winning horse – and he won!

The truth is we are already righteous, and when we get to heaven we will be no more righteous then we are now! When we begin to believe this truth, the Holy Spirit will translate that positional righteousness into a practical righteousness in our lives. But as long as our testimony is, "Lord I fall so short, I aint nothing but a sinner who sins every day." We will remain so in our daily lives. The greatest thing about this is when we see righteousness in our daily lives God has to get all of the glory.

Con:

1. Justification as we have looked at it, including forgiveness is a mind boggling stunning treasure. A Pardon, *just-as-if-I'd-never sinned*; and Imputed righteousness, *just-as-if-I'd-always-done-everything-right.*

2. Thus the barrier of the Sin Debt has long since been removed.

3. An article in *USA Today* caught my attention. It noted that the American Psychological Association has published new research exploring the rise of perfectionism in young people. Compared to prior generations, today's college students are harder on themselves, more demanding of others, and report higher levels of social pressure to be perfect.

The study examined over 40,000 college students who took a special survey between 1989 and 2016. The more recent students scored higher in all three forms of perfectionism. Between 1989 and 2016, the scores for socially prescribed perfectionism—or perceiving the excessive expectations of others—increased by 33 percent. Other-oriented expectations—putting unrealistic expectations on others—went up 16 percent, and self-oriented perfectionism—our irrational desire to be perfect—increased 10 percent.

One of the lead researchers concluded:

"Today's young people are competing with each other in order to meet societal pressures to succeed and they feel that perfectionism is necessary in order to feel safe, socially connected and of worth." Unfortunately, perfectionism can lead to anxiety, clinical depression, anorexia, and other health issues.[130]

We can say two thing, one is in order not only to feel safe, but to be safe in the eyes of a holy God one must be perfectly righteous.

Two, the only way to reach that perfection, is not by striving, but by receiving Christ's Pardon and Imputation of His Righteousness. The

---

[130] Adapted from Sean Rossman, "Millennials strive for perfectionism more than past generations, study says," USA Today (1-4-18).

only alternative is anxiety, depression, and ultimately eternal hell.

Joseph Parker:

My age would wither away before the growing tale was well begun. I owe all to Christ. There is nothing mine but my hateful sin. He found me; he loosed my bond; he paid my debt; he sounded the depths of all my woe; he ransomed me with blood!"... How poor my best return! How mean my gifts! How weak my service! But as he met me in the helplessness of my sin, so will he meet me in the imperfection of my work. He will make it worthy with his own merit; he will complete it by his own might; he will sanctify it by his own holiness. The blood of Christ![131]

II. REDEMPTION.

There was a bullfighter who lived from 1917 to 1947 known as Manolete. He was perhaps the greatest bullfighter who ever lived. He killed hundreds of bulls, he himself was badly gored a

---

[131] Parker, Joseph. Ephesians to Revelation (The People's Bible Book 26) (Kindle Locations 5104-5106). Pioneer Library. Kindle Edition.

dozen times. His last battle was against the bull, named Islero, who had gored a horse and nearly killed its rider. As Manolete thrust the sword over the bull's horns and between his shoulders, the bull caught Manolete in his upper thigh, and hurled the bullfighter high into the air. Both bullfighter and bull died. When his death was announced in the newspapers, one reporter summed up the fight with these words, *"He killed dying and he died killing."* Yes, even in his death, he conquered.

The Lord Jesus died on that cross, but, in the process, He defeated Satan and rose from the dead to tell about it. We are talking about our Lord removing the barrier of Satanic Dominion, or what we call Redemption. Satan is a defeated foe!

See, Col. 2:15/Heb. 2:14/Jam. 4:7/1 Jn. 3:8; 4:4.

There are various words translated redemption, redeem, etc., that are found 132 times in the Old Testament and 22 times in the New Testament. The essential idea is "freedom by payment of a price."

Hal Lindsey:

The word "redemption" was a very familiar word in the first century since nearly half the world was involved in slavery in one way or another. The sweetest word a slave could hope to hear was the word "redemption". Since one of the major barriers between God and man is man's slavery to Satan, the New Testament writers have freely used the concept of redemption to describe the work of Christ on the cross which has reclaimed man from Satan's clutches.[132]

Christ's death as a ransom appears (Matt. 20:28; Mark 10:45; 1 Tim. 2:6).

A. *Person.*

Note: The background is related to the laws of redemption as found in the Old Testament; you might begin by looking at Lev. 25:24-34 (related to property) and Lev. 25:47-55 (as related to

---

[132] Liberation of Planet Earth, Hal Lindsey, p. 102.

persons). In addition, the book of Ruth gives us a wonderful example of this. Keep in mind, this book is a Back to the Basic, not meant to be an in-depth study.

1. The person who redeems must be *Acceptable*.

A kinsman (Lev. 25:48-49/Ruth 2:20; 3:12-13). The Lord Jesus fulfilled this requirement when He became Man, related to Israel (Mat. 1:1ff) and related to the whole human race (Lu. 3:23-38).

2. He also had to be *Agreeable.*

See Ruth 3:13, as to our Lord see Heb. 10:5-10/Jn. 10:17-18.

3. He must be *Able* to pay the price.

Look at Ruth 4:6, our Lord alone was able to redeem (1 Pet. 1:18-19).

One of the great heroes in African-American history is a woman named Harriet Tubman, a slave in Maryland who escaped to Philadelphia over the famous "Underground Railroad" and then became one of its most successful conductors in the years leading up to the Civil War. Mrs. Tubman became known as "Moses" for her work in helping bring slaves to freedom. Altogether, she made nineteen trips back to the South and led about three hundred slaves from bondage to freedom. It was said that she worked between trips to get enough money to pay whatever it took for these slaves to reach freedom. The work of the Underground Railroad was a process of redemption, taking people out of slavery and setting them free no matter what the cost.[133]

She is a faint picture of what the Lord Jesus did in setting us free from Satanic Dominion.

B. *Place.*

Let's get an overview picture of what we might call the slave market of humanity:

1. The *Slave Maker.*

---

[133] Evans, Tony. Theology You Can Count On: Experiencing What the Bible Says About... God the Father, God the Son, God the Holy Spirit, Angels, Salvation... (Kindle Locations 15656-15660). Moody Publishers. Kindle Edition.

As we have already seen, it was Adam who turned his God-given dominion over to Satan (Rom. 5:12). It is hard for us to believe that the entire human race is born in a broken sinful state.

In seems like another lifetime, but I was stationed in Germany for several years. I read about Polish Pottery that was popular. The Polish pottery capital of the world is Boleslawiec. At one big factory, you will see a huge pile of Polish pottery – it is damaged and discarded.

You might protest, surely in such a large pile there must be a lot of pottery worth having. But if you looked through it all day you would find that every single plate, every platter, every pitcher, every bowl, every mug, and every tea cup and saucer would have some fracture or blemish that made it only fit for the garbage heap.

The truth is that all of humanity is like that pile of broken Polish pottery. There is not a single person who is righteous, who does good, who even seeks God. Every one of us are born sinners and unfit to stand in the presence of a holy

God – regardless of the self-righteous polish that we often wear.

2. The *Slave Master.*

Again, we have seen that it was turned over to Satan (Jn. 12:31). And the entire world, outside of believers in Christ, is under his influence (1 Jn. 5:19).

Let's keep in mind what a terrible Master Satan is, one who is cruel and hateful!

In the early Eighteenth Century, England had what is known as the debtors prisons of this time – a time in which something as small as a debt of just two pounds could get a person thrown in jail.

The Fleet Debtors Prison in London was the very worst.

In 1728 Thomas Bambridge paid the sum of 5,000 pounds to be the warden of this prison. He charged prisoners for staying in his jail. The more they paid the better their chances of survival. If prisoners paid enough they might even get their own cell and something palatable to eat. Those who had nothing to pay were forced to live in the most horrific conditions – most of them perishing from Diphtheria, Smallpox, and other deadly diseases. Bambridge not only charged the inmates for living space, but for food and even for the shackles that the prisoners were forced to wear.

Thomas reminds me of Satan, who is called a murderer (Jn. 8:44), a liar (Jn. 8:44), a confirmed sinner (1 Jn. 3:8), and accuser (Rev. 12:10), and an adversary (Job 1:12). And just look at how he treats those he enslaves, he inflicts them with physical diseases (Mt. 9:32-33) and mental derangement (Mt. 17:15), etc.

C. *Price.*

1. Required a *Special Birth*.

A slave cannot redeem a slave! This is why the virgin birth is so important, our Lord had to bypass the sin nature. We have looked at this and you can go back and refresh your memory.

2. It also required a *Sacrificial Death.*

The blood of Christ was the purchase price (1 Pet. 1:18-19; 3:18). Swindoll notes:

Redemption is God's act of paying the ransom price to release us from our bondage of sin. Held hostage by Satan, we were shackled by the iron chains of sin and death. Like a loving parent whose child has been kidnapped, God willingly paid the ransom for you. And what a price He paid![134]

D. *Product.*

1. To *Buy* - Agoradzo.

Agorazo, meaning "to buy in the market" (agora means "market"). Man in his sin is considered under the sentence of death (John 3:18-19; Rom. 6:23), a slave "sold under sin" (Rom. 7:14), but in the act of redemption purchased by Christ through the shedding of His blood (1 Cor. 6:20; 7:23; 2 Pet. 2:1; Rev. 5:9; 14:3-4).

---

[134] Swindoll, Charles R.. The Owner's Manual for Christians: The Essential Guide for a God-Honoring Life (p. 229). Thomas Nelson. Kindle Edition.

The basic idea is to purchase or to *buy*.

A Caution: We must *not* conclude that the price was paid to Satan. God never owes Satan anything! Man is ransomed from the righteous claims of another; it is God who has satisfied God's claims in man's place.

This redemption is not paid for by the Lord Jesus and some sort of commitment on the believers part! It is a gift to be received not something given because of our good works, merit, or promises to live right. Again, Hal Lindsey writes:

"The redemption that Jesus made available to men at the cross is a love gift with no strings attached. We're not used to receiving things without someone wanting something in return, so it's hard to really grasp the nature of this fantastic offer of a free salvation. In the back of many peoples' minds is the thought that there must be a hidden gimmick somewhere. No one gives something for nothing! But let me assure you, there's no fine print in the contract of salvation. It doesn't even say that we have to give Him ourselves. All we're asked to do is to *take* the pardon He's graciously offered us and then begin to enjoy our freedom."[135]

2. To say *Bye-Bye* - Exagoradzo.

Exagorazo, meaning "to buy out of the market" which adds the thought not only of purchase but removal from sale (Gal. 3:13; 4:5; Eph. 5:16; Col. 4:5), indicating that redemption is once for all;[136]

We say bye-bye to the slave market forever!

3. The *Battle Cry* – Lutroo!

Lutroo, "to let loose" or "set free" (Luke 24:21; Titus 2:14; 1 Pet. 1:18). The same idea is found in the noun form lutrosis (Luke 2:38; Heb. 9:12), another similar expression epoiesen lutrosin (Luke 1:68), and another form used frequently, apolutrosis, indicating freeing a slave (Luke 21:28; Rom. 3:24;

---

[135] The Liberation of Planet Earth, Hal Lindsey, p. 108.
[136] Chafer, Lewis Sperry; Walvoord, John F.. Major Bible Themes (p. 61). Zondervan. Kindle Edition.

8:23; 1 Cor. 1:30; Eph. 1:7, 14; 4:30; Col. 1:14; Heb. 9:15; 11:35).[137]

We are free from Satanic Dominion (Col. 1:13). We can submit to God and resist the Devil and he must flee (Jam. 4:7) based on his defeat at the cross!

Martin Luther King Jr. gave his *I Have a Dream* speech in 1963, at the March on Washington. At the end of that speech he said:

When we allow freedom to ring-when we let it ring from every city and every hamlet, from every state and every city, we will be able to speed up that day when all God's children, black men and white men, Jews and Gentiles, Protestants and Catholics, will be able to join hands and sing in the word's of the old Negro spiritual, "Free at last, Free at last, Great God almighty, we are free at last."

The truth is that the gospel is offered to all – Democrats and Republicans; black, white, Hispanic, whoever; Jews and

---

[137] Chafer, Lewis Sperry; Walvoord, John F.. Major Bible Themes (pp. 61-62). Zondervan. Kindle Edition.

Gentiles; Protestants and Catholics; all who will admit that they are a sinner and receive the Lord Jesus Christ as their Savior – only then will a person truly be free at last, and it will all be because of the Great God Almighty!

Con:

1. Redeemed how I love to proclaim it! The Person, Place, Price, and Product – we have been bought, and have said good bye to the slave market, and our battle cry is We are free at last, free at last, thanks to the Lord Jesus, we are free at last.

2. The problem is, Satan does not want us to grab a hold of this truth, he wants to bluff us into thinking that he is a larger than life foe, who we should be terrified of.

3. I have watched many of those old scary monster movies in my day. When I was a kid they scared me half to death. I watched Frankenstein meets the Wolfman and didn't sleep for a week! The other day I watched, for the first time in years, and to tell you the

truth those monsters not only were no longer scary but I found myself laughing throughout the movie, as I wondered if these were what I was so terrified of!

¹² "How you are fallen from heaven, O Lucifer, son of the morning! *How* you are cut down to the ground, You who weakened the nations! ¹³ For you have said in your heart: 'I will ascend into heaven, I will exalt my throne above the stars of God; I will also sit on the mount of the congregation On the farthest sides of the north; ¹⁴ I will ascend above the heights of the clouds, I will be like the Most High.' ¹⁵ Yet you shall be brought down to Sheol, To the lowest depths of the Pit.

Notice vv. 16-17

¹⁶ "Those who see you will gaze at you, *And* consider you, *saying:* '*Is* this the man who made the earth tremble, Who shook kingdoms, ¹⁷ Who made the world as a wilderness And destroyed its cities, *Who* did not open the house of his prisoners?' Isaiah 14:12-17

Don't get me wrong, if we fight Satan in our own strength we will get hurt, but if we claim all that is ours through Christ the Devil's threats will appear to be ridiculous!

III. REGENERATION.

In the second century, Celsus, an adversary of Christianity, complained:

"Jesus Christ came into the world to make the most horrible and dreadful societies; for he calls sinners, and not the righteous, so that the body he came to assemble is a body of profligates, separated from good people, among whom they before were mixed. He has rejected all the good, and collected all the bad."

The church father Origen replied:

"True, our Jesus came to call sinners— but to repentance. He assembles the wicked— but to convert them into new men...We come to him covetous, he makes us generous; lascivious, he makes us chaste; violent, he makes us meek..."[138]

There is nothing more radically life changing as regeneration! So let's look at this wonderful work of God that takes place within every believer.

A. Description.

1. Biblically.

The actual word is used only twice in the Bible. One is related to the Millennial kingdom.

²⁸ So Jesus said to them, "Assuredly I say to you, that in the regeneration, when the Son of Man sits on the throne of His glory, you who have followed Me will also sit on twelve thrones, judging the twelve tribes of Israel. Matthew 19:28

The other is related to our subject today.

⁴ But when the kindness and the love of God our Savior toward man appeared, ⁵ not by works of righteousness which we have done, but according to His mercy He saved us, through the washing of

---

[138] J. B. Sumner, The Evidence of Christianity, Derived for its Nature and Reception (London: J. Hatchard and Son, 1824), 402.

regeneration and renewing of the Holy Spirit, 6 whom He poured out on us abundantly through Jesus Christ our Savior, 7 that having been justified by His grace we should become heirs according to the hope of eternal life. Titus 3:4-7

2. Theologically.

It is the act of God whereby He imparts new life to the one who believes in Jesus Christ as Savior.

Grudem notes, "We did not choose to be made physically alive and we did not choose to be born — it is something that happened to us; similarly, these analogies in Scripture suggest that we are entirely passive in regeneration."[139]

26 ***I will*** *give* you a new heart and put a new spirit within you; **I** will take the heart of stone out of your flesh and **give you** a heart of flesh. 27 **I will** put My Spirit within you and cause you to walk in My statutes, and you will keep

---

[139] Grudem, Wayne A.; Grudem, Wayne A.. Systematic Theology: An Introduction to Biblical Doctrine (p. 699). Zondervan. Kindle Edition.

My judgments and do *them.* Ezekiel 36:26-27

¹² But as many as received Him, to them He gave the right to become children of God, to those who believe in His name: ¹³ who were born, not of blood, nor of the will of the flesh, nor of the will of man, but of God. John 1:12-13

¹⁸ Of His own will He brought us forth by the word of truth, that we might be a kind of firstfruits of His creatures. James 1:18

⁵ not by works of righteousness which we have done, but according to His mercy He saved us, through the washing of regeneration and renewing of the Holy Spirit, Titus 3:5

The movie *The End of the Spear*, tells the story of Nate Saint and four other missionaries who were murdered by the Waodani people of South America. However, in a testament to forgiveness, the families of the slain missionaries later returned to the tribe, eventually winning many of them to Christ.

Nate Saint's son, Steve, was asked: "So you've had a history of reconciliation [with the Waodani] over the years, but there wasn't a specific moment of reconciliation?" He replied:

It was a developing thing, but I think that the point of reconciliation really was with Mincaye [the man who killed Steve's father] and my Aunt Rachel. In her journal she once wrote:

"Tonight when I was sleeping in the hammock I heard a noise. Somebody was walking around in the dark."
Mincaye called out to her and squatted by her fire, wanting to talk.
He said, "You said that Waengongi, the Creator, is very strong."
Aunt Rachel said: "Mincaye, he is very strong. He made everything here, even the dirt."
Mincaye said: "You said that he could clean somebody's heart. My heart being very, very dark, can he clean even my heart?"
Aunt Rachel said, "Being very strong, he can clean even your heart."
She wrote that Mincaye got up and walked away, but that the next morning

he came back excited. He said: "Star, what you said is true. Speaking to God, he has cleaned my heart. Now it's waatamo—it's clear like the sky when it has no clouds in it."[140]

Regeneration is not to be confused with some outward reformation, Robert McGee notes:

Regeneration is not a self-improvement program, nor is it a cleanup campaign for our sinful natures. Regeneration is nothing less than the impartation of new life. Paul stated in Ephesians 2:5 that we were once dead in our sins, but we have since been made alive in Christ. Paul also wrote about this incredible transformation process in his letter to the young pastor Titus (Tit. 3:3-7). Regeneration is the renewing work of the Holy Spirit that literally makes each believer a new person at the moment trust is placed in Christ as Savior. In that wondrous, miraculous moment, we experience more than swapping one set of standards for another. We experience what Jesus called a new birth (John

---

[140] Amanda Knoke, Decision (January 2006), p. 20.

3:3–6), a Spirit-wrought renewal of the human spirit, a transforming resuscitation that takes place so that the Spirit is alive within us (Rom. 8:10).[141]

It is a total inner transformation, Louis Berkhof notes:

Regeneration consists in the implanting of the principle of the new spiritual life in man, in a radical change of the governing disposition of the soul, which, under the influence of the Holy Spirit, gives birth to a life that moves in a Godward direction. In principle this change affects the whole man: the intellect . . . the will . . . and the feelings or emotions."[142]

Regeneration turns on the light so to speak! Hal Lindsey notes:

Every spring the whole earth gives testimony to the truth of regeneration as it emerges from its wintry slumber and comes forth with fresh, green

---

[141] McGee, Robert. The Search for Significance: Seeing Your True Worth Through God's Eyes (Kindle Locations 1846-1848). Thomas Nelson. Kindle Edition.
[142] Louis Berkhof, Systematic Theology (Grand Rapids: Eerdmans, 1941), 468.

vegetation from the soil. What has been dead for a time now comes back to life.

But as great a phenomenon as it is to put a kernel of corn into the ground and then watch new life spring forth from the dead kernel, the greater miracle of regeneration of the human spirit has been made possible because of Christ's substitutionary death on the cross. The moment we place our trust in that death in our behalf, the Holy Spirit of God impregnates our death human spirits with the eternal life of God and we're reborn spiritually...When Adam and Eve were created, they were given a human spirit that enabled them to commune with God...[then man sinned and thus experienced spiritual death...Sometimes it's been mistakenly thought that the human spirit doesn't exist in us until we've been reborn...[But] I believe the spirit has continued to exist in men right from the day Adam sinned, but what we inherit from him is a spirit void of its ability to communicate with God so in every real sense it's dead...Actually it's much like a lamp to which the electricity is turned off. It doesn't cease being a lamp just because it isn't functioning the way it should...The Bible pictures the unregenerate man as "walking in darkness."...But at the heart of God's plan to regenerate men was His intention of restoring the light to the darkened spirits of men...So when a person is born again, the light really goes on inside him.[143]

The point is that this is not a surface work but an inner transformation. The problem with religion is that it never gets to the heart of the matter – our desperately sick hearts!

Snow can be a problem, it has to be removed from parking lots, roads, etc. But what to do with all that removed snow? They just pile it up. In Massachusetts the other year they had a lot of snow and so the piles of snow were huge. But then, the weather turned unseasonably warm and those pure white piles turned out not to be so pure! I read:

---

[143] The Liberation of Planet Earth, by Hal Lindsey.

The fury of the sun revealed the snow to be strewn with, literally, tons of trash. Snow plows had scooped up traffic cones, bicycles, discarded trash bags, and loads of debris in their haste to move the snow into 70-foot piles. And now, under the heat of the sun, the true character of the snow is being revealed. And it's not a pretty sight.[144]

That is a picture of man's self-righteousness, it looks good on the outside but inside it is nothing but trash. So God crucifies that old self, but then does a work within and gives us a new heart that really is pure!

3. Figuratively.

a. It is compared to a Birth.

³ Jesus answered and said to him, "Most assuredly, I say to you, unless one is born again, he cannot see the kingdom of God." ⁴ Nicodemus said to Him, "How can a man be born when he is old? Can he enter a second time into

---

[144] (Information from Doyle Rice, Wait, what? There's still snow in Boston?!, USA Today, May 28, 2015, http:// www.usatoday.com/ story/ weather/ 2015/ 05/ 28/ boston-snowpile/ 28089509/).

his mother's womb and be born?" 5

Jesus answered, "Most assuredly, I say to you, unless one is born of water and the Spirit, he cannot enter the kingdom of God. 6 That which is born of the flesh is flesh, and that which is born of the Spirit is spirit. 7 Do not marvel that I said to you, 'You must be born again.' John 3:3-7 See, John. 1:12-13.

They call it "the born again beach." Here's how a British newspaper described the "rebirth" of a lost beach:

An Irish beach that disappeared more than 30 years ago has returned to an island off the County Mayo coast. The sand at Dooagh, Achill Island, was washed away by storms in 1984, leaving only rocks and rock pools. But after a freak tide around Easter this year, hundreds of tons of sand were deposited around the area where the beach once stood, recreating the old 300-metre stretch of golden sand.

Local people are using the word "miraculous" to describe the beach's renewal. An official for the areas tourism board explained why pilgrims are flocking to the site:

> We live in a dark world these days so I think that is why there has been so much interest in Dooagh beach since the story broke. For something like our beach to come back gives people hope. It's a good news story and one where nature has done something benign for a change.[145]

If people would only know the miracle of the new birth! I have quoted from Hal Lindsey often, I love his testimony:

> Despondently I flipped over to another part of the New Testament - John, Chapter Three. As I glanced down the page, I was intrigued by a conversation Jesus had with a man who was looking for answers about God, just as I had been for years. The man's name was Nicodemus, and Jesus told him that unless he was born again, he could never understand the kingdom of God or enter it. "What's all this about being born again?" I asked myself. "If there's

---

[145] JJ McNamara, "'It gives people hope': born-again Irish beach captures world's attention," The Guardian (5-10-17).

anything I need, it's to be born all over again. I was surely born wrong the first time."

The truth is that we all were, and what a thrill to be given a new life, to be born into the very family of God.

b. It is compared to a Resurrection.

13 And do not present your members *as* instruments of unrighteousness to sin, but present yourselves to God as being alive from the dead, and your members *as* instruments of righteousness to God. Romans 6:13

4 But God, who is rich in mercy, because of His great love with which He loved us, 5 even when we were dead in trespasses, made us alive together with Christ (by grace you have been saved), 6 and raised *us* up together, and made *us* sit together in the heavenly *places* in Christ Jesus, Ephesians 2:4-6

That dead spirit, is made alive and indwelt by, God Himself! Remember God is Spirit and we must worship Him in spirit and in truth (Jn. 4:24). We now have the capacity to fellowship with

Him, a resurrected mind to know Him; emotions to love Him; and a will to obey Him.

Botanists have discovered that there is the power of ancient seeds to germinate, sprout, and produce a "resurrected" plant. Archeologists discovered the 2,000-year old seeds of the Judean date palm in the palace of King Herod at the Dead Sea fortress of Masada. From one of these ancient seeds a date palm was produced in 2005.

A hard, dead seed is resurrected to life! I don't know all of how this works, but a dead spirit is resurrected back to life in regeneration.

c. It is compared to that of a New Creation.

¹⁷ Therefore, if anyone *is* in Christ, *he is* a new creation; old things have passed away; behold, all things have become new. 2 Corinthians 5:17

Those old things, everything we were in Adam, has been crucified with Christ (Rom. 6:6-7).

London businessman Lindsay Clegg told the story of a warehouse property he was selling. The building had been empty for months and needed repairs. Vandals had damaged the doors, smashed the windows, and strewn trash around the interior. As he showed a prospective buyer the property, Clegg took pains to say that he would replace the broken windows, bring in a crew to correct any structural damage, and clean out the garbage. The new buyer said, "Forget about the repairs, when I buy this place, I'm going to build something completely different. I don't want the building; I want the site."

Regeneration is not a patch up job, or some kind of improvement program for our old self, the old life is over and we are new creatures in Christ.[146]

B. Distinctive feature.

1. It is Instantaneous.

This is revealed by the fact that these passages are in an aorist tense (Jn. 1:12-13, etc.). This is not a process or

---

[146] Ian L. Wilson, Barrie, Ontario. Leadership, Vol. 4, no. 3.

gradual thing but something that takes place at a moment in time. I was not saved the week of May 5th through the 11th, I was saved at a moment in time, instantaneously on the 7th of May, 1974, at about 8:00 p.m.

2. It is not Inclusive.

What I mean by stating that it does not *remove* the old sin nature (1 Jn. 1:8). We are saved from the sin nature's power (Rom. 8:13), but not from its presence. And the old nature is NOT turning into the new nature! The old nature is never salvaged but crucified (Gal. 2:20; 6:15). Billy Graham writes:

Salvation is not just repairing the original self. It is a new self created of God in righteousness and true holiness. Regeneration is not even a change of nature or a change of heart. Being born again is not a change— it is a regeneration, a new generation. It is a second birth. "Ye must be born again." There is nothing about the old nature that God will accept. There is no soundness in it. The old nature is too weak to follow Christ... Jesus, knowing that it was impossible to change, patch up, and reform, said you must have a total new birth, "Ye must be born again."[147]

C. *Demonstration.*

1. By an *Inability* to sin.

I understand that when we sin, while we are accountable for it, it does not come from the new nature (Rom. 7:17, 20/1 Jn. 3:9). The new nature always desires to do God's will, and the Holy Spirit gives us the power to put those desires into our daily lives (Gal. 5:16). The real you never sins! Again let's not think that this means we are not responsible or accountable when we choose to let the old nature have its way. We are and when we sin we are to confess and forsake it (1 Jn. 1:9). But it is transforming to realize that I have a new nature that has never been tainted by sin. Watchman Nee notes:

What is "in Christ" cannot sin; what is in Adam can sin and will do so whenever

---

[147] Graham, Billy. Peace with God: The Secret of Happiness (Kindle Locations 2550-2552). Thomas Nelson. Kindle Edition.

Satan is given a chance to exert his power. So it is a question of our choice of which facts we will count upon and live by: the tangible facts of daily experience or the mightier fact that we are now "in Christ."[148]

2. It gives us an *Ability* to perceive the spiritual realm.

As one put it:

It's called the "sixth sense," faith. Faith is the eyesight of the spirit. It causes us to reach out to God and to know Him. Faith enables us to believe that when God says He'll do something for us, He will. The body has its five senses that make the material world real...But the intimate knowledge of God can only be known through the sixth sense, faith...Faith is such a misunderstood concept. I often hear people praying for more faith, but strictly speaking, that's a wrong prayer. Once you've been born again and had your sixth sense restored to your spirit, you now have all the faith you can ever get...But faith needs an

---

[148] Nee, Watchman. The Normal Christian Life (p. 66). CLC Publications. Kindle Edition.

object in order for it to function, and Jesus is that object, revealed to us through His Word.[149]

We will look at this later...

3. It gives us eternal *Security.*

It gives us *eternal life*, which by definition must never come to an end, or it would not be eternal. If God offered 50-year life only, I would take it, but He never offers anything but eternal life (Jn. 5:24; 10:27-28/1 Jn. 2:25; 5:11-13).

In the Military Intelligence world of Classified and Unclassified information, there is a firm rule that governs everything. It is this: Unclassified material can be bumped up a notch to Confidential, Secret, and Top Secret classifications. But, once the document has been designated "Classified," it cannot be lowered back down to an "Unclassified" status.

I read that you can type a document on an "Unclassified" computer, save it to a

---

[149] The Liberation of Planet Earth, Hal Lindsey.

compact disk (CD), and then upload the document onto a "Secret" computer. But, after you have done that you cannot remove the original CD from the secure site where the exercise took place. It is now marked "secret."

Documents can move up in classification, but they can never move back down.

Of course, man can and does violate such rules, but the principle of eternal life is like that, only unalterable. Once you go from dead to eternal life – you can never go back to dead! Once you go from lost to saved, you can never go back to unsaved. Regeneration is irreversible! See, Phil. 1:6/2 Tim. 2:13/Heb. 13:5-6/etc.

Con:

1. So, the Salvation includes Justification; Redemption; and Regeneration. There is one more we will look at next, the Relocation.

2. Have we been transformed from the inside? Do you have new desires that really want to follow the Lord Jesus? As

one put it, "If we are, what we have always been, then we are not saved."

3. Vicki Hicks, of Sydney, Australia, has a duck, named Ducka, it apparently will eat anything. It was acting weird and Vicki was shocked to see the duck coughed up a nail! She rushed the duck to the Avian Reptile and Exotic Animal Hospital in West Sydney and X-Rays confirmed her fears. Ducka had swallowed a small toolbox-worth of nails, screws, hooks, and other metal objects – 21 pieces of metal in all.[150]

Doctors could remove all the sharp metal objects from Ducka's belly, but they could not remove her appetite for the wrong type of food or metal.

We have to be honest, what we desire, reveals what kind of nature we have. Regeneration gives us a new nature and thus new desires. If someone claims to be saved, but then still loves the same old sins, and are never bothered by self-

---

[150] (Information from http://www.dailytelegraph.com.au/ newslocal/ macarthur/ ducka-thehttp:// www.dailytelegraph.com.au/ newslocal/ macarthur/ ducka-the 1227086692966).

centered living, that person still has the nature of sin.

Peter talking about false teachers, who were in the church, writes:

[20] For if, after they have escaped the pollutions of the world through the knowledge of the Lord and Savior Jesus Christ, they are again entangled in them and overcome, the latter end is worse for them than the beginning. [21] For it would have been better for them not to have known the way of righteousness, than having known *it,* to turn from the holy commandment delivered to them. [22] But it has happened to them according to the true proverb: *"A dog returns to his own vomit,"* and, "a sow, having washed, to her wallowing in the mire." 2 Peter 2:20-22

No, these are not people who were saved and then lost, but were never saved to begin with.

IV. RELOCATION.

A. Positional Truth – In Christ.

Positional truth is true of every believer, by way of Divine declaration. There are certain truths we must know about positional truth: Hal Lindsey writes:

My new position in Christ gives me a *total* identification with Jesus in God's eyes. As He looks at the Son, He looks at me in the same way because He sees me in the Son and the Son in me. If I took a grimy piece of paper and inserted it into the pages of a book and closed it, that paper would be totally identified with the book and we would no longer see it, only the book...What becomes true of the One becomes true of the other.

So, Positional truths are:

- Positional truth is *Imperceptible* at the time of salvation – you don't feel it or experience it. To be set apart from sin unto God is not something you feel when you are saved. For example, one does not feel forgiven or feel like a saint, or chosen, etc.

- Positional truth cannot be *Improved* upon – it is not progressive, it is not related to growth or getting better. We will be no holier in heaven then we are right now positionally. It is true there is a progressive and ultimate sanctification in our experience. But that is not to be confused with positional truth.

- It is *Impossible* to mix any trace of human merit to Positional truth – it is not given on the basis of merit. Remember these blessings are given to every believer, and every believer is saved by grace.

- It cannot be *Impaired* by time or failure or sin. It is totally irreversible. Our behavior cannot undo it.

- It is imparted to our understanding only by divine revelation. We know it because it has been revealed in the Bible. We would not know that we stand perfectly holy before God, unless God's Word declared it to be so.

- It is Imputed by God alone – without any help from the believer at all. We looked at the fallacy of the idea that

"God helps those who help themselves." We are removed from Adam and placed into Christ by God's power alone!

- It is Imperative to count these things as true by faith, in order to enjoy them.

I go into this in my book, *A Manual for Survival*.

All of this is related to the fact that we are in Christ, which includes all that we have looked at and much more:

Chosen (Eph. 1:4)
Saints (1 Cor. 1:2)
Believers (Eph. 1:1)
Adopted (Eph. 1:5)
Accepted (Eph. 1:6).
Redeemed (Eph. 1:7)
Co-crucified (Gal. 2:20)
Forgiven (Eph. 1:17)
Loved (Rom. 5:8)
Complete (Col. 2:10)
New creatures (2 Cor. 5:17)
Raised and seated with Christ (Eph. 2:6)
United (Jn. 17/Eph. 4)
Regenerated (Tit. 3:5)

No Condemnation (Rom. 8:1)
Every blessing (Eph. 1:3)
Eternal life (1 Jn. 5:11-13)
Child of God (Jn. 1:12)
Righteous (2 Cor. 5:21)
Reconciled (2 Cor. 5:18)

I doubt if this list is exhaustive, and I hope you understand this book is a fly-over, just a brief look at the basics.

B. Practical Faith – Christ in you.

As we experience fellowship with God, we will actually experience some wonderful things in our daily lives:

Walking in the Spirit (Gal. 5:16)
Fruit of the Spirit (Gal. 5:22-23)
Prayer life (Jude 20)
Manifested presence of God (Jn. 14:21)
Witnessing (Ac. 1:8)
Overcoming temptation (Rom. 8:13)
Spiritual growth (2 Cor. 3:17-18)
Warfare (Eph. 6:10)
Worship (Jn. 4:24)
Desire for God's Word (1 Pet. 2:2)
Inner enablement (Eph. 3:16-19)
Faithfulness in giving (2 Cor. 9:6-8)

Singing, thanksgiving, submitting (Eph. 5:18-21)
Attending church (Heb. 10:24-25)
Using our spiritual gifts (1 Cor. 12)
Forgiving others who offend us (Mt. 18)

Again, this is only a limited list, but will all be experienced as we walk under the controlling power of the Holy Spirit.

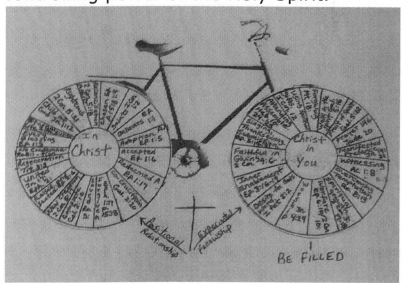

Chapter Five

THE STIPULATION OF MAN

Intro:

1. The Bar-tailed Godwit is a medium sized bird, about the size of a seagull. It has a long, skinny beak, and as it feeds on the Mud flats of New Zealand, it becomes inordinately fat. Now these birds make the longest non-stop flights of any bird. Satellites have tracked females with transmitters taking non-stop flights from Alaska to New Zealand. This return route of their annual migration is nearly 8,000 miles long, from the northern reaches of the North Pacific to the southern extremes of the South Pacific. It's the equivalent of flying from London to Los Angeles and overshooting LA by 1,000 miles. The bar-tailed godwit makes this amazing journey in eight days, without ever stopping to eat, drink, or rest along the way. [(Information from: https://www.youtube.com/ watch?)]

I read where someone said this is physically impossible! That is what faith does! It places its full confidence in God to do what we could never do. Salvation is impossible!

²⁵ When His disciples heard *it,* they were greatly astonished, saying, "Who then can be saved?" ²⁶ But Jesus looked at *them* and said to them, "With men this is impossible, but with God all things are possible." Matthew 19:25-26

2. Faith in the Lord Jesus brings about what is humanly impossible – salvation by the power of God.

3. Therefore it is extremely important that we understand what faith is, and what it is not. Let's look at the one stipulation for salvation.

Trans: Let's review where we have been:

I. The Situation.
A. God's Perfection.
B. God's Creation.
C. God's Demonstration.
II. The Separation.
A. Standard of Deity.
B. Sin Debt.
C. Satanic Dominion.
D. Spiritual Death.

III. The Solution.
A. Representation.
B. Incarnation.
C. Substitution.
D. Satisfaction.
IV. The Salvation.
A. Justification.
B. Redemption.
C. Regeneration.
D. Relocation.
V. The Stipulation.

Ryrie notes:

Salvation is always through faith, not because of faith (Eph. 2: 8). Faith is the channel through which we receive God's gift of eternal life; it is not the cause. This is so man can never boast, even of his faith. But faith is the necessary and only channel (John 5: 24; 17: 3). Normally the New Testament word for believe (pisteuō) is used with the preposition eis (John 3: 16), indicating reliance or confident trust in the object. Sometimes it is followed by epi, emphasizing the trust as laying hold on the object of faith (Rom. 9: 33; 10: 11). Sometimes it is followed by a clause that introduces the content of the faith (10: 9). The verb is used with a dative in Romans 4: 3. But whatever the form, it indicates reliance on something or someone.[151]

This is extremely important! Because if we get what faith means wrong, say add to it, we turn the gospel of grace into a works salvation, which is really NO salvation at all!

A. The *Meaning* of Faith.

The *Substance* of believing.

We have made faith too complicated, some have so many strings attached to faith that it could choke a large elephant! But it is compared with such simple things like:

- Receiving (Jn. 1: 12).

- Drinking (Jn. 4: 14).

- Eating (Jn. 6: 40 with v. 54), and

- Looking (Jn. 3: 14-15).

---

[151] Basic Theology, A popular Systematic Guide to Understanding Biblical Truth by Charles Ryrie, p. 377.

Some try to make faith a synonym for "commit" but those examples of drinking, eating, looking are not related to commitment but of appropriating or taking what is there.

It involves three basic concepts:

- *Intelligence.* We have to understand the gospel and that can only be done through the illumination of the Holy Spirit (1 Cor. 2: 14). He alone can convince us that we are sinners under God's just and holy wrath (Rom. 3: 23; 6: 23); that the Lord Jesus Christ is the God/man who died in our place (Rom. 5: 8); and then rose from the dead (Rom. 10: 9-10/1 Cor. 15: 3-6). Moreover, that He is the *only* way of salvation. It all begins with intelligence, we must first hear the gospel as the Holy Spirit gives us understanding of what we hear (Ac. 18: 8/ Rom. 10: 14/ Eph. 1: 13/ 1 Cor. 15: 3-4).

If you go to a doctor and he examines you and then tells you that you have a fatal disease – you now know you have a problem.

- Intelligence has to lead to *Acceptance*. When one hears the gospel, they have to accept it as the truth.

Again if you go to the doctor and he tells you, you have a tumor that will kill you if it is not removed, you have to make a choice. Do you believe him or not? Some are simply unwilling to believe (Mt. 23: 37). Refusing to accept that we are sinners and that Jesus is the only way of salvation will ultimately lead to eternal judgment.

- Intelligence leads to Acceptance which leads to *Reliance.*

If you go to the doctor and he finds you have a tumor; and you accept that to be true; it does you no good unless you rely upon the Doc to remove it. The substance of faith in the gospel of Christ will always include intelligence that leads to acceptance that leads to reliance. Michael Cocoris notes that, "Thus faith is the recognition of truth, the reception of truth, and the reliance upon truth."[152]

Anything short of intelligence, acceptance, and reliance falls short of saving faith.

Charles Hodge writes:

That faith, therefore, which is connected with salvation, includes knowledge, that is, perception of the truth and it's qualities; assent or persuasion of truth of the object of faith; and trust, or reliance. The exercise or state of mind expressed by the word faith, as used in the scriptures is not mere mental assent or mere trust, it is the intelligent perception, reception, and reliance on the truth as revealed in the gospel."[153]

We must understand faith is not a work, but to trust in the work of another, the Lord Jesus Christ. It is only as good as its object, which is the Person and Work of the Lord Jesus Christ in His death, burial, and resurrection. It is not faith in

---

[152] Evangelism: A Biblical Approach, by G. Michael Cocoris, p. 76, Moody Press, 1984.
[153] Commentary on the Epistle to the Romans, by Charles Hodge, p. 29.

faith but faith in Jesus Christ. Salvation is all of grace, there can be no human work required to receive it (Eph. 2:8-9/ Rom. 4:4-5; 11:6). It is not something we do, but believe it has already been done through the Lord Jesus Christ (Jn. 6:28-29). We receive it as a gift! Next Christmas, when someone gives you a gift, open your wallet and try to pay for it – see how that goes! If you have to pay for it, then it's not a gift (Rom. 10:1-4).

As Spurgeon often said, "Let's not make a Christ out of our faith."

Lewis Sperry Chafer gives a good definition of faith:

To turn voluntarily from all hope in one's own merits, and take an expectant attitude toward God, trusting Him to do a perfect work of salvation based on the merits of Christ alone.

I heard Billy Graham give this illustration many years ago:

Years ago, a tightrope walker named Charles Blondin, went across Niagara Falls, walking on a wire. He went back and forth. He even filled a wheelbarrow with bricks and took that across. A crowd gathered, and he asked one of them, "Do you believe I could do that with you?" The man agreed that he could. Then Blondin said, "Hop on in, and I'll carry you across." The man said, "No way!" You see, he did not really believe. He believed in his mind that Blondin could take him across; he wanted him to in his emotions, but he would not commit himself to Blondin and trust him to take him across. Saving faith involves our mind, emotion, and will.

B. The *Mistake* of Front loading.

Joseph Dillow writes:

Front loading the gospel means attaching various works of submission and obedience on the front end and including them in the conditions for salvation... Faith is redefined to include submission, and a man becomes a Christian not by "hearing" and "believing" but by believing and promising God he will submit his life to Christ... their view is that a man must resolve to turn from all known sin and follow Christ absolutely. It seems that works enter through the front door... In their preoccupation with means, they have forgotten that God has already told us what the means of salvation are and what they are not. Works are not a means, whether on the front end or on the back end. The only means necessary for obtaining salvation is faith and faith alone.[154]

Let us look at some things that are smuggled into the idea of faith:

- It is not faith plus works.

The passage they use is James 2:23-24:

"And the Scripture was fulfilled which says, *"Abraham believed God, and it was accounted to him for righteousness."* And he was called the friend of God. 24 You see then that a man is justified by works, and not by faith only."

---

[154] Dillow, Joseph. The Reign of the Servant Kings: A Study of Eternal Security and the Final Destiny of Man (Kindle Locations 354-356). Paniym Group, Inc.. Kindle Edition.

What James is really saying is that man can only see faith when it is demonstrated by works and that is true, but God sees faith immediately because He alone sees the heart of man. While faith does produce works, works are the results not the cause of faith (Eph. 2:8-10).

James points to Abraham's demonstration of faith when he offered up Isaac, recorded in Gen. 22. However, God had already declared Abraham righteous nearly 40 years before by faith alone as proven by Gen. 15:6! See, Rom. 4:1-5.

So it took Abraham 40 years to produce this work which man can see, but God saw it the moment Abraham believed. An example of this is seen in Lot, he had very little outward fruit that revealed inward faith, but God calls him righteous because He could see a regenerated heart (2 Pet. 2:7-8).

You cannot mix faith and works without losing faith (Rom. 11:5-6).

- Faith plus repentance?

Repentance means a *change of mind* not as some say, a promise to stop sinning, or even a willingness to stop sinning or to live right. Repentance is not even turning from sin; you cannot do that until you are saved! As one notes:

In the New Testament, repentance is definitely *not* turning from sin. It makes a distinction between repentance and turning. There is another Greek word for turning (epistrephō) and it is never translated "to repent" (Wilkin, dissertation, p. 11).
Acts 26:20 clearly demonstrates that repenting and turning are two different things. Paul says that the Gentiles should "repent **and** turn to God" (literal translation).[155]

Berkhof notes, "Scripture, repentance is wholly an inward act, and should not be confounded with the change of life that proceeds from it. Confession of sin and

---

[155] Cocoris, G. Michael. Repentance: The Most Misunderstood Word in the Bible (Kindle Locations 179-182). Grace Gospel Press. Kindle Edition.

reparation of wrongs are fruits of repentance"[156]

Luke 17:1-4 is an illustration that proves the point. Jesus teaches that if a man repents seven times in one day, he is to be forgiven seven times. There is no question that there is genuine repentance here—the whole point assumes that the repentance is genuine. Yet this genuine repentance did not affect the man's lifestyle!

It simply means a *change of mind*!

Chafer says, "The word (repentance) means a change of mind" (Chafer, vol. 3, p. 372).

Ryrie states, "In both the Old and New Testaments repentance means 'to change one's mind'"[157]

Baker writes, "It (repentance) refers to reconsidering or changing the mind after an action has taken place" (Baker, p. 411).

---

[156] (Berkhof, p. 487).

[157] (Ryrie, So Great Salvation, hereafter SGS, p. 92).

Erickson, who pours more into the word, admits that "literally" it means, "to think differently about something or have a change of mind" (Erickson, p. 937).

Alfred Plummer calls repentance "an inward change of mind."

Westcott says, "It follows, therefore, that 'Repentance from dead works' expresses the complete change of mind—of spiritual attitude—which leads the believer to abandon these works and seek some other support for life."

R. A. Torrey said, "What the repentance, or change of mind, is about must always be determined by the context" (Torrey, p. 355).

Many Greek scholars have also concluded that repentance means a change of mind.

One Greek lexicon says that the Greek word translated "repent" means "to change one's mind or purpose" and "repentance," means "after-thought" (Abbott-Smith).

A. T. Robertson, the great Greek scholar, defines "repent" as a "change (think afterwards) [of] their mental attitudes" (see his Word Pictures in the New Testament).

Julius R. Mantey, who co-authored the famous A Manual Grammar of the Greek New Testament (known as "Dana and Mantey") says, "It means to think differently or have a different attitude toward sin and God, etc." (Mantey, Basic Christian Doctrine, p. 193).

Often times it is confused with another Greek word, which means remorse. Repentance is not feeling sorry for our sin. As one noted:

In the New Testament, repentance is definitely not being sorry for sin. It makes a distinction between remorse and repentance. There is another Greek word for regret (metamelomai). It appears five times in the New Testament (Mt. 21:29, 32; 27:3; 2 Cor. 7:8; Heb. 7:21). This word describes "sorrow for something done and wishing it undone," but "forgiveness of sins is nowhere promised" for it (Trench, p.

258). Judas was "remorseful" (Mt. 27:3), but he did not get saved. On the other hand, the Greek word for repentance (metanoia) "does not properly signify sorrow for having done amiss" (Trench, p. 257). Esau shed tears, but it didn't change anything (Heb. 12:16-17). Paul plainly demonstrates that sorrow and repentance are two different things. He says, "Your sorrow **led to** repentance" (2 Cor. 7:9). Sorrow may lead to repentance; sorrow may accompany repentance, but sorrow and repentance are two different things... In Acts 2, the Jews regretted what they did to Christ. They were "cut to the heart" and asked, "What shall we do?" (Acts 2:37). It was **after their regret** that Peter said, "Repent" (Acts 2:38), which shows that regret is different than repentance.[158]

D. L. Moody used to say the inquirer is "not to seek for sorrow, but for the Savior."

---

[158] Cocoris, G. Michael. Repentance: The Most Misunderstood Word in the Bible (Kindle Locations 160-162). Grace Gospel Press. Kindle Edition.

Gill says, "Tears of repentance will not wash away sin; notwithstanding these, iniquity remains marked before God; Christ's tears themselves did not take away, nor atone for sin; His blood must be shed, and it was shed for the remission of it; and that is the only meritorious cause of it" (Gill on Lk. 24:47).

Harry Ironside said, "Nowhere is man exhorted to feel a certain amount of sorrow for his sins in order to come to Christ."

I remember reading Josh McDowell's testimony, he said after he received Christ he felt like throwing-up! He said, "What have I gotten myself into!" But I think we would all agree he got saved!

The word repent occurs forty-six times. Thirty-seven of these times, God is the one repenting (or not repenting). If repentance means sorrow for sin or turning from sin, God would be a sinner!

The problem is not with repentance which is clearly necessary for salvation but making it mean something that it really doesn't mean.

So what do we change our mind about? Hal Lindsey says it well:

Repentance, as it relates to Christ means to change our minds about Him, who He is and what He's done to provide forgiveness and deliverance from our sins. When we place faith in Jesus as having taken our place personally on the cross and borne the penalty due our sins, then we're automatically repenting, because we couldn't accept Him in this way without having had to change our minds in some way concerning Him.

The essence of the issue is this: you can repent and not believe; but can't believe and not repent. This is why in the gospel of John, which was expressly written to bring people to new life in Christ, the condition "believe in Christ is stated ninety-nine times. But the word "repent" isn't used at all in the book.[159]

---

[159] The Liberation of Planet earth, Hal Lindsey.

Try to find repentance mentioned in a key passage related to salvation, I am talking about Romans 4, it is not there! Or try and find it in the book of Galatians. Michael Cocoris observes:

The most detailed book in the Bible on salvation is the book of Romans. The chapter in Romans on what one must do to be saved is Romans 4, but Romans 4 does not contain the words "repent" or "repentance." In fact, the word "repentance" only occurs once in the book of Romans (Rom. 2:4) and there it is a virtual synonym for faith. The only book in the Bible written to defend the Gospel is Galatians. Neither the word "repent" nor the word "repentance" makes an appearance in that book at all.[160]

To be sure, we would include repentance in the requirement for salvation, but it must be rightly understood. It is interesting to study how the Word of God used the word repentance:

---

[160] Cocoris, G. Michael. Repentance: The Most Misunderstood Word in the Bible (Kindle Locations 95-98). Grace Gospel Press. Kindle Edition.

1. Repentance is not sorrow for sins, it can lead to repentance but it is not in and of itself repentance.

[9] Now I rejoice, not that you were made sorry, but that your sorrow led to repentance. For you were made sorry in a godly manner, that you might suffer loss from us in nothing. 2 Corinthians 7:9

2. Repentance is not always a lasting change.

[1] Then He said to the disciples, "It is impossible that no offenses should come, but woe *to him* through whom they do come! [2] It would be better for him if a millstone were hung around his neck, and he were thrown into the sea, than that he should offend one of these little ones. [3] Take heed to yourselves. If your brother sins against you, rebuke him; and if he repents, forgive him. [4] And if he sins against you seven times in a day, and seven times in a day returns to you, saying, 'I repent,' you shall forgive him." Luke 17:1-4

3. Repentance's root and fruit must be distinguished.

⁸ Therefore bear fruits worthy of repentance, Matthew 3:8

Lenski notes:

Repentance cannot be meant by "fruits"..."Fruits" indicate an organic connection between themselves and repentance just as the tree brings forth the fruit that is peculiar to its nature...[repentance] is invisible; hence we judge its presence by the Fruits which are visible.[161]

So first, comes repentance, a change of mind, and then comes the outward fruit. Repentance is the root and a change in conduct is the fruit. Obviously, the fruit is not part of the root!

4. Repentance/faith is two sides of one coin.

²¹ testifying to Jews, and also to Greeks, repentance toward God and

---

[161] R.C.H Linski, The Interpretation of St. Luke's Gospel [Minneapolis: Augsburg Publishing House, 1961, p. 188.

faith toward our Lord Jesus Christ. Acts 20:21

In Acts 20:21, repentance and faith are united by one article. Therefore, repentance and faith are not two steps to salvation; they are not temporally successive. They cannot be separated; but they ought to be distinguished. One can repent and not exercise faith; but to exercise saving faith always involves repentance. The Bible declares up to 150 times that salvation is by faith alone. When repentance related to salvation is mentioned without faith, faith is always assumed.

5. Repentance in various contexts:

a. Repentance because of *Storms*, but when the storm is over it is business as usual. Example: Pharaoh (Ex. 9:27).

b. Repentance because of the *Sword*, but when threat of death was passed, it was back to life as before. Example: Balaam (Num. 22:34).

c. Repentance can be *UnSuccessful* because God refused to acknowledge it. Example: Achan and Esau.

d. Repentance that is just face *Saving,* done only with men in mind. Example: Saul (1 Sam. 15:24).

e. Repentance of *Scorning* God's sovereignty. Example: Job (Job. 40:3-; 42:1).

f. Repentance of a *Sinning* Saint. Example: David (Psa. 51).

g. Repentance of a lost *Sinner.* Example Prodigal son (Lu. 15:1-2, 20).

h. Repentance that is *not Sincere.* Example: Judas (Mt. 27:4-5).

It can get complicated, but the bottom line is that it must not be made as a requirement for salvation, it must not be explained to the lost sinner that he must stop sinning *before* he can be saved. Repentance is a *change of mind*, about who we are, a sinner; and about the Lord Jesus Christ, the only one who can save us based on His death, burial, and resurrection.

What is the big deal you ask? First, if you add anything we do to salvation we end up unsaved! Two, if we add anything to it we share in God's glory and God will not tolerate that (Isa. 42:8). Let us say one of my deacons; Steve Hicks buys me a brand new truck. And I pull two cents out and give it to him and say, "Here this will help pay for the truck!" Later another deacon, Gary Cash says, "Wow, that is a wonderful truck!" And I say, "It sure is, Steve and I bought it!" I do not think Steve would appreciate that. And, God does not appreciate or accept our two cents added to salvation.

- It is not faith plus Lordship.

We live in a world where "fake news" has become part of our vocabulary. I came across this the other day:

People are confused about the credibility of "news" and where it comes from, according to a global report.

Fifty-nine percent of people surveyed for the 2018 Edelman Trust Barometer said they were unsure what they see in the media is true and what isn't, while nearly seven in 10 said they worry about fake news being used as "a weapon."

Almost two-thirds (63 percent) said the average person does not know how to tell good journalism from rumor or falsehoods. The report surveyed people in 28 countries.

"In a world where facts are under siege, credentialed sources are proving more important than ever," Stephen Kehoe, global chair of reputation at Edelman, said. "There are credibility problems for both platforms and sources. People's trust in them is collapsing." [cnbc.com/2018/01/22/nearly-70-percent-of-people-are-worried-about-fake-news-as-a-weapon-survey-says.]

Well there is also fake faith! Faith in faith; faith in works to save; faith in the ability to change your life so God will accept you; faith in one's ability to make Jesus Lord of every area of your life in order to bring about salvation; faith in water baptism to secure conversion. Praise God we have the Word of God to tell us what is really required to be saved.

Hal Lindsey writes:

"Lordship salvation is a very subtle form of human merit which some add to "faith" as a condition of salvation...who can say at this moment, no matter how long he's been a believer, that he has *everything* in his life under the lordship of Jesus?...As long as we're still in this world, the flesh, and the devil are still out to get us, there's not much chance that there'll be a time in our lives when *everything* is under Christ's Lordship.... So how can we make an unbeliever responsible to do something as a condition of salvation that we're still not able to do?...But worse than that, they're subtly adding "works" to faith which nullifies grace...The scriptural teaching on this issue is that we must recognize Jesus as Lord in the sense that He's not a mere man, but the Lord from heaven who became a man to die for our sins."

All right, let us consider the following:

1. Jesus Christ is *Already* LORD.

He is already Lord! And it is nothing but a straw man to say that those of us who do not believe in Lordship salvation deny that truth. The issue is not whether He is Lord or not, but whether making Him Lord of our lives is a requirement to be saved. The truth is no lost person has the power to make Him Lord in order to merit salvation. In fact, if we were honest how many of us believers are 100% yielded to His Lordship? Take Peter, he did not yield totally to the Lordship of Jesus after he was saved. Read Mt. 26:69-75/Acts 10:14! Gal. 2:11. How about John Mark? Hardly! Look at Acts 15:38. Was Paul always yielding to the Lordship of Christ? Read Rom. 7:14-23. How about that bunch of believers at Corinth! How about you and me? I tell you He is firmly sitting on His sovereign throne regardless of what anybody does, thinks, or says.

2. That one does not have to *make Him Lord* in order to be saved is *Affirmed* by people who were saved without yielding to His Lordship!

Take Lot, we could read the Old Testament for the rest of our lives and find no proof that he ever yielded to God. He was about as self-absorbed as any person you can think of, but God says he was righteous in His sight! See 2 Pet. 2:7-8.

How about those saved at Ephesus.

Ryrie notes:

It concerns those who were converted at Ephesus during Paul's third missionary journey (Acts 19)...These converts came out of a background of the worship of Diana (of which worship Ephesus was the center). An important part of this worship included the superstitious dependence on magical words, charms, and sayings. These were based on letters, which were on the crown, girdle, and feet of the statue of Diana in the temple at Ephesus. Magical incantations were compiled in books, and charms were worn as amulets by the Ephesians. This, is the kind of superstitious background from which the Christians were converted in Ephesus.

In Acts 19:18-19 we are told that more than two years after Paul had first gone to Ephesus, "Many also of those who had believed kept coming, confessing and disclosing their practices. And many of those who practiced magic brought their books together and began burning them in the sight of all; and they counted up the price of them and found it fifty thousand pieces of silver."

It is important to know the tense of the word *believed.* It is a perfect tense, indicating that those who burned their books that day had believed before that time; that is, sometime during the more than two years Paul had been in Ephesus (see vv. 8 and 10). In other words, they did not burn their books of magic as soon as they had become believers. As believers, they had continued to practice and be guided by the superstitious magic of their heathen background... In case I have not been crystal clear about the import of this example, let me say it again. There were people at Ephesus who became believers in Christ knowing that they should give up their use of magic but who did not give it up, some of them for as long as two years after they had become Christians. Yet their unwillingness to give it up did not prevent their becoming believers. Their salvation did not depend on faith plus willingness to submit to the lordship of Christ in the matter of using magical arts. Their salvation came through faith alone even though for months and years afterward many of them practiced that which they knew to be wrong.[162]

3. Salvation is by grace and thus must be *Apart* from anything that man can do (Jn. 6:28-29/Rom. 11:5-6/Eph. 2:8-9/Tit. 3:5/etc.)

4. We must *Ascertain* what the word LORD means.

Again, Ryrie is helpful:

To be sure, Lord does mean Master, but in the New Testament it also means God (Acts 3:22), owner (Luke 19:33), sir (John 4:11), man-made idols (1 Cor. 8:5), and even one's husband (1 Peter

---

[162] Charles C. Ryrie, *Balancing the Christian Life*, (Chicago: Moody Press, 1969), WORD*search* CROSS e-book, 179-180.

3:6)... the title Lord, which meant "Jehovah-God" to the Jewish mind, became attached to this Man Jesus in the preaching of the apostles, then there was division. Such division would not have been so sharp if Lord Jesus meant merely "Sir Jesus" or "Master Jesus"; but if it meant "God Jesus" or "Jehovah Jesus," then one can account for the division and debate over that kind of claim. If Lord means God and Lord Jesus then means the God-Man... There is nothing unique in Christ's relationship with His followers if that is all Jesus the Master means. Even the leaders of cults claim this. But what religion, other than Christianity, has a savior who claimed to be both God and Man in the same person? If Lord in the phrase Lord Jesus means Master, then the claim to uniqueness is absent. If Lord in the phrase Lord Jesus means Jehovah-God, then Jesus is unique, and this is the very heart of the message of salvation in Christianity... what did cause division among the people was His claim to be God as well. Not a man who claimed to be master, but a man who said he was God is what angered them.

The Jews clearly said on one occasion, "For a good work we do not stone You, but for blasphemy; and because You, being a man, make Yourself out to be God" (John 10:33). The offense is the God-Man, not the Master-Man. Why is this such a crucial matter in our salvation? It is for the simple reason that no other kind of savior can save except a God-Man. Deity and humanity must be combined in order to provide a satisfactory salvation. The Savior must be a man in order to be able to die and in order to be identified with the curse on man. And He must be God in order that that death be effective for an infinite number of persons…The same emphasis is seen in Romans 10:9: "That if you confess with your mouth Jesus as Lord…you shall be saved." It is the confession of Jesus as God and thus faith in the God-Man that saves from sin. This is the same point that Peter drove home on the day of Pentecost when he said: "Therefore let all the house of Israel know for certain that God has made Him both Lord and Christ—this Jesus whom you have crucified" (Acts 2:36). Jesus the Man had been proved by the resurrection and ascension to be Lord, God and Christ, the Messiah. They had to put their faith in more than a man; it had to be in One who was also God and the promised Messiah of the Old Testament.[163]

Robert P. Lightner:

"The question is not, "Is Jesus Christ Lord?" Of course He is!...The gift of salvation must be received, but it is apart from any human work or contribution of any kind. Sinners are saved by grace through faith alone. These views – the absolutely free gift view and the Lordship view – cannot both be right. They are mutually exclusive. The Bible teaches one or the other or neither, but it cannot teach both without contradicting itself...Christ is called Lord (Greek, *kurios*) many times in the New Testament...Those who hold to faith only salvation have no problem with this data. It is hard to imagine anyone wishing to be known as evangelical who would ever want to

---

[163] Charles C. Ryrie, *Balancing the Christian Life*, (Chicago: Moody Press, 1969), WORD*search* CROSS e-book, 182-183.

question that Jesus Christ is Lord. That has never been the issue with them. The issue is whether or not God requires the sinner to promise Him that he will make the Lord Christ sovereign master, the Lord over his entire life all the rest of his life, before He will save him?...When Scripture calls Jesus "Lord" it ascribes full and absolute deity to Him. He is sovereign...Unless He is God the Sovereign One, He could not have atoned for sin...But accepting Jesus for who He claimed to be – the Lord God who died as man's substitute – is not the same as promising Him complete surrender and dedication of one's entire life. The latter involves human effort or work and the former does not...The term Lord in Ac. 16:31 –or anywhere else it is used of Christ [including Rom. 10:9-10) – does not mean Master over one's life. Rather it is a descriptive title of who He is – the sovereign God...One Greek Scholar [B. F. Westcott] stated what confessing Jesus as Lord means: "To recognize divine sovereignty in One who is truly man, or in other words, to recognize the union of the Divine and human in one person."

The Jews had no problem calling Jesus Master, that was nothing new they had all kinds of masters but the real hold up was calling the Lord Jesus God, that they would not do. By the way, the context of Romans 9-11 is related to Israel!

Archibald Thomas Robertson notes:

"No Jew would do this [calling Jesus Lord] who had not really trusted Christ, for *kurios* in the LXX is used of God. No Gentile would do it who had not ceased worshipping the emperor as *kurios*. The Word *kurios* was and is the touchstone of faith."[164]

Lightner continues:

Lord applied to Jesus, means He is God and therefore the sovereign One. Evangelicals on both sides of the lordship issue agree – no one can have Christ as a substitute for sin and become a child of God who does not acknowledge Him as such. Lordship salvation people go a step further and

---

[164] Archibald Thomas Robertson, *Word Pictures in the New Testament* (Nashville: Broadman Press, 1931), 389.

say the sinner must turn his entire future life over to Jesus as Lord before he can receive forgiveness of sin. Nowhere in Scripture is making Jesus lord of one's life a requirement to receive salvation from the Savior...The Lordship view confuses *becoming* a Christian with *being* a Christian...The lordship view adds to the Gospel of the grace of God what Scripture does not...The gospel of God's saving grace must not be adulterated, not even by evangelicals.[165]

Lord is most often the concept of Jesus as Deity. B. B. Warfield writes:

The full height of this reverence may be suggest to us by certain passages in which the term "Lord" occurs in citations from the Old Testament, where its reference is to Jehovah, though in the citations it seems to be applied to Jesus..."Make ready the way of the Lord, make His paths straight" (Isa. 3:4), and applies it to the coming of John the Baptist whom he represents as

---

[165] Sin, the Savior, and Salvation, Robert P. Lightner, Th.D, What about Lordship Salvation, Thomas Nelson Publishers, Nashville, 1991.

preparing the way for Jesus' manifestation....On the other hand, in passages like Luke 1:17, 76, although the language is similar, it seems more natural to understand the term "Lord" as referring to God Himself, and to conceive the speaker to be thinking of the coming of Jehovah to redemption in Jesus without necessary identification of the person of Jesus Jehovah...who is Jehovah – to identify the person of Jesus with Jehovah is significant.! We should never lose from sight that outstanding fact that to men familiar with the LXX and the usage of "Lord" as the personal name of the Deity there illustrated, the term "Lord" was charged with associations of deity, so that a habit of speaking of Jesus as "the Lord," by way of eminence, such as is illustrated by Luke and certainly was current from the beginning of the Christian proclamation (Luke 19:31), was apt to carry with it implications of deity, which, if not rebuked or in some way guarded against, must be considered as receiving the sanction of Jesus Himself.[166]

---

[166] Benjamin B Warfield, The Lord of Glory [New York: American Tract

J. Gresham Machen notes:

When the early Christian missionaries, therefore, called Jesus "Lord," it was perfectly plain to their pagan hearers everywhere that they meant to ascribe divinity to Him and desired to worship Him."[167]

The bottom line is that when the Bible says Jesus Christ is Lord, it is a claim that He is God. And, as the God-man, He is our Savior. He is able to save us and give us eternal life when we trust in Him, and Him alone to do so (Jn. 1:12).

5. We do not have to be *Afraid* that if we do not put the pressure on they will not change! When one is saved, as we have seen, they become a new person indwelt by the Holy Spirit. They are changed! After we are saved, by the power of the Holy Spirit, He will deal with the need to yield to His lordship (Rom. 12:1-2). Every believer has both the desire and the power to yield to the

---

Soceity, 1927], p. 105-106.
[167] J. Gresham Machen, The Origin of Paul's Religion [New York: The MacMillian Co., 1921], p. 306.

Lordship of Jesus Christ, and yes, even with that we all fall short!

When will we learn we do not change people by making them promise and vow to do something, but by giving them the gospel of grace which is trusting God to change people's hearts.

[11] For the grace of God that brings salvation has appeared to all men, [12] teaching us that, denying ungodliness and worldly lusts, we should live soberly, righteously, and godly in the present age, [13] looking for the blessed hope and glorious appearing of our great God and Savior Jesus Christ, Titus 2:11-13

Michael Cocoris shared this experience:

Several years ago, I preached a gospel message. After the service, a sensual-looking young lady said to me that she wanted to trust Christ, but she had a problem. She explained that she was living with a man who was involved with the underworld. She was afraid, and she was certain that if she did that he would kill her. I urged her to admit the fact that she was a sinner and trust in Jesus

Christ, and Him alone, for salvation. She then asked, "Do I have to stop the affair?" I explained that one does not have to stop sinning in order to be saved, but that candidly, if she trusted Christ, God would tell her that was a sin, and she should stop. She concluded that she would have to stop the affair in order to go to heaven. I insisted that that was not exactly right, but she didn't get the message.

Finally, I went to the blackboard and drew a circle. In the circle I wrote the word "salvation." I drew an arrow to the circle and on top of the arrow wrote "faith." I then drew another arrow, away from the circle, and entitled it "stop sinning." I explained that the *means* of salvation was faith. The result would be that God would tell her to stop sinning, and she should. But she was trying to turn it around and say that the means of salvation was to stop sinning, and that was simply not the case.

She finally got it. She agreed to trust in Christ and let God deal with the fellow. She did just that. Sometime later she broke up with the fellow. He did not kill her. On the contrary, she married another man, is the mother of several children, and is happily serving the Lord in her local church.

What must I do to be saved? The Biblical answer is, "Believe on the Lord Jesus Christ, and you shall be saved." (Ac. 16:31).[168]

- Not faith plus baptism.

There are many reasons why we do not include water baptism as part of how to be saved. The thief on the cross was not baptized; yet he was assured of being in Paradise with Christ (Luke 23: 43); The Gentiles in Caesarea were baptized *after* they were saved (Acts 10: 44– 48); Jesus Himself did not baptize (John 4: 1, 2)— a strange omission if baptism were necessary for salvation; Paul thanked God that he baptized very few of the Corinthians (1 Cor. 1: 14– 16)— an impossible thanksgiving if baptism were essential for salvation; Approximately 150 passages in the NT state that salvation is by faith alone.

---

[168] Lordship Salvation is it Biblical? Michael Cocoris, Redencion Viva, 1983. p. 19-20.

Sometimes people use Acts 2:38 to prove that water baptism is part of salvation, "Repent, and let every one of you be baptized in the name of Jesus Christ for the remission of sins; and you will receive the gift of the Holy Spirit." Here is from my book on the book of Acts:

The view I personally hold is that "and be baptized, every one of you in the name of Jesus Christ" is parenthetical:

- The verb makes a distinction between singular and plural verbs and nouns. The verb "repent" is plural and so is the pronoun "your" in the clause "so that your sins may be forgiven" [lit. "unto the remission of your sins."]. Therefore the verb "repent" must go with the purpose of forgiveness of sins. On the other hand the imperative "be baptized" is singular, setting it off from the rest of the sentence.

- This concept fits with Peter's proclamation in Acts 10: 43, in which the same expression "sins may be forgiven" occurs. There, it is granted on the basis of faith alone. Notice - PETER NEVER ADDS THE "AND BE BAPTIZED" WHEN DISCUSSING FORGIVENESS AGAIN. Check it out, he always offers forgiveness without any mention of being baptized, indicating that the phrase "and be baptized" is parenthetical. Acts 3: 19; 5: 31; 10: 43; 13: 38; 20: 21; 26: 18/ Lu. 24: 47.

It would be like me saying, "The storm last night blew down a tree, hey did you see that deer that just crossed the street, it also blew some of the roof off my house." The part about the deer is parenthetical. Every time I mention the storm, I leave out the part about the deer, because it is not my main point. If I were to mention the deer every time I told the story, it would not be parenthetical. So why does Peter not mention the part about being baptized when he talks about forgiveness of sin, in the rest of the book of Acts? It's parenthetical!

- In Luke 24: 47 and Ac. 5: 31, the same writer [Luke], indicates that repentance results in the remission of sins.

The truth is salvation is by grace through faith in Jesus Christ plus nothing.

CONCLUSION:

There you have it! Not exhaustive but hopefully foundational, designed to give us a firm footing in a shaky world.

Andrew Klavan is a popular writer of mysteries—some of which have been made into movies (1999's *True Crime* and 2001's *Don't Say a Word*). He was recently interviewed in *World* magazine about how his writing interacts with his Christian faith. In the process, he described his conversion to being a follower of Christ:

"My life has been more like one of those Outward Bound programs where they drop you far from home and you have to make your way back with a piece of string and a matchbook. I was born and raised a Jew and came up in that wonderful secular intellectual tradition that teaches you to analyze everything.

God kept coming into my life, and I kept disproving him—I was very good at it!

Fortunately, I could also disprove the foundations of my disproof. Eventually I saw that the pillars of the secular consensus—scientism, materialism, rationalism—were all made of sand. Whereas the deeper I went into the experience of God, the more I found...life in abundance."[169]

I have found these basic truths have allowed me to experience the life abundant in Christ.

Check Lists that have blessed me:

Manifested *Presence* (Ex. 32/Isa.64).

- No *Thought* of merit outside of Christ (Lu. 18: 9-14/Rom. 4:5).

- Do not *Tolerate* sin (1 Cor. 4: 4; 10:13/ 1 Jn. 1: 9; 2:1).

- Render *Total* obedience by the power of the Holy Spirit (Jn. 14: 21/1 Cor. 4:4/Jam. 4:8).

---

[169] Marvin Olasky, "Too nice for vice?" World (2-10-07), pp. 32-33.

- *Talk* to Him all the time. This is what the old preachers called practicing the presence of God (Ac. 2: 25/ 1 Thess. 5: 17).

- *Take* Him at His word (Rom. 8: 8/ Gal. 4:6/1 Cor. 3: 16/ Col. 1: 27/ Rev. 2: 1; 3: 20).

- *Travail* in prayer to clear the atmosphere (2 Cor. 10/ Jam. 4:7).

- *Treasure* His Word (Psa. 1/ Josh. 1: 8).

- *Trust* Him even in darkness (Isa. 50: 10-11)

- Don't *Tell* Him what to do, just set your sail (Jn. 3: 8).

- *Think* humbly (Psa. 34: 18; 51: 17/ Isa. 57: 15; 66: 2/ 2 Cor. 1, 10).

Supernatural *Power* (1 Cor. 2:4-5/2 Cor. 4:7/Eph. 5:18; 6:10/Gal. 5:16).

Provisions (Psa. 23/37:25/Mt. 6:33/Ro. 8:32/2 Cor. 9:6-7/Phil. 4:19).

Love for His *Providence* (Dan. 4/Book of Job/2 Sam. 3:18/Hab. 3:17-19/Ro. 8:28).

Phobia – (Josh. 1:9/Prov. 29:25/Isa, 41:10/2 Tim. 1:7).

Protection (Eph. 6:10-18/2 Cor. 10:3-6/Jam. 4:7).

Pride crushed (Prov. 16:18/1 Pet. 5:5-6).

Stop *Playing* God ((Mt. 7:1/2 Cor. 4:5).

Review *Positional* truth: D.C.F.T.E.

- *Deeply* loved no matter what because God has been propitiated.
- *Completely* forgiven through the blood of Christ.
- *Fully* pleasing to God by way of the imputed righteousness of Christ.
- *Totally accepted* in Christ.
- *Entirely* a new creature.

Preparation for eternity:

- *Starve* the flesh (Ro. 13:14).
- *Strengthen* the inner man (Eph. 3:16).
- *Stay* in step with the Spirit (Gal. 5:16).
- *Stimulations*: *Ruling* (2 Tim. 2:11-13); *Rewards* (W.C.L.S.D. = Witnessing; Caring for the flock; Longing for His return; Suffering rightly; Discipline of dying to self); *Recognized* (Mt. 25:21); *Return* glory to God (Rev. 4:11); Avoid *Regret* (1 Jn. 2:28).

Promote the Lord Jesus (1 Cor. 10:31/Gal. 2:20/Phil. 1:21/1 Pet. 4:10-11).

Expect answered *Prayer* Mt. 7:7/Jam. 5:16/1 Jn. 5:14-15).
Expect *Persecution* (2 Tim. 3:12).

People – *List* of saved people, may I feed, lead, and Intercede for them; *Lost*, may I win somebody to Christ.

Psalm 23 – review it:

- The Phenomenal – The LORD...

- The Perpetual – is...
- The Personal – my...
- The Pastoral – shepherd...
- The Principle of satisfaction – I shall not want...
- The Provisional – He makes me lie down in green pastures...
- The Peaceful – He leads me beside still waters...
- The Prodigal – He restores my soul...
- The Possible – He guides me in the paths of righteousness for His name's sake...
- When life turns Painful – Yea, though I walk through the valley of the shadow of death, I will...
- The Practical – You prepare a table before me in the presence of...
- The Plentiful – My cup runs over...
- The Pleasurable – Surely goodness and mercy shall follow me all...
- The Promotional – And I will dwell...

M & M's

- *Manifested* Presence.
- *Magnify* God.
- *Mighty* anointing.

- *Mindful* not to grieve, quench, or resist the Holy Spirit.
- *Momentum* – don't lose it! Obedience leads to more obedience and disobedience makes disobedience easy and inevitable.
- *Ministry* – send visitors and new members.
- *Members* – pray for by name.
- *Many* may be saved.
- *Make* Satan flee through by union with the Lord Jesus Christ.
- *Money* – enough to pay my bills.
- *Maintain* my health.
- *Mind* to be clear and remember things.
- *Movement* during the invitation.
- *Music* – may it be spiritually uplifting.
- *Moistened* eyes, brokenness.
- *Make* no needless purchases.
- *My* books might minister to someone.

Principles of Grace from James:

- *Turn in* your resignation – "Submit to God" (Jam. 4:7a).

- *Turn down* the devil – "Resist the devil and he will flee from you"
- *Tune into* the supernatural – "Draw near to God and He will draw near to you."
- *Turn away* from sin – "Cleanse your hands, you sinners; and purify your hearts, you double minded."
- *Turn on* the tears – "Be miserable and mourn and weep; let your laughter be turned into mourning and your joy to gloom."
- *Tune out* your ambitions for greatness – "Humble yourselves in the presence of the Lord, and He will exalt you."
- *Turn off* your tongue – "Do not speak against one another….:

Activating God's Presence (Ephesians 3:14-21):

- The *Unemployment* of self – "For this reason I bow my knees to…"
- Inner *Enablement* – "to be strengthened with might through His Spirit in the inner man"

- Leading to an *Enthronement* – "that Christ may dwell in your hearts through faith"
- Leading to *Enlightenment* – "may be able to comprehend...love of Christ which passes knowledge"
- Leading to a God *Environment* – "may be filled with the fullness of God"
- *Encouragement* to believe all of this – "Now to Him who is able..."

Praying through the Lord's Prayer

- *Family* – "Our"
- *Father* – "Father"
- *Far* above us – "in heaven"
- *Fear* – "Hallowed be Your name"
- *Future* – "Your kingdom come..."
- *Food* – *Physical* "Give us our daily bread; *Spiritual* "Your will be done, on earth as it is..." (Jn. 4:34).
- *Forgiveness* – "And forgive us..."
- *Freedom* from sin – "And do not lead us into temptation"
- *Fighting* against the evil one – "but deliver us from evil."
- *Fantastic* – "For Yours is the..."

Dealing with Temptation

- *Affirm* God's Promise (1 Cor. 10:13)
- *Abide* in Christ (Jn. 15:)
- *Assimilate* God's Word (Josh. 1:8).
- *Ask* for help (Mt. 6:13).
- *Artillery* (Eph. 6:18)
- *Abstain* completely (1 Thess. 4:1-8).
- *Appetite* factor – sin leads to sin (Jn. 8:34).
- *Alternative* focus – replace sinful habits with godly ones (Prov. 23:7).
- *Aware* of the consequences of sin. **Mr. Palmer:**
  -**M** = misery.
  -**r** = responsibility to glorify God, sin always dishonors God.
  -**P** = loss of peace, power, manifested presence, etc.
  -**a** = sin is against God's Agape (love).
  -**l** = loyalty to Satan! That is what sin really is.
  -**m** = ministry will be negatively affected.
  -**e** = eternity, a loss of rewards.

-**r** = reality, God's way is always best.
- *Aggressiveness* is called for (Mt. 5:30).
- *Audibly* rebuke the Devil (Lu. 4:4, 8, 10-11).
- *Affections* must be dethroned, live by faith (Rom. 1:17).
- *Acknowledge* God's goodness has already given us what is good for us (Psa. 84:11).
- *Accept* responsibility – do not excuse, rationalize, or blame others for our sin (1 Jn. 1:9).
- *Apathy* must be rejected. When we sin, get back into fellowship and press on (Phil. 3:13). Never quit!

Armor of God (Eph. 6:10-18)

- A *Strengthening* – "be strong..."
  -By the *Trinity* (Father, Jer. 32:17); Son (Phil. 4:13); Holy Spirit (Ac. 1:8).
  - For the *Ministry* (1 Cor. 2:4-5).
  -Against *Iniquity* (1 Cor. 10:13).

- A *Standing* – "stand...stand..."
  -In *Intimacy* (Hab. 3:17-19).

-In my *Identity* (Gal. 2:20).
-In *Victory* (Rom. 8:37/1 Cor. 15:57/2 Cor. 2:14).
-In *Ministry* (1 Cor. 15:58).

- A *Struggling* – "against the wiles of the devil..." (2 Cor. 10:3-6/Jam. 4:7/1 Pet. 5:8/ 1 Jn. 4:4).

- A *Suiting up* – "put on the whole armor of God..."

  -*Reality* (Belt of truth), Mt. 16:18; 18:20/Rom. 8:32/Heb. 13:5-6. Jesus (Jn. 14:6).
  -*Conformity* (Breastplate of righteousness), Rom. 4:5/Rom. 13:11-14. Jesus (2 Cor. 5:21).
  -*Tranquility* (shoes of peace), Eph. 1:11/Rom. 8:28/Rom. 5:1/Isa. 26:3/2 Tim. 1:7. Jesus (Eph. 2:14).
  -*Dependency* (Shield of faith), Prov. 3:5-6/Rom. 4:20-21/Heb. 11:6. Jesus (Heb. 12:2).
  -*Mentality* (Helmet of salvation), Rom. 12:2. -*Eternity*, 1 Thess. 5:8/Jn. 14:1-3/1 Thess. 4:16-

18/Heb. 10:35-39. Jesus (1 Cor. 2:16/Col. 1:27).
-*Authority* (Sword of the Spirit), Josh. 1:8/2 Tim. 3:16-17/Heb. 4:12. Jesus (Jn. 1:1).
-*Artillery* (praying...), Mt. 7:7-8/Jn. 16:24/Jam. 5:16/ 1 Jn. 5:14-15. Jesus (Heb. 7:25).

FOLLOW-UP ESPECIALLY FOR NEW CHRISTIANS

Eternal Security

Intro: Notice that *Assurance of*

Salvation is not the same as *Eternal Security*. Every believer is eternally secure, but not all have assurance that they are eternally secure. Eternal Security means that once a person is truly saved, they will remain saved eternally.

I. First, the *Biblical Teachers* taught this truth.

A. The Lord *Jesus* taught this truth (Jn. 5:24).

B. *John* taught this truth (1 Jn. 2:25).

Observation: If the believer was saved for 200 years and then lost, what he had was 200-year life not eternal life. Eternal life by definition means that it cannot come to an end. We must also understand that "Eternal Life" is more than just length of time, it also speaks of abundancy and intimacy with God (Jn. 17:3). The lost person will live forever, but they are never said in the Bible to have Eternal Life.

C. *Jude* taught this truth (Jude 24-25).

D. *Paul* taught this truth (Rom. 8:1).

E. *Peter* taught this truth (1 Pet. 1:3-6).

II. Furthermore, some *Biblical Truths* to think about.

A. God's *Unconditional Promises*.

"^{27} "My sheep hear My voice, and I know them, and they follow Me; ^{28} and I give eternal life to them, and they will never perish; and no one will snatch them out of My hand." John 10:27-28

One might object, "Ok, He will not take us out of His hand, but we can take our self out of His hand!" This does not take into account the Biblical image presented - we are not only in His hand but part of His hand!

"For we are members of His body, of His flesh and of His bones." Ephesians 5:30

"For I am confident of this very thing, that He who began a good work in you will perfect it until the day of Christ Jesus." Philippians 1:6

"If we are faithless, He remains faithful, for He cannot deny Himself." 2 Timothy 2:13

"5 Let your character or moral disposition be free from love of money [including greed, avarice, lust, and craving for earthly possessions] and be satisfied with your present [circumstances and with what you have]; for He [God] Himself has said, I will not in any way fail you nor give you up nor leave you without support. [I will] not, [I will] not, [I will] not in any degree leave you helpless nor forsake nor let [you] down (relax My hold on you)! [Assuredly not!] 6 So we take comfort and are encouraged and confidently and boldly say, The Lord is my Helper; I will not be seized with alarm [I will not fear or dread or be terrified]. What can man do to me?" Hebrews 13:5-6 (AMP)

"There are three negatives before the word, making the promise one of triple assurance. It is, "I will not, I will not I will not let you down."[170]

B. God's *Unlimited Power* to back up those promises.

"5 Then a voice came from the throne, saying, "Praise our God, all you His servants and those who fear Him, both small and great!" 6 And I heard, as it were, the voice of a great multitude, as the sound of many waters and as the sound of mighty thunderings, saying, "Alleluia! For the Lord God Omnipotent reigns! Revelation 19:5-6

"The English word "omnipotent" comes from the Latin 'omnis' meaning "all." God is all powerful, meaning "That quality of deity means God is all powerful and can do anything that is consistent with His Nature." [The Moody Handbook of Theology, Paul Enns].

C. God's *Unquenchable Love* for His children.

"6 For while we were still helpless, at

---

[170] Wuest Word Studies, Kenneth Wuest.

the right time Christ died for the ungodly. 7 For one will hardly die for a righteous man; though perhaps for the good man someone would dare even to die. 8 But God demonstrates His own love toward us, in that while we were yet sinners, Christ died for us. 9 Much more then, having now been justified by His blood, we shall be saved from the wrath of God through Him. 10 For if while we were enemies we were reconciled to God through the death of His Son, much more, having been reconciled, we shall be saved by His life." Romans 5:6-10

If God loved you as a lost person, one who was without any strength; ungodly; still sinning; and enemy of God, how much more does He love you now that you have been forgiven of all your sins (Col. 2:13) and imputed the very righteousness of Christ (Rom. 4:6-8)?

See, Rom. 8:31-39.

D. God's *Unquestionable Answer* to the prayer of the Son of God.

Jn. 17:9-1215, 20.

Trans: Therefore we are eternally secure because of God's totally Unconditional promises which are far too many to list; also due to His Unlimited power to keep those promises; and His Unquenchable love which cannot be quenched by our faults, failures, and sins; and finally, we take courage in the Unquestionable answer to His prayer specifically for our security.

III. Finally, the *Trinity is Behind* our security.

A. God the *Father* is the *Planner of* our salvation.

"3 Blessed be the God and Father of our Lord Jesus Christ, who has blessed us with every spiritual blessing in the heavenly places in Christ, 4 just as He chose us in Him before the foundation of the world, that we would be holy and blameless before Him. In love 5 He predestined us to adoption as sons through Jesus Christ to Himself, according to the kind intention of His will, 6 to the praise of the glory of His grace, which He freely bestowed on us in the Beloved." Ephesians 1:3-6

If God's plan were to fail, then God Himself would be a failure! Such a thought is obviously unthinkable!

B. God *the Son is the Provider* of our salvation.

"In Him we have redemption through His blood, the forgiveness of our trespasses, according to the riches of His grace." Ephesians 1:7

- He is our Advocate. 1 Jn. 2:1

Observation: The term Advocate means "a defense attorney" in a court of law. Jesus Christ is our defense attorney before the Father.

Question: Why? Why do we need a defense attorney in the presence of God the Father? Most people think that it is to keep the Father from condemning us, but He has already been propitiated (1

Jn. 2:2). Propitiation means "to turn away wrath by the satisfaction of violated justice." The reason we need an advocate is not to protect us from the Father, He isn't mad anymore! It is due to the continual accusations of the Devil (Rev. 12:10/ Job 1:1,6-12; 2:1-6). Keep in mind that Jesus does not plead our innocence but His nailed scared hands.

- He is our Intercessor. Lu. 22:31-32/Heb. 7:25

- His salvation is a free gift. "being justified as a gift by His grace through the redemption which is in Christ Jesus;" (Romans 3:24). The word gift is "dorean" and is the same word used in John 15:25, "But they have done this to fulfill the word that is written in their Law, 'THEY HATED ME WITHOUT A CAUSE.' They hated Jesus without a cause - if you lived a trillion years you could not think of one legitimate reason to hate Jesus.

And if you lived a trillion years you could not think of one legitimate reason why God should save you! That's why it had to be a gift!

- The sin debt has been paid in full!

"13 When you were dead in your transgressions and the uncircumcision of your flesh, He made you alive together with Him, having forgiven us all our transgressions, 14 having canceled out the certificate of debt consisting of decrees against us, which was hostile to us; and He has taken it out of the way, having nailed it to the cross." Colossians 2:13-14

"In the days of the great dominion of Rome law was built on the assumption that every Roman citizen owed Caesar perfect allegiance and obedience to his laws...If any citizen broke one of his laws. The offender would soon find himself standing before the courts or Caesar himself. If the man were found guilty of breaking the law and sentenced to prison, an itemized list was made of each infraction and its corresponding penalty...It was technically called a "Certificate of Debt." When the man was taken to his prison cell, this Certificate of Debt was nailed to the cell door so that anyone passing by could tell that the man had been justly condemned and could also see the limitation of his punishment...When the man had served his time and was released, he would be handed the yellowed, tattered Certificate of Debt words "Paid in Full" written across it. He could never again be imprisoned for those same crimes as long as he could produce his canceled Certificate of Debt. But until the sentence was paid, that Certificate of Debt stood between him and freedom...A Certificate of Debt was prepared against every person who would ever live, listing his failure to live in thought, word, and deed in accordance with the law of God. This death sentence has become a Debt of Sin which has to be paid, either by man, or if possible, someone to take his place...Jesus cried "My God, My God, why have you forsaken Me?" In that instant God had taken the Certificate of

Debt of every human being from the beginning of mankind until the close of history, and nailed it to the cross, making Jesus responsible and guilty for each one!...The victorious cry on the cross was the Greek word, *tetelestai* (Jn. 19:30). Let that burn like a firebrand into your mind, because that's the exact same word that a Roman judge would write across a released criminal's Certificate of Debt to show that all his penalty had been paid and he was free at last. In the mind of God, "Paid in Full" has been written with the blood of Jesus Christ across the Certificate of Debt of every man who will ever live. We can never be condemned for all these things again."[171]

Common sense illustration: How many of your sins were future WHEN Jesus died for you on the cross? All of them! You were not even born yet. How could God deal with your future sins that were not yet committed? Because God is omniscient - knowing everything past, present, and future, actual and possible at one time. Isa. 46:9-10/etc. What is

---

[171] Amazing Grace, Hal Lindsey.

the only way that God can forgive your sins? At the cross, by the blood of Christ (Heb. 9:22). Jesus' glorified body has no blood (Lu. 24: 37-39/ 1 Cor. 15:50). Therefore, if He didn't pay for sins on the cross, he cannot pay for sins, since it is only through His shed blood! But He did pay for all sins at the cross making every person SAVEABLE, but not actually saved until they personally receive Jesus Christ as their savior by faith (Jn. 1:12).

The Point - since Jesus paid for ALL of your sins, ALL of your sins are forgiven the moment you believe in Jesus Christ. Since ALL your sins, past; present; and future were an issue to a Holy God, therefore He must deal with them all or He could never save you in the first place. If you say God saved someone, and then they later commit a particular sin that causes them to be lost, the truth is that the sin was just as real to God when He saved that person in the first place. The basic problem with those who deny eternal security is that their God is too small!

A Problem - then why are we told to confess our sins (1 Jn. 1:9)? Not in order to secure our forgiveness in a judicial sense. We confess known sin to restore fellowship in a parental sense. We no longer relate to God, as believers, as a criminal before a Judge; but as a child before a Father.

C. God the *Holy Spirit is the Power* of our salvation.

"13 In Him, you also, after listening to the message of truth, the gospel of your salvation—having also believed, you were sealed in Him with the Holy Spirit of promise, 14 who is given as a pledge of our inheritance, with a view to the redemption of God's own possession, to the praise of His glory." Ephesians 1:13-14

"Do not grieve the Holy Spirit of God, by whom you were sealed for the day of redemption." Ephesians 4:30
Regeneration - spiritual birth like physical birth is irreversible (Jn. 1:12-13)

Indwelling of God's Spirit is permanent (Jn. 14:16)

Spirit Baptism is a one-way trip! (1 Cor. 12:13)

Con:

So What?

"3 If You, LORD, should mark iniquities [keep an itemized account], O Lord, who could stand? 4 But there is forgiveness with You, That You may be feared [reverently trusted]." Psalm 130:3-4

If you think that God can love you one minute and then cast you into hell, it is impossible to trust Him. All believers are eternally secure regardless of what they believe, but that is very different from the peace and joy of having assurance of salvation and a close intimate walk with God.

The Bible

I. THE *MIRACLE* OF THE BIBLE.

- Written over a period of a 1,500-year span. Moses wrote the first book of the Bible, Genesis about 1400 B.C., and the apostle John the last book, Revelation, about 96 A.D.

- Written by some 40 authors, from every walk of life:

Moses, a political leader, trained in the universities of Egypt.
Peter, a fisherman.
Amos, a herdsman.
Joshua, a military General.
Nehemiah, a cupbearer.
Daniel, a Prime Minister.
Luke, a Doctor.
Solomon, a King.
Matthew, a tax collector.
Paul a former Rabbi.
Just to name a few...

- Written in different places:

Moses in the wilderness.

Jeremiah in a dungeon.
Daniel on a hillside and Palace.
Paul in prison
John in exile on Patmos
Etc.

- Written at different times: both in times of peace and war.

- Written in three languages:

Hebrew, the major portion of the Old Testament; *Aramaic*, in Ezra 4:8-6:18; 7:12-26/ Dan. 2:4-7:28/ Jer. 10:11; and *Greek* in the New Testament.

The miracle is that even though the Bible was written over a large period of time by men who did not know each other, and had very little in common, there is a definite unity of mind from Genesis to Revelation! There are no discrepancies, contradictions, or disagreements when all the facts are known. That makes this a miracle Book.

II. THE *MECHANICS* OF THE BIBLE:

A. Bible – the English word Bible is derived from the Greek word *biblion*, which means "book" or "roll." The name comes from *Byblos,* which denotes the papyrus plant that grew in marshes or river banks, primarily along the Nile River. Writing materials were made from papyrus plants. Eventually, the plural form *biblia* was used by Latin speaking Christians to denote all the books of the Old and New Testament (Dan. 9:2).

B. Scripture – the Greek word is *graphe,* which means "writing." In the Old Testament, this writing was recognized as carrying great authority (2 Kings 14:6/ 2 Chronicles 23:18/Ezra 3:2/Nehemiah 10:34). The writings of the Old Testament were eventually collected into three groups called the Law; Prophets; and Writings and consisted of the 39 books of our Old Testament (Lu. 24:44).

In the New Testament, the Greek verb *grapho* is used about 90 times in reference to the Bible, while the noun form *graphe* is used 51 times, almost exclusively of Holy Scriptures. The term the Scriptures designates collectively all the parts of the Scripture (Matthew 21:42; 22:29; 26:54/Luke 24:27, 32,

45/John 5:39/ Romans 15:4/2 Peter 3:16) or individual parts of the Scripture (Mark 12:10; 15:28/John 13:18; 19:24, 36/Acts 1:16; 8:35/Romans 11:2/2 Timothy 3:16). The phrase The Scripture says, is a synonym for quoting God Himself (Romans 4:3; 9:17; 10:11/Galatians 4:3/I Timothy 5:18). 2 Timothy 3:16 declares that all the Scriptures are God breathed, inspired by God (2 Peter 3:16).

C. Old and New Testament – the Hebrew word for testament is *berith* meaning Covenant or agreement. The Greek word is *diatheke* and means covenant. The Old Covenant is preparation for Jesus' coming, the Law showed man was a sinner, the animal sacrifices showed how God would forgive sin through His perfect substitute, the Lord Jesus Christ (John 1:29). The New Covenant is the fulfillment of the Old Covenant.

III. THE *MESSAGE* OF THE BIBLE.

- The Lord Jesus Christ (Luke 24:27/John 5:39, 46/Acts 26:22-23; 28:23).

- There are also many other themes: sin; redemption; kingdom; faith; etc.

- The Kingdom of God is a very important theme in helping us understand our Bible:

In the Old Testament the Kingdom is *Promised*; in the Gospels it is *Proclaimed* and rejected; in the New Testament epistles it is *Postponed*; and in the book of Revelation it is *Presented.*

I also believe it is impossible to understand the need for a future earthly kingdom without understanding the importance of the Abrahamic Covenant as the foundation for all proceeding covenants and how this covenant has not yet been totally fulfilled.

Palestinian	New	Davidic
Cov.	Cov.	Cov.
(Dt.30)	(Jer. 31)	(2 Sam.7)
Land	Seed	Blessing

The Abrahamic Covenant is the foundation, which promised a land, seed, and a blessing.

IV. *MANY* WAYS TO ORGANIZE THE BIBLE:

If we organized it in bookshelf form:

History section: Law of Moses - Genesis; Exodus; Leviticus; Numbers; Deuteronomy. Joshua; Judges; Ruth; 1 & 2 Samuel; 1& 2 Kings; 1 & 2 Chronicles; Ezra; Nehemiah.

Poetry: Job; Psalms; Proverbs; Ecclesiastes; Song of Solomon.

Prophecy: Major Prophets - Isaiah; Jeremiah; Lamentations; Ezekiel; Minor Prophets -Daniel; Hosea; Joel; Amos; Obadiah; Jonah; Micah; Nahum; Habakkuk; Zechariah; Malachi.

Biography: Matthew; Mark; Luke; John.

History: Acts

Paul's Letters: Romans; 1 & 2 Corinthians; Galatians; Ephesians;

Philippians; Colossians; 1 & 2 Thessalonians; 1 & 2 Timothy; Titus; Philemon.

Other Letters: Hebrews; James; 1 & 2 Peter; 1 & 2 & 3 John; Jude.

Prophecy: Revelation.

It is helpful to organize the whole thing in a time frame and in relationship to other books:

Job, for example was written during the time period of the book of Genesis...

Ruth, was written during the period of the book of Judges...

Psalms, was written during the period of 1 & 2 Samuel...

Esther, during the time of Ezra...

Therefore if you are studying the Psalms, it is helpful to know 1 & 2 Samuel for background material.

The book of Acts comes alive when you realize it in relationship to other books.

Early church growth, which takes place in Jerusalem and Judah are covered in Acts 1-12, during which time the book of James was written...

Paul's First Missionary Journey is found in Acts 13-14, in which the book of Galatians was written...

Paul's Second Missionary Journey, is depicted in Acts 16-18, both 1 & 2 Thessalonians was written then.

Paul's Third Missionary Journey found in Acts 19-21, during that time 1 & 2 Corinthians and Romans was written...

We have Paul's first Prison term, found in Acts 22-28, when Philemon; Colossians; Ephesians; and Philippians were written...

The book of Acts ends, but not Paul's life, he is released at which time 1 Timothy and Titus is written...

He has a second prison term, in which he is beheaded and his last letter is 2 Timothy.

Knowing this background is vital for understanding the background of the epistles.

You can get an overview of the Bible to help you get a handle on it:

- *Roots* of the Nation of Israel, Genesis.
- *Redemption* of the Nation, Exodus.
- *Requirements* for the Nation, Leviticus.
- *Refusal* of the Nation, Numbers.
- *Reminder* to the Nation, Deuteronomy.
- *Reception* of the Nation, Joshua.
- *Rebellion* of the Nation, Judges.
- *Remnant* of the Nation, Ruth.
- *Rulers* of the Nation, 1 Sam-2 Kings.
- *Retrospection* in 1 & 2 Chronicles.
- *Restoration* in Ezra.

- *Reconstruction* in Nehemiah.

- *Remnant* that did not return to Jerusalem in Esther.

- *Rhythm* of the Nation – Job about *Suffering;* Psalms abut *Singing;* Proverbs about *Sayings;* Ecclesiastes about *Searching;* Song of Solomon about *Sharing.*

- *Revealers* of God's Word – Pre-exilic Prophets : Joel; Jonah; Amos; Hosea; Micah; Isaiah; Nahum; Zephaniah; Habakkuk; Jeremiah. Exilic Prophets: Daniel; Ezekiel; Obadiah. Post-exilic Prophets: Haggai; Zechariah; and Malachi.

Anyway, we need to realize that the Bible comes from God. God Revealed His Word to the authors of the Bible and enabled them to write those words down; and then by His Sovereign power preserved them for us today.

This Bible is therefore from God and is our authority; our boss; our Control Tower. We flew to Nicaragua from Rogers, AR. To do that, the pilot needed to be under the authority of the control tower. The pilot had a limited vantage point. He could not see underneath or above the airplane. Even with all of their instruments, they cannot see all the weather conditions that they will encounter during their flight. The folks in the control tower provide pilots with help, direction, and guidance that they will need. The Word of God is the control tower for the Christian. Where we have only a limited vantage point, God's Word can communicate to us what we would not know by ourselves.

We must believe that the Bible is from God and is our authority! If the Bible teaches a doctrine then we teach that doctrine; if the Bible commands something then we are to obey those commands; we have all played Simon says! We need to learn to play the Bible says.

There is a game show called, *Who Wants to Be a Millionaire?* People are asked questions and if they give the right answers they can become rich. If you do not know the answer you are given what they call "lifelines." That means they can call a *friend* and ask them what is the answer to the question; or they can ask the *audience* to help and go with what the majority have to say. In life we have one reliable lifeline – it is not what we think or what friends think or what the majority thinks – our lifeline is the Bible! It tells us what God has to say! What's our lifeline? Is it our personal opinion, preferences or feeling? It must be God's Word!

Illumination must also come from God (1 Cor. 2:9-12/Heb. 3:7-8).

The Holy Spirit is the *Source* of the Scriptures (2 Tim. 3:16-17).

The Holy Spirit also allows us to make *Sense* out of the Bible (John 16:13-15).

I wear glasses because without them I cannot read the Bible. The older I get, it seems that the print of my Bible is getting smaller. I have to squint in order to see. But when I put glasses on, I can read the Bible with ease. The Holy Spirit is like glasses. He allows us to see what the Bible really means.

The Holy Spirit will only help us if we are willing to *Submit* to what we read (John 7:17/Heb. 5:14).

Anne Sullivan, who tutored Helen Keller who was deaf, dumb, and blind, said, "I saw clearly that it was useless to try to teach her language or anything else until she learned to obey me. I have thought about it a great deal, and the more I think, the more certain I am that obedience is the gateway through which knowledge comes."

Prayer is needed

We must pray before, during, and after we study the Bible (Psa. 119:18).

When a woman is pregnant we say, "She is expecting." Prayer keeps us in an attitude of expecting – we are expecting God to speak to us through His Word, we are expecting Him to give birth to a sermon! Prayer keeps us in touch with God, and keeps our hearts open to God.

V. THE *MINIMUM* IN BIBLE STUDY.

A. *Observation* is our part.

- Observation by *Reflecting*, we need to pay attention to what the Bible is actually saying. *Sir William Osler* was a physician. He was always trying to impress upon his students the importance of observation. Once he held up a bottle which contained a urine sample. He told the students that sometimes it is possible by testing to determine what disease a patient suffered. He then dipped a finger into the fluid and then into his mouth. He then passed out that bottle and told them to taste of that bottle *as he* had done. As the bottle was passed among the students, they reluctantly sampled the contents. When they were finished he said, "Gentlemen, now you can appreciate the importance of observation. If you would have been observant you would have noticed that I put my index finger into the bottle, but my middle finger into my mouth!"

- Observation requires much *Reading.* Let the Bible tell us what it is saying. We must not come to the Bible with our own ideas. We must be open to what it is saying, not what we want it to say. Many are like the old man who was hard of hearing. One day while they were sitting on the porch, his wife said to him, "I love you." He said, "What did you say?" She repeated, "I love you!" He looked with scorn and said, "Well, I'm tired of you too!"

- Read it *Repeatedly*.

We simply cannot read it too much. When John G. Mitchell, of Multnomah School of the Bible, was pastor of the First Presbyterian Church in Tacoma, Washington, he heard Dr. G. Campbell Morgan preach. The man knew his text, and young Mitchell was impressed. In fact, he asked the visiting Bible teacher how he understood Scripture so well. "If I told you, you wouldn't do it," Morgan said. "Just try me," Mitchell insisted. The veteran preacher replied, "Before I study a book, I read it fifty times." Beloved, if you want to learn God's

Word, then read and re-read the Bible repeatedly.

Therefore, observation requires *Reflecting and Reading.* We need to think, to meditate on God's Word (Josh.1:8/Psa. 1). Like a coffee percolator – the water goes up a small tube and drains down through the coffee grounds. It goes through this cycle until the coffee and water are one.

- Read it *Reflectively.*

Discover the key word, the *main theme* - What one word would sum up the passage? Write out in one sentence what a passage is saying.

Next, we should make an outline of the entire book we are studying. And then an outline of the passage before us.

Now, we just slowly *work through the passage, getting a subject and an outline.*

B. Interpretation.

- *Context.* The Context of what goes before and what comes after the passage we are studying. The overall context or what dispensation is the passage found in? A dispensation is related to the different ways that God relates to mankind. Like different administrations among various Presidents.

Overall view of Dispensations:

Perfection (Innocence) – Gen. 1:26-3:6
Permissiveness (Conscience) – 4:1-8:14
Protection (Human Government) – Gen. 8:15-11:32
Promise – Gen. 12:1-Ex.18:27
Precepts (Law) – Ex. 19:1-Ac.1:26
Patience (Church) – Ac. 2-Rev. 4
Power (Kingdom) – Rev. 20:

Pattern for each Dispensation:

They begin with a new *Revelation*.
There is a *Requirement*.
There is a *Rejection* of that requirement.
There is therefore *Retribution*.

- *Cross-references.* The best commentary on the Bible – is the

Bible! I recommend that you get a *Strong's Concordance*:

Warning: You have to consider the Context in order to understand the meaning of a word. Studying a word without considering the context is worthless.

You can study the word *ice* for days and all you know is that it is "frozen water." But is it? Somebody might be dealing in *ice*, a slang term for cocaine! In that context it has nothing to do with frozen water. The mob might decide to *ice* someone, a slang to take that person's life. One might be about to *ice* a cake – frosting! An offended friend might be as cold as *ice*.

Take the word *trunk* – is it a tree trunk; a trunk in the attic; a trunk of a car; etc. The meaning of words must be determined by the context. Take the word *lion* in the scriptures – only when you are talking about an animal, will studying the word be helpful. It can be a reference to *Babylon* (Jer. 4:7); or the nation of *Israel* (Ezk.19:2); or an analogy for Satan (1 Pet. 5:8); and even Jesus Christ Himself (Rev. 5:5).

Take the word *Run* – if you just study the word you might come up with the definition of walking fast. But the word is used of not only a man running, but of one's nose running; a washing machine running; running the pool table; leaving a faucet running, running for office; etc.

For example take the word *ekklēsía*; a called out assembly has to be identified by its context:

It can be referring to an assembly of Jewish people (Ac. 7:38).
It can refer to a pagan assembly (Ac. 19:32, 39, 41).
It can refer to the Body of Christ, which includes all believers from Pentecost to the Rapture (Col. 1:18).
It can refer to a local church (1 Cor. 1:2).

- *Cultural* setting. Looking at the *original* situation. Question: What did the text mean to the biblical audience? Getting the Principle is vital to making the passage relevant. So when Paul commands "Be not drunk with wine, but be filled with the Spirit" (Eph. 5:18), we realize that the command is not limited to wine. The principle goes beyond wine; it would include things like any alcohol, drugs, etc.

The cultural setting involves:

Political culture:

Why did King Belshazzar offer the third position in the Babylonian kingdom to Daniel instead of the second position? History sources reveal that at that time Belshazzar was only second in command. His father Nabonidus was out of the country so the best he could offer Daniel was the third spot.

Religious culture:

Moses commanded "not to cook a young goat in its mother's milk." (Ex. 23:19; 34:26/Deut. 14:21) He did this because according to archeological discoveries it was a pagan ritual practiced by the Canaanites.

Economic culture:

Job 22:6 Eliphaz accused Job of having "taken pledges from you brother for no reason." The background is that if someone owed someone money they could not pay. The one owed the money could take the debtors coat as a pledge of future payments, but must return it at night so the person could use it as a blanket and keep warm. Truth is, Job was not guilty of doing this but was being falsely accused (31:19-22).

Legal culture:

In 2 Ki. 2:9 Elisha asked Elijah to give him a "double portion of his spirit." Was he power hungry? Was he asking for twice as much power? No, he was simply requesting to be his successor. The firstborn in a family was given a double share of his father's estate (Deut. 21:17).

Agricultural culture:

Why would Amos call the women of Bethel "cows of Bashan?" These cows, located northeast of the Sea of Galilee, were known for having an easy life of grazing their way to fatness. The woman of Bethel had become wealthy and lazy! Amos 4:1

Clothing culture:

What does the Bible mean when it tells us to "gird up the loins of our minds?" 1 Pet. 1:13 In that day when a man worked or ran or engaged in battle he tucked his robe into his sash so he could move freely.

Domestic culture:

What did the man in Lu. 9:59 mean by saying "let me go bury my father first?" It did not mean that his father had just died. The man felt obligated to take care of his father until he died, no doubt so he would get his father's inheritance. He was willing to put Jesus on the back burner for several years.

Geographical culture:

What is significant about the message to the Laodicean church being lukewarm, not hot or cold? He is comparing them to the water supply. Water was piped into Laodicea from Heirapolis about 6 miles away. When the water left the hot springs in Heirapolis it was hot, but by the time it reached them it was lukewarm.

The bottom line is that understanding the culture is vital to understanding what the Bible is saying. For example, Mt. 17:24-27 seems extremely odd, I have been fishing for years and have never caught one with money in its mouth. The fish in the passage is a tilapia, a fish that actually carries its eggs in its mouth. If the young fish become frightened, they head for mother's mouth for protection. Often the mamma fish will pick up an object to prevent the babies from invading her mouth. That day by God's providential moving this fish picked up a shekel that was obviously on the bottom of the lake. There are various helps in explaining the cultural background. Many Commentaries give helpful insight; Today's Handbook of Bible Times & Customs; Harper's Encyclopedia of Bible Life; The New Manners and Customs of Bible times; etc.

Also, some cultural practices are temporary and others are still binding. When the Bible says greet one another with a holy kiss it is not still a normal thing. In our culture, a warm handshake is comparable...

How to have a Quiet time:

1. **Make it a *Priority*** – a firm decision to set aside a time daily to seek God.

2. **Have a specific *Place*** – a room, a chair, a place of solitude.

3. **Have a *Plan*** – same time, same place, every single day.

4. **Bring some *Paper*** – a notebook to write down thoughts, impressons, insights, promises, etc.

5. **Have a *Program*:**

Singing – get a small hymnbook and sing out loud to the Lord.

Scripture:

Any examples to follow...
Any exhortations...
Any promises to claim...

Any sin to confess and forsake...
Any new thought about God...
Any principle to apply to our life, family, job, church, community, or nation...
What specific changes do I need to make...
How exactly will I make them...
What scripture can I memorize to summarize this truth...
What illustration will help me remember it...

Speaking:

Pray for God's manifested Presence.
Pray that the Lord Jesus will be Promoted.
Pray for supernatural Power to do the will of God.
Pray for daily Provisions.
Pray for Protection.
Pray for People.
Pray God will crush our Pride.
Pray for Purity.

Reviewing Positional truth – We are
Deeply loved no matter what; Completely forgiven; Fully pleasing; Totally accepted in Christ; Entirely a

new creature; Adequately empowered by God's Spirit; etc.

- *Considering* words. We need to consider the Dictionary meaning of a Word. This can be discovered by looking at various translations; or by getting a Bible dictionary; and getting into original languages.

Discovering the grammatical tenses, etc. This is not always possible without the right kind of tools and training but don't worry about it! It's like watching a movie in black and white versus watching a movie in color. It might be more pleasing to watch it in color, but you get the same movie even if it's in black and white.

An important thing to watch for is *pronoun changes.* Pronoun Change is often the key that unlocks the door to understanding a passage.

- Commentaries. If you can get some commentaries, they can be helpful, unless they become a crutch to where you cannot study without them.

So all of this is under Interpretation – Context, Cross-reference; Culture; and Considering words.

Questions

Bombard the text with questions: Who? What? Where? When? Why? How? So What? Write down the questions and seek to answer them, but at this stage asking is more important than answering them. Who are these people in my passage? What is the basic purpose of the passage? Where did all of this take place? When did they take place? Etc. I have watched a kid's show many times with my grandkids called Curious George; it's about a monkey whose curiosity is always getting him into trouble. Our trouble is a lack of curiosity!

Integration

The theological framework puts the passage in light of the overall teaching of the Bible. Systematic theology is an organized study of all the passages that relate to a Biblical subject.

Imagination - write the passage out in your own words.

Injection – we need to inject the gospel into every sermon.

Incubation – sleep on it! Give the Holy Spirit time to do His work. Brood over the Scriptures, and He will birth some wonderful ideas.

Application

General:

Examples to follow?
Exhortations to obey?
Promises to claim?
Sin to confess or forsake?
Error to avoid?
Any new principles to apply?
Any new thoughts about God?

Specific:

How does this apply to my life; family; work; church; community; and Nation?
What specific changes do I need to make?
How exactly will I go about making this change?

What verse could I memorize that would best summarize this truth?
What illustration can I use to help me remember this truth?
What hymn would help me remember this truth?

I have bought many Muscle and Fitness magazines through the years, though not in recent years. I used to love to read those articles on how to lift weights, as long as I was lifting my weights! From time to time I quit lifting and guess what, during those times I lose interest in those magazines, I never even open them. But the moment I start lifting weights, I start reading them again. Why? Because I knew I was going to apply what I read. It is the same with the Bible! If you are not applying the Word of God to your life, you will lose all interest in God's Word. It is obedience to God's Word that compels us into God's Word and really causes us to be educated in the things of God.

Implementation

We must have a determination to obey. Sometimes we pastors are the most guilty of not applying the Word of God. It reminds me of a doctor, a lawyer, and a preacher who went hunting together. A deer jumped out in front of them and all shot at it. The deer immediately went down. When they came to it there was no bullet hole! They begin to argue about which one shot the deer. About that time a game warden came by and asked what the problem was. They explained it to him and he examined the deer. He said, "It was the preacher who killed the deer." The doctor asked, "How do you know?" He said, "Because the bullet went in one ear, and out the other!" We must not allow God's Word to simply go in one ear and out the other.

Illustration - Find an illustration that will help you to remember this truth.

Invocation - Find a hymn that will help you worship this truth.

Interaction - Share your study with someone.

You may not have access to many commentaries and other books. Just remember the words of John Bunyan who wrote *Pilgrim's Progress*:

"Although you may have no commentaries at hand, continue to read the Word and pray; for a little from God is better than a great deal received from a man. Too many are content to listen to what comes from men's mouths, without searching and kneeling before God to know the real truth. That which we receive directly from the Lord through the study of His Word is from the 'minting house' itself. Even old truths are new if they come to us with the smell of heaven upon them."

I would recommend that you make a copy of the quick overview. Run it off on colored paper using extra thick paper. That makes it easy to find and will last much longer then just normal paper.

Quick Overview:

Inspiration – that the Bible is God breathed.

Illumination – the revealing ministry of the Holy Spirit.
Intercession – from beginning to end it must be bathed in prayer.
Investigation – (Observation) Reading and Reflecting.
Identification – of a Theme and Outline.
Interpretation – Context; Cross-references; Cultural setting; Considering words; Consultation; Commentaries.
Interrogation – bombard the text with questions.
Integration – what is the theological framework.
Imagination - write out the passage in your own words.
Injection – of the gospel.
Incubation – to brood over the scriptures until the Holy Spirit births a communication to your spirit. Involves contemplation, prayer, meditation.
Implication – (Application) how does this apply to my life?
Implementation – a determination to obey.
Illustration - to help remember this truth.
Invocation – find a hymn that relates to your passage.

Interaction – share your study with someone.

Prayer

I. A few *Prerequisites* for Prayer.

A. A *Personal* relationship with Christ (Jn. 9:31/Eph. 2:13).

B. A *Continual* fellowship with Him (Psa. 66:18/ Isa. 59:1/Jam. 4:3).

C. An *Unshakable* confidence in God's Person and Promises (Heb. 11:6/ Jam. 1:5-6).

D. A *Total* dependency upon the Holy Spirit (Rom. 8:26/Heb. 10:19).

E. A *Habitual* trust in the merit of Jesus Christ. To pray "in Jesus' name is to present all that He is on our behalf (Jn. 14:13-14; 16:23-24/Eph. 2:18/ Heb. 10:19).

F. A *Radical* willingness to obey God's will and Word (1 Jn. 5:14).

II. The *Reasons* why we pray.

A. To Glorify God (1 Cor. 10:31).

B. It is Commanded (Lu. 18:1/1 Thess. 5:17).

C. To get eternal Results (Jer. 33:3/Jam. 5:16).

D. To Prepare us for God's work (Ac. 1:13014; 4:29).

E. To find God's Will (Jam. 1:5).

F. To pray for the Salvation of the lost (Rom. 10:1/1 Cor. 3:6-9).

G. To Engage in spiritual warfare (2 Cor. 10:/Eph. 6:).

III. The *Requirements* for effective prayer.

A. *Persistence* (Lu. 18:1-8/1 Thess. 5:17).

B. *Resistance* (Jam. 4:7).

C. *Relevance* (Mt. 6:11; 7:7-8). Not vague prayers but for a specific thing.

D. *Insistence* (Gen. 32:26).

IV. The *Rudiments* of prayer.

A. Praise – for who He is (Psa. 145-150).

B. Thanksgiving – for what He has done (Phil. 4:6/Col. 4:2).

- Material blessings.
- Physical blessings.
- Spiritual blessings.
- Relational blessings.
- Tribulational blessings.

C. Confession of known sin (1 Jn. 1:9).

Admit it; Quit it; and Forget it.

D. Supplication (1 Tim. 2:1).

- Intercession – for others.
- Petition – for ourselves.

V. The *Road blocks* to prayer.

A. *Prominent* prayer (Mt. 6:5).

B. *Pretense* in prayer (Mt. 23:14).

C. *Particular* unconfessed sin.

VI. A *Recognition* of our Lord's Praying.

A. It *Commenced* with Prayer (Lu. 3:21-22).

B. It *Consisted* on prayer (Mk. 1:35-38/Lu. 5:15-16; 6:12-13).

C. It *Consummated* with prayer (Mt. 26:39/Lu. 23:34, 46).

D. It *Continues* in prayer even now (Heb. 7:25).

VII. A few things to *Remember.*

A. Our physical position is not important (Neh. 9:4-5/Ezra 9:5/1 Chron. 17:16-27/ Ex. 34:8/Jn. 17:1).

B. God always answers prayer.

- Direct answer – ask and receive.
- Delayed answer – ask and receive in a different way than we expected.
- Denial – ask and the answer is no, a no answer is NOT no answer!

C. God is not limited to miracles, he can heal by way of medicine, etc.

D. Prayer must be couple with Scripture (Ac. 6:4).

VIII. Prayer and *Reflection*.

- *Review* past blessings.
- *Reflect* upon God's greatness.
- *Remember* God's promises.
- Make *Requests.*

IX. Prayer and some concluding *Rules.*

A. The *Target* of prayer – God's will and glory.

B. *Trust* factor – prayer is a mystery, we must trust God, we do not have a clue what He is up to. We must say with Job,

"Though He slay me, yet will I trust Him."

C. The *Train tracks* – think of a powerful locomotive, it needs tracks to run on. Prayer is laying down the tracks for the power of God.

D. *Third Time* is a charm – our Lord prayed three times in the Garden; Paul asked that his thorn would be removed three times.

E. Need for *Tenacity.*

F. The adversity seeks to *Thwart* us.

- Makes us feel *Tired* during our times of prayer.
- Raises up people to *Take* a stand against us.
- Seeks to interfere with our appointed prayer *Time*.
- Brings a *Thick* cloud to block God's manifested presence.
- *Tries* to cut off funds and support.
- Puts the *Thought* in our mind that prayer does not do any good.

G. *Thank* God that our prayers have been answered by faith.

X. *Run* through the Lord's Prayer (Lu. 11:1-4).

A. For the *Glory* of the *Father*. 11:2

1. *Intimacy* – "Our Father" (Lu. 15:11).

2. Right *Mentality* – "Hallowed be your Name" (Lu. 5:1-8).

3. *Prophecy* – "Your kingdom come" (1 Thess. 4:16-18).

4. *Conformity* – "Your will be done" (Mt. 26:38).

B. For the *Good* of the *Family*. 11:3-4

1. *Necessity* – "Give us this day our daily bread" (Mt. 6:33).

2. *Expectancy* – "And forgive us our sins as we..." Forgiven people are expected to forgive (Mt. 18:21/Eph. 4:32).

3. *Vulnerability* – "Lead us not into temptation" (1 Cor. 10:12-13).

Be Filled with the Holy Spirit

I. Definition.

A. Biblically – it means "to be under the full influence of; to be wholly occupied with; to be controlled by."

B. Theologically – Lu. 5:26; 6:11/Jn. 16:6/Ac. 5:3; 6:5).

II. Description. Eph. 5:18

A. Imperative Mood – a commandment.

B. Present Tense – continuous action.

C. Passive voice – the believer is acted upon by the Holy Spirit.

III. Illustration – getting drunk!

A. Common usage – Lu. 1:15/Ac. 2:4, 13, 15/ Eph. 5:18.

B. Contrast – which is more sinful? Getting drunk or being filled? Neither!

C. Comparison – just as getting drunk transforms a person so does being filled.

IV. Invitation on how to be filled.
A. *Confess* all known sin (1 Jn. 1:9).

- Pride – an exalted feeling in view of our success or position or gifts or talent.
- Anger – which is often excused as righteous indignation. It is a touchy, over sensitive disposition, which refuses to be contradicted or confronted.
- Self-will – a stubborn, unteachable spirit which manifests itself in arguments, sarcasm, critical spirit, harshness, and the like.
- Fear – a fear of man which causes one to be silent about Jesus, a shrinking from your spiritual duties, a compromising spirit so as not to offend anyone.
- Jealous disposition – secret spirit of envy shut up in your heart, and

unpleasant sensation in view of the prosperity of another.
- A dishonest, deceitful spirit – the evading of the truth, covering up of the truth. Leaving a better impression of ourselves than what is strictly truth. Always having to exaggerate the facts to make us look good.
- Unbelief – discouraged in times of pressure, a focus on our own performance instead of the promises of God.
- Self-righteousness – always having to defend ourselves and prove that we are right.
- Up and down emotionally – living in extremes, one day deliriously happy and the next suicidally sad.
- Talkative – always having to dominate every conversation, having to be the center of attention.
- Lust – an over emphasis on sex, or always having to buy something, never being satisfied with what we have.
- Laziness – not giving our all for the Lord on your job, sleeping in on

Sundays instead of going to the house of worship, just serving the Lord half-heartedly.
- Unforgiveness – holding a grudge against someone, always nursing hurt feelings. Avoiding certain people because they did something to us in the past.
- Intemperate in eating and drinking – also called gluttony.
- Filthy talk – cursing, inappropriate jokes, etc.
- Refusing to give thanks in all things – always complaining, always wishing things were different.
- Poor prayer life – always too busy to pray.
- Neglected Bibles – no devotions, no meditation on God's Word, no personal Bible study or memorization of the Scriptures.

This is just a sample list but enough to get us thinking.

B. *Count* ourselves as dead to the sin nature (Rom. 6).

C. *Consider* ourselves alive in our new nature (Rom. 7/1 Jn. 3:9).

D. *Crown* Jesus Lord (Rom. 12:1-2).

E. Be ready for Satanic *Conflict*! (Jam. 4:6/Eph. 6:10-/2 Cor. 10/1 Pet. 5:8).

"When yielding our lives to God, instead of the great manifestation of peace and joy of the Spirit we anticipated, we are troubled at finding one totally different. We come instead into a place of struggle, and of soul agony; a consciousness of fierce resistance, of keen suffering; of turmoil, uncertainty and distress. Instead of light is darkness; instead of peace a dire unrest; instead of fullness a seeming utter spiritual void and barrenness in our souls; instead of advance, an apparent backward step. All the while continues this sense of intense, awful, inward suffering, which we can neither define, describe, nor understand, save that it is so utterly diverse from our expectation as to throw us into almost hopeless confusion. Yet this experience is absolutely normal, explainable, and to be expected in every yielded life. Let any believer who comes into this crisis be not confounded, or discouraged thereby, for it is sure evidence that God is going to bring you into a place of fullness for which your heart yearns." (McConey)

F. Consent to the Holy Spirit's control by confident faith (Eph. 5:18 with 1 Jn. 5:14-15).

G. *Continue* with instant confession (so as not to grieve the Spirit) and immediate obedience (so as not to quench the Spirit).
"An airplane can fly either by instruments or visual sight. However, if one enters a storm, he must rely on instruments. One pilot wrote, "The turbulence was so strong that I got the distinct feeling that we were banking to the left. But the artificial horizon, which shows the plane is banking or level, clearly indicated that we were climbing straight and true. For the first time since I could remember, my sense of equilibrium and feelings were deceiving me. I felt as if we were going to crash

and had to keep fighting the urge to pull back on the controls. It took all of my strength of will and concentration to keep from reacting to the false signals my physical senses were giving me. I realized that believing the flight instruments in spite of my feelings meant life or death."

As we cope with the daily challenges of life we are tempted to follow our feelings and human reasoning stead of God's Word. This will seem to work until we hit storm. Then the very self-confidence that we have developed through years of trusting our own human resources and abilities will actually hinder our total dependency upon God alone. Remember walking in the Spirit means that by faith not sight we believe God's promises to be the truth."

The Church

I. The *Marked* beginning of the church.

A. For starters, there is no indication that the church began in the Gospels. It only is mentioned in Mat. 16:18 and 18:17. Both of these are looking to the future. Jesus said, "I will build my church" which is a future indicative, demanding a future fulfillment.

B. Furthermore, the church is dependent upon Christ's death (Ac. 20:28); resurrection (Eph. 1:20-21) and ascension (4:7-12).

C. Finally, the baptism of the Holy Spirit was necessary for the church to exist.

1. The church is the body of Christ (Col. 1:18/Eph. 1:22-23).

2. We enter into that body by Spirit baptism (1 Cor. 12:13).

3. Therefore, whenever, Spirit baptism first took place, is also when the church first began. Let's keep in mind that it was Jesus Christ who sent the Holy Spirit (Jn. 7:39) and so the Spirit's work of baptizing is the *immediate agent* that effects placing people, when they believe, into the body of Christ, and the ascended Christ is the *ultimate agent*

because He sent the Spirit (Jn. 14:17. So it is correct to say both He (Jesus) will baptize you as well as the Holy Spirit will baptize you (1 Cor. 12:13). Both speak of the same experience.

4. Now the promise for this baptism, which places us into the body of Christ, is given in Mat. 3:11 and is repeated in Acts 1:5. Both promises are in a future tense but in Ac. 1:5, it adds, "not many days from now" an obvious reference to the Day of Pentecost. It is true that Acts 2 does not specifically mention baptism, however Ac. 11:15-16 looking back to Pentecost does. Peter says, "...the Hoy Spirit fell upon them (Gentiles), just as He did upon us (Jews) at the beginning (Day of Pentecost). And I remember the Word of the Lord, how he used to say, "John baptized with water, but you shall be baptized with the Holy Spirit" (compare with Ac. 1:5).

Question: Does this baptism give the believer special power? No! Look at the Corinthian church, they were *all* said to be baptized, indwelt, and endowed with every spiritual gift, and yet, called carnal.

Question: Where does the power come from? The filling of the Holy Spirit.

Question: Because it says that the Apostles laid the foundation of the church, does it mean that the church began with their appointment to apostleship? No, Eph. 2:20 gives no mention of *when* they laid the foundation. The Apostles cannot be equated with that because they existed *before* the church began and are *now* no longer here, yet the church is.

Question: Is the view that the church was started on Pentecost held by many? It is held by such men as W. A. Criswell, Charles Swindoll, Charles Stanley, Adrian Rogers, Billy Graham, Charles Ryrie, Scofield, Hal Lindsey, and many others.

II. The Meaning of the local church.

A. Unbiblical terms.

1. Building – the church is not a physical building.

2. Denomination – the church is not Baptist, Methodist, etc.

3. State – the church was actually persecuted by the state not part of it.

4. Israel – is not the church (1 Cor. 10:31/Rom. 9-11).

5. Kingdom – the future earthly reign of the Lord Jesus in the Millennial is not the church.

B. Biblical Meaning and Usage.

1. The Meaning.

It comes from a word meaning "to call" and a prefix "out of", it is referring to those called out of or from this world.

2. The Usage:

a. Secular Greek – in Athens the ekklesia signified the constitutional assembly which met on previously fixed dates and did not need to be specifically summoned, much like our modern day legislature.

b. Septuagint – meaning assembly or gathering of people (Gen. 49:6/Psa. 26:5/Deut. 9:10).

c. New Testament Scriptures:

- Used of an unruly mob (Ac. 19:32, 32).
- Of a lawful assembly of citizens (Ac. 19:39).
- Of the community of Israel (Ac. 7:38).
- Of the local church (1 Thess. 1:1/Col. 1:1/etc.).

III. The *Make-up* of the local church.

A. Definition.

The local church is an assembly of professed believers in Christ who observe the ordinances and organization of Scripture related to the church.

B. Description:

1. *Open* Assembly – from the word ekklesia.

2. *Organization.*

a. Pastor (elder, overseer or bishop, shepherd are all used interchangeably (Ac. 20:17-18/Tit. 1:5, 7).

(1) Primary Passage: Eph. 4:11-12).

(2) Particular duties:

- Oversee (1 Tim. 3:1).
- Protect (Tit. 1:9)
- Maintain Biblical qualifications (1 Tim. 3:1-6/Tit. 1:5).
- Correct or reprove (1 Thess. 5:12).
- Pray for the flock (Jam. 5:14).
- Teach (1 Tim. 3:2)
- Lead (Heb. 13:7, 17, 24).

We might say he is to feed, lead, and intercede.

b. Deacons – to assist the pastor and serve the congregation (Ac. 6/1 Tim. 3:8-13).

3. *Ordinances.*

a. Definition – a visible expression, commanded by Christ to be performed by His church.

b. Description.

(1) Water Baptism (Mt. 28:19-20).

It is a public identification with Christ by immersion (Jn. 3:23/Ac. 8:38-39) baptize means "to dip, or immerse") into water for those who have *already* placed their faith in Christ.

(2) Lord's Super (Mt. 26:26-29/1 Cor. 11:23-34). It is a reminder of Christ's death and return.

4. The *Operation* of the Local Church.

a. The Motive – to glorify Christ (1 Cor. 10:21).

b. The Ministry – how we glorify Him.

- Exalt God in worship (Jn. 4).
- Edify believers (Eph. 4).
- Evangelize the lost (Mt. 28).

c. The Means.

- Spiritual gifts (1 Cor.12/Rom.12/Eph. 4/1 Pet. 4).
- Material gifts (1 Cor. 16:1-2/Heb. 7:1-2/1 Cor. 9:7-14/2 Cor. 9:6-7/Gal.6:6). Under the Old Covenant people gave to get a blessing (Mal. 3:10-11); under the New Covenant we give because we have received all God's blessings (Eph. 1:3).
- Physical presence (Heb. 10:24-24).

Witnessing

I. Every believer is *Responsible* to be a personal soul-winner (Mt. 4:19/Ac. 1:8; 8:1, 4/Rom. 1:14-16/2 Cor. 5:17-21).

A. Soul winning is to include follow-up (Mt. 28:19-20).

B. It involves both planting (sharing the gospel) and watering (prayer). 1 Cor. 3:5-6).

C. It is not to be confused with the gift of evangelism (Eph. 4:11-12).

D. We should expect various responses (Mt. 13:18-23).

E. Only the Holy Spirit can convict and convert (Jn. 1:12-13; 16:8-11/1 Cor. 3:5-6).

II. Every believer has a two-fold *Responsibility.*

A. To witness by our lives (Mt. 5:16).

B. To witness by our verbal speech (Ac. 4:4/Rom. 10:17/Gal. 3:2).

III. Every believer needs a Ready plan.

See the gospel presentation for an example.

A. Find your natural approach.

1. Some are naturally *confrontational*, like Peter or John the Baptist (Ac. 2:36).

2. Others are more *intellectual*, like Paul (Ac. 17).

3. Many are *testimonial*, like the blind man in John chapter nine.

4. Some are *relational* witnesses (Mk. 5:19).

5. There are *invitational* types like the woman at the well (Jn. 4).

6. Other are the *ministerial* or serving type like Dorcas (Ac. 9).

B. Memorize the gospel passages.

IV. *Reason* for being a personal soul-winner.

A. Love of Christ for us (2 Cor. 5:14).

B. It is commanded (Mt. 28:19-20).

C. People are lost without Christ (Jn. 4:35).

D. It brings rewards (1 Thess. 2:19/ Prov. 11:3).

E. We are debtors and ambassadors (Rom. 1:14/2 Cor. 5:17-21).

V. Two common *Reactions* to overcome.

A. Fear – God's answer for this is Spirit-filled boldness (Ac. 4:24-31/2 Tim. 1:7).

B. Lack of knowledge – remember a man with experience is never at the mercy of a man with an argument. We do not have to out-argue or convince the lost, but simply share with them the gospel and how it has saved us.

VI. Expect *Resistance.*
Satan will always oppose the gospel (2 Cor. 4:2-3/Mt. 16:18).

VII. Handling *Rejection.*

A. Do not argue. You can win an argument and lose your fish in the process!

B. Be positive – there is no value in being mean and nasty.

C. Be generous and sincere with your compliments. If one rejects the gospel today but shows they are sincerely seeking answers, encourage them in their pursuit. Have prayer for them that they will have their eyes opened to the gospel.

D. Be honest – if you do not know the answer to a question, just say I do not know but will search it out and get back with you.

Gospel Presentation:

Let me ask you one of the most important questions you will ever ponder.

Have you come to a place in your life where you know for certain that if you died you would go to heaven?

The only answer to that question is, yes, no, or I don't know. Take a moment and think about it. A follow up question would be:'

If you were standing before God right now and He were to ask, "Why should I let you into my perfect heaven?"

What do you think you would say? You might say, "I go to church. I try to live a good life. I try to keep God's law." Such responses are sincere, and I appreciate your honesty. Most would probably say, "I don't know what I would say." Well, would you like to know? Then read the following carefully.

God Really Does Love You

"For God so loved the world, (put your name here), that He gave His only begotten Son, that whoever believes in Him should not perish but have everlasting life" (John 3:16).

It is natural to question this claim; we tend to wonder how God could love us with all of our problems and hang-ups, yes, you can say it – with all of our sins. My wife and I have had two children. When they were born they did nothing for us! And after they were born, for the first several months they kept us up all hours of the night; we had to change their diapers and feed them. I think most of you know what I'm talking about. However, we did love them. Why? I suppose it was because we had something to do with them being in this world. They are our children; they even looked a little like us – poor kids! You need to realize that God is the one who had everything to do with your coming into this world. Without God you would not even exist! He is the Creator and Sustainer of life. He, in fact, created you in His image and loves you even though you have done nothing to deserve it.

So What's a Fella to Do?

Have you ever felt that your life lacked purpose and meaning? Have these thoughts ever crossed your mind:

- Where did I come from?
- Why am I here?
- Where am I going?

God knows the answer to these questions. He created you with a definite purpose in mind.

"The thief does not come except to steal, and to kill, and to destroy. I have come that they may have life, and that they may have it more abundantly" (John 10:10).

An abundant life is a life of purpose, meaning, and fulfillment. That is what God offers you. This brings up an unavoidable question—what happened! If He loves us and has this great purpose for our life, then why are both concepts so foreign to us? The answer is both profound and very simple.

Sin Separates!

We are all sinners, "for all have sinned and fall short of the glory of God" (Rom. 3:22). We are a sinner by birth. God created Adam and Eve and put them in a garden with only one commandment; they were not to eat of a certain tree. They disobeyed God by taking a bite, and thus they sinned. Now what kind of babies are two sinful people capable of having? It is the law of biogenesis—like produces like. This is why there is no need to teach children how to tell a lie, but only to teach them positive things like telling the truth. They know how to lie naturally!

The reason for that is that we are all born with a sin nature inherited from Adam.

"Therefore, just as through one man sin entered the world, and death through sin, and thus death spread to all men, because all sinned" (Rom. 5:12).

We are also sinners by behavior. Have you not sinned? The Bible commands us to love God with all our heart, mind, and soul. Have you always done that? Have you ever done that? Have you ever told a lie? Have you ever wanted to? God not only looks at our deeds but at our desires. The Bible clearly declares we have all sinned.

So What?

Here is the answer to the so-what question.

"For the wages of sin is death, but the gift of God is eternal life in Christ Jesus our Lord" (Rom. 6:23).

What we have earned from our sin is death. Death means separation.

- There is spiritual death—the separation of the spirit/soul from God. "And the LORD God commanded the man, saying, 'Of every tree of the garden you may freely eat; but of the tree of the knowledge of good and evil you shall not eat, for in the day that you eat of it you shall surely die'" (Gen. 2:16–17). The day they ate of it they did not physically die; that took place many years later. But God said *in the day* you eat of it you will die. They died spiritually that very day.

- There is also physical death—the separation of the spirit/soul from the body. "And as it is appointed for men to die once, but after this the judgment" (Heb. 9:27). The fact that everybody dies physically is proof positive that everyone is spiritually dead. If we were not sinners, we would not die. The statistics are rather impressive; one out of every one person dies!

- If you die physically while you are spiritually dead, you will die eternally. Eternal death is the eternal separation of the spirit/soul/body from God's goodness, grace, mercy, and blessings. It is to be fully conscious and live in a place the Bible calls the lake of fire. "Then Death and Hades were cast into the lake of fire. This is the second death. And anyone not found written in the Book of Life was cast into the lake of fire" (Rev. 20:14–15).

Question: How can you say one moment that God loves me and then in the next that He condemns me?

Well let us imagine putting on a judge's robe and sitting on the bench. Then the unthinkable happens. Your son, whom you love very much, is brought before you, guilty of a capital offense! The penalty for his crime is death, and the evidence is clear as to his guilt. Would you sentence him to death? If you were a just judge, you would, not because you no longer love him, but in spite of your great love for him. God is holy, righteous, and just, as well as a God of love. This looks like bad news! However, the very word *gospel* means good news, so where is this good news?

Jesus Christ Is God

"In the beginning was the Word, and the Word was with God, and the Word was God" (John 1:1).

This is a great mystery, but the Bible teaches that God became God/man. "And the Word became flesh and dwelt among us, and we beheld His glory, the glory as of the only begotten of the Father, full of grace and truth" (John 1:14).

Jesus Christ the Substitute

The Lord Jesus Christ lived a perfect life and then died in your place. "But God demonstrates His own love toward us, in that while we were still sinners, Christ died for us" (Rom. 5:8 NKJV).

Let us put our judge robe back on for a minute. Imagine after sentencing your boy to be executed, taking off your robe and then voluntarily offering to die in his place. That would make you just and loving at the same time. That is what Jesus Christ actually did for us. We do not understand all of this but must accept it by faith. I do not understand electricity, but I still do not live in the dark. I do not understand how the digestive system works, but I still eat. I do not understand how a brown cow eats green grass and produces white milk. You do not have to understand everything to be saved—just that you are a sinner and that Jesus Christ died for your sin.

He Is Not Here, He Has Risen

"For I delivered to you first of all that which I also received: that Christ died for our sins according to the Scriptures, and that He was buried, and that He rose again the third day according to the Scriptures, and that He was seen by Cephas, then by the twelve. After that He was seen by over five hundred brethren at once, of whom the greater part remain to the present, but some have fallen asleep" (1 Cor. 15:3–6).

By rising from the dead, He proved that He paid for all of our sins. If He had not, death would have held Him. It also proved that He had no sin of His own. If He had, He would have stayed dead like everybody else.

One Way Only

We have all seen *One Way Only* signs, and so it is with the way of salvation. There is only one person who can save. "Jesus said to him, 'I am the way, the truth, and the life. No one comes to the Father except through Me'" (John 14:6).

You can line up every one of us on the West Coast with plans to swim to Hawaii, and no doubt, some would swim a lot farther than others. Nevertheless, we would all have one thing in common: nobody would make it! It is impossible for anybody to swim from the West Coast to Hawaii. And it is just as impossible for sinful man to make his way to a Holy God on his own without experiencing God's wrath. What one needs is a boat to get them from the West Coast to Hawaii. Moreover, the only salvation boat is the Lord Jesus Christ. That Jesus is the only way to be saved is as true as $2 + 2 = 4$. There is only one answer to that equation, and there is only one way to be saved.

"Nor is there salvation in any other, for there is no other name under heaven given among men by which we must be saved" (Acts 4:12).

Facts

These are only facts. Giving mental assent to these facts is not enough to save anyone. It is not enough to give intellectual assent to these facts. We must believe and thus receive Christ.

"But as many as received Him, to them He gave the right to become children of God, to those who believe in His name" (John 1:12).

Faith

Facts must be wedded to faith. So, what do we mean when we say believe or place your faith in Christ?

Faith involves mind, emotion, and will.

Years ago, a tightrope walker named Charles Blondin, went across Niagara Falls, walking on a wire. He went back and forth. He even filled a wheelbarrow with bricks and took that across. A crowd gathered, and he asked one of them, "Do you believe I could do that with you?" The man agreed that he could. Then Blondin said, "Hop on in, and I'll carry you across." The man said, "No way!" You see, he did not really believe. He believed in his mind that Blondin could take him across; he wanted him to in his emotions, but he would not commit himself to Blondin and trust him to take him across. Saving faith involves our mind, emotion, and will.

Amazing Grace

You likely have heard the song, "Amazing Grace." We are saved by grace through faith in Jesus Christ. Now faith is not a work—faith is to believe in the work of another. "For by grace you have been saved through faith, and that not of yourselves; it is the gift of

God, not of works, lest anyone should boast" (Eph. 2:8–9).

Dr. Gerstner: "Christ has done everything necessary for his salvation. Nothing now stands between the sinner and God but the sinner's good works. Nothing can keep him from Christ but his delusion that he does not need Him—that he has good works of his own that can satisfy God. If men will only be convinced that all their righteousness is as filthy rags; if men will see that there is none that does good, no, not one; if men will see that all are shut up under sin—then there will be nothing to prevent their everlasting salvation. All they need is need. All they must have is nothing. All that is required is acknowledged guilt. But alas, sinners cannot part from their virtues. They are imaginary, but they are real to them. So grace becomes unreal. The real grace of God they spurn in order to hold on to the illusory virtues of their own. Their eyes fixed on a mirage; they will not drink real water. They die of thirst in the midst of an ocean of grace."

Repentance is a synonym for faith; it is like heads and tails of *one* coin. Repentance is not making a vow you will stop sinning, nor is it a change of life. You cannot stop sinning or change your life until God saves you! I have fished most of my life and I have never cleaned a fish before I caught it. Repentance is a *change of mind*, about who you are, a sinner; and about the Lord Jesus Christ, the only one who can save you based on His death, burial, and resurrection.

Good Enough Is Not Good Enough

The religious leaders of Jesus' day prayed three times a week, fasted twice a week, never missed going to the house of worship, and memorized the Old Testament (Luke 18:9–12). Yet, Jesus said that if you are not more righteous then they, you are not going to make it!

"For I say to you, that unless your righteousness exceeds the righteousness of the scribes and Pharisees, you will by no means enter the kingdom of heaven (Matt. 5:20).

Then he says something rather startling:

"Therefore you shall be perfect, just as your Father in heaven is perfect" (Matt. 5:48).

Did you know Jesus said it takes perfect righteousness to get to heaven? We all know that nobody is perfect! How then can we be perfectly righteous before a perfectly righteous God?

"For He made Him who knew no sin to be sin for us, that we might become the righteousness of God in Him" (2 Cor. 5:21).

The truth is, there is only one person who lived a perfect life, and that was Jesus Christ. You see, the good news is that not only did Jesus die on the cross in our place, to offer us forgiveness of all our sins, He also offers us His perfect righteousness, placed on our account! The only sin Jesus ever knew was ours; the only righteousness we will ever know is His.

Never the Same!

Salvation is not an external thing. When you receive Jesus Christ as your Savior, He makes you a new creature within!

"Therefore, if anyone is in Christ, he is a new creation; old things have passed away; behold, all things have become new" (2 Cor. 5:17).

And the Holy Spirit takes up permanent residence within you.

"And because you are sons, God has sent forth the Spirit of His Son into your hearts, crying out, 'Abba, Father'" (Gal. 4:6).

Thus, you now have the desire (new nature) and the power (indwelling Holy Spirit) to live for God. You are positionally changed from being in Adam to now being in Christ, and experientially changed because the inner transformation of regeneration and salvation begins the process of progressive sanctification, which ultimately leads to glorification.

"For it is God who works in you both to will and to do for His good pleasure" (Phil. 2:13).

While we still have an old sin nature though Satan is opposing us every step of the way, we must grow in the grace and knowledge of the Lord Jesus. It is also true that our entire life is different! If we are what we've always been, we are not saved. I know that I am saved because on the seventh of May, 1974, I received the Lord Jesus Christ as my Savior and also because I have never gotten over it! And it is not that we are trying to be saved. If I asked you, "Are you an elephant?" You would not say, "Well, I'm trying to be!" You either are an elephant or you're not. No one who is trying to be saved understands salvation. *You are either saved or you're not!* You are saved because you have had a personal, life-changing encounter with the Lord Jesus Christ at a point in time. It is a matter of trusting not trying.

So Are You Ready to Be Saved?

If this is something you want to do, then here is a suggested prayer; the words are not what's important but what's in your heart. If God is dealing with you, then cry out to Him:

Lord Jesus, I need you. Thank you for dying on the cross for my sins. I cannot save myself. I cannot even help you save me. But the best I know how, I confess that I am a sinner and believe that the Lord Jesus Christ died on the cross for my sins and rose from the dead. I open the door of my life and receive you right now as my Savior. Come in and make me the kind of person you want me to be.

If you just received the Lord Jesus Christ as your Savior, then you are saved! This promise is based on the authority of God's Word.

"But as many as received Him, to them He gave the right to become children of God, to those who believe in His name" (John 1:12)

A list of my other books: Go to Amazon.com and type in Johnny A Palmer Jr.

Genesis: Roots of the Nation Vol. 1
Genesis: Roots of the Nation Vol. 2
Genesis: Roots of the Nation Vol. 3

Exodus: Redemption of the Nation. Vol. 1
Exodus: Redemption of the Nation. Vol. 2
Book of Leviticus
Book of Judges
First Samuel
Second Samuel
Book of Job
Jonah, God of the Second Chance
Nahum, the God who is good and angry
The Gospel of Mark: the servant.
The Gospel of Luke Vol. 1
The Gospel of Luke Vol. 2
The Gospel of Luke Vol. 3
The Gospel of Luke Vol. 4
The Book of Acts
Ephesians: A Manual for Survival
Jude: Hey Jude
Revelation: The Revelation of Jesus Christ
A Manual for Revival
Practical Principles for Studying the Bible
Read Limit 30 mph
Proclamations from a Politically Incorrect Prophet
Elvis Wellness
Awake for the Dawn is About to Break

Rewards of Rejecting Christ
Which Messiah will you Meet?
GPS-23
Spiritual Survivor Man
A Father's Day Message
A Mother's Day Message
I'm For Life
Double Solitaire with the Trinity
Fuel – The Lord's Prayer
Practical Principles for Bible Study
The God of the Second Chance
1 Peter, Grace that gets us through the Grind of life
Back to the Basics